Collateral Knowledge

Collateral Knowledge

Legal Reasoning in the
Global Financial Markets

ANNELISE RILES

THE UNIVERSITY OF CHICAGO PRESS   CHICAGO AND LONDON

ANNELISE RILES is the Jack G. Clarke Professor of Far East Legal Studies, professor of anthropology, and director of the Clarke Program in East Asian Law and Culture at Cornell University. She is the author of *The Network Inside Out* and editor of *Rethinking the Masters of Comparative Law* and *Documents: Artifacts of Modern Knowledge.*

The University of Chicago Press, Chicago 60637
The University of Chicago Press, Ltd., London
© 2011 by The University of Chicago
All rights reserved. Published 2011.
Printed in the United States of America
20 19 18 17 16 15 14 13 12 11   1 2 3 4 5

ISBN-13: 978-0-226-71932-0 (cloth)
ISBN-13: 978-0-226-71933-7 (paper)
ISBN-10: 0-226-71932-4 (cloth)
ISBN-10: 0-226-71933-2 (paper)

Library of Congress Cataloging-in-Publication Data

Riles, Annelise.
    Collateral knowledge : legal reasoning in the global financial markets / Annelise Riles.
        p.   cm.—(Chicago series in law and society)
    ISBN-13: 978-0-226-71932-0 (cloth : alk. paper)
    ISBN-10: 0-226-71932-4 (cloth : alk. paper)
    ISBN-13: 978-0-226-71933-7 (pbk. : alk. paper)
    ISBN-10: 0-226-71933-2 (pbk. : alk. paper)   1. Security (Law)   2. Derivative securities—Law and legislation.   3. Over-the-counter markets—Law and legislation.
4. Financial risk management.   5. Derivative securities—Japan.   6. Over-the-counter markets—Japan.   I. Title.   II. Series: Chicago series in law and society.

    K1100.R55 2011
    346′.0922—dc22

                                                                    2010036689

♾ This paper meets the requirements of ANSI/NISO z39.48-1992 (Permanence of Paper).

広和とザビエへ

Contents

Acknowledgments

It has been more than twelve years since this project began. This book draws upon seventeen months of fieldwork conducted in Tokyo between summer 1997 and fall 2001 followed by frequent research visits in the years that followed. Research and writing were supported by the American Bar Foundation, a Howard Fellowship, an American Council of Learned Societies Fellowship, a residential fellowship at Girton College, Cambridge, and research grants from the Social Science Research Council, the Japan Foundation, and the National Endowment for the Humanities. During that time, I held visiting positions at the University of Tokyo Faculty of Law, the Department of Anthropology at Keio University, and the Institute of Social Science at the University of Tokyo. I am grateful to each of these institutions for their hospitality, and in particular to professors Yoshiko Terao, Satoshi Tanahashi, and Yuji Genda, respectively, for making each of these affiliations possible.

I am deeply indebted to the staff of the Bank of Japan, and to the staff of the bank at which I conducted fieldwork for so generously sharing their time and knowledge with me. At the Bank of Japan, I especially thank Masatoshi Okawa for his early and enthusiastic support of my project and for first drawing my attention to payment systems as a research topic. In order to protect the confidentiality of informants, I have refrained from attributing statements or thanking them by name here. Only where the identity of a particular individual or institution is a matter of public knowledge, that is, where it has been reported in the press and individuals or institutions have identified themselves with a particular act in public settings or government filings, have I identified them as such here. This limitation on sourcing conforms to disciplinary ethical practices for ethnographic research. I deeply regret that this means that I cannot thank them by name here. However, I hope that this book captures a small fraction of all that I have learned from them.

I am fortunate to work in an exciting field, and this project bears the imprint of so many colleagues whose work I admire greatly. For comments, criticism, and assistance of many kinds, I thank Richard Abel, Greg Alexander, Ron Allen, Marietta Auer, Nathaniel Berman, Lisa Bernstein, Don Brenneis, Cynthia Bowman, Bob Burns, Richard Buxbaum, Bruce Caruthers, Rebbecca Chang, David Charney, Abe Chayes, Jon Cisterno, John Comaroff, Marianne Constable, Susan Coutin, Charlotte Crane, Tony Crook, Zhiyuan Cui, Martha Fineman, Bryant Garth, Anna Gelpern, Yuji Genda, David Gerber, Carol Greenhouse, Jane Guyer, David Haddock, Laura Hein, Doug Holmes, Alan Hyde, Iris Jean-Klein, Naoki Kasuga, David Kennedy, Karen Knop, Doug Kysar, Mitchel Lasser, Jessica Leight, Jing Leng, Amy Levine, Jim Lindgren, George Marcus, Bill Maurer, Ralf Michaels, Curtis Milhaupt, Fabian Muniesa, Kunal Parker, Sol Picciotto, Alain Pottage, Jeff Rachlinski, Hugh Raffles, Mark Ramseyer, Adam Reed, Tom Riles, David Ruder, Alvaro Santos, Kim Scheppele, Pierre Schlag, Vicki Schultz, Susan Shapiro, Marshall Shapo, Carol Silver, David Snyder, Nomi Stolzenberg, Marilyn Strathern, Mark Suchman, Richard Swedberg, Veronica Taylor, Yoshiko Terao, Chantal Thomas, David Thompson, Mark Tushnet, William Twining, Takashi Uchida, Frank Upham, Mariana Valverde, David Van Zandt, Ahmed White, David Wilkins, and Zhu Suli, as well as the many audiences that have endured early versions of the argument over the years.

Over its lifetime, this project has benefited from help from numerous brilliant and dedicated research assistants, including Leticia Barrera, Jane Campion, Jessica Clarke, Aya Eguchi, Matt Erie, Marie-Andrée Jacob, Sergio Lattore, Amy Levine, Yuko Masunaga, Elisabeth Olds, Guillaume Ratel, Anna-Marie Slot, Tatiana Thieme, Yoko Tokunaga, Saiba Varma, and Shiori Yamamoto.

At the University of Chicago Press, John Tryneski managed the manuscript with patience and acumen. I owe a special debt to the manuscript's anonymous reviewers, whose insightful critical comments substantially improved the project. I also owe my deepest thanks to my assistant at the Cornell Law School, Donna Hastings, whose patience, professionalism, and generosity of spirit is a daily source of inspiration to me. For eight years she has endured this project and no doubt will be at least as glad as I am to see it go.

Over the last twelve years, our families in the United States and Japan have tolerated the many oddities of our life choices and have always been there for us, at any moment of need. Most recently, the addition of a new member to our family has created many more such quotidian moments, and they have done everything they can, chipped in everywhere along the way to help us do our best, in all the dimensions of our lives. Thank you.

Four years ago, Xavier came into our lives, and with a bang not a whimper. His patience, understanding, and desire to see the success of a project that continually fights for Mama's attention stuns me, even if to date our explanations of what his parents do strike him as a little odd. For the last few months, I have been spurred on by his daily greeting of "Where's my book, Mama?" Here it is, my love.

Finally, thanks is not nearly enough—it is just not an adequate register—for marking the influence of my husband and intellectual partner Hirokazu Miyazaki's influence on this work. From the beginning, this was a collaboration, and although it results in two separate monographs, we have grown through the issues together. I simply want to mark the joy of this trajectory, and also the impact of his fierce and unwavering faith in me, and in the wider endeavor. He is never fooled, and his criticism can be devastating but it is always spot on. Watching him at the craft of ethnographic research—engaging others with dog-headed tenacity and the passionate joy of the hunt, but with true tenderness and empathy for others, and creativity in response—renews my faith in the discipline daily and has taught me so much about friendship besides.

Although in all cases the argument differs substantially from what has appeared elsewhere in print, small portions of some chapters have appeared in previous publications. Those publications include the following: "The Anti-Network: Private Global Governance, Legal Knowledge, and the Legitimacy of the State," 56 *Am J Comp Law* 3 (2008): 605–30; "Collateral Expertise: Legal Knowledge in the Global Financial Markets," *Current Anthropology* 51, no. 6 (2010); "Is the Law Hopeful?" in *Hope in the Economy*, ed. Hirokazu Miyazaki and Richard Swedberg (forthcoming); "Comparative Law and Socio-legal Studies," *Oxford Handbook of Comparative Law*, ed. Reinhardt Zimmerman and Mathias Reimann (Oxford: Oxford University Press, 2006), 775–814; "A

New Agenda for the Cultural Study of Law: Taking on the Technical-ities," *Buffalo L Rev* 53 (2005): 973–1033; "Property as Legal Knowl-edge: Means and Ends," *Journal of the Royal Anthropological Institute*; "Real Time: Unwinding Technocratic and Anthropological Knowledge," *American Ethnologist* 31, no. 3 (2004): 1–14.

Private Governance, Global Markets, and the Legal Technologies of Collateral

Everywhere one turns today industry experts, government officials, and members of the media are decrying the weak legal, analytical, and ethical foundations of the global swap markets. But if swaps are seen as economically irrational, financially dangerous, and prone to ethical abuse, another dimension of the same market has emerged as solid, respected, and even morally and ethically empowered, what George Soros recently referred to as "motherhood and apple pie" (Soros 2009). That element is collateral. Collateral seems to have survived the tectonic shifts in market ideologies of the last few years with its reputation intact when so much else of what once was unquestionable dogma—free markets, self-regulation, the innate brilliance and rationality of derivatives traders—now seems like a quaint mythology from a strange other world.

At first glance, it is an unlikely winner of popularity contests. Collateral rather is a technical little sideline item, something on the margins, tangential . . . *collateral*. An early treatise defines it as both a technical matter of arcane property law, and as something of an afterthought in market practice:

> "Collateral security" is a separate obligation, as the negotiable bill of exchange or promissory note of a third person, or document of title, or other representative of value, endorsed where necessary, and delivered by a debtor to his creditor, to secure the payment of his own obligation, represented by

an independent instrument. Such collateral security stands by the side of the principal promise as an additional or cumulative means for securing the payment of the debt. . . . "Collateral," in the commercial sense of the word, is a security given in addition to a principal obligation, and subsidiary thereto. (Colebrooke 1883, 2–3)

And yet, I will suggest in this book that as a motif collateral tells us much about what law is like in global markets. In recent years, social theorists have advanced important critiques of the global spread of the neoliberal political and antiregulatory agenda and its relationship to late modern forms of global capitalism epitomized by the financial markets (Comaroff and Comaroff 2001). What is often overlooked in these debates is that the global spread of neoliberalism is, at its most concrete, usually a set of legal practices: the global diffusion of particular legal models that embody free-market ideals (Graziadei 2006). Often these reforms come in standardized packages promoted by international financial institutions, as when international lending institutions impose on many developing countries a standard law reform menu of new property rights regimes, new bankruptcy laws, and new corporation and labor laws as a condition of borrowing. But equally often, powerful global industry associations promote law reform projects central to their interests in multiple jurisdictions around the world. In all these concrete moments of neoliberal reform, law is itself collateral—on the sidelines, somewhat of an afterthought. Its style at first glance is more staid and buttoned down than flashy and innovative—and yet in moments of crisis one begins to see its sustaining role, from the margins of the market. So maybe tracing all that happens, all that is produced, and debated, and wished for and lost, under the banner of "collateral" can give us a new appreciation for how legal thought shapes markets. Maybe also, as an ambassador from that old discredited world of unfettered free marketeering, it can help us to understand private market governance in more subtle ways, beyond either dogmatic devotion or dogmatic denunciation.

Over-the-counter (OTC) derivatives trading is a form of trading, generally limited to large financial institutions, in which market participants enter into agreements to make an exchange, or "swap"—one currency for another, for example—at some future date. They do this in order to "hedge" against a certain kind of risk—for example, the risk of fluctuating exchange rates—or to "speculate" on such fluctuations.[1] The number of participants in these markets—mostly financial institutions and investment entities such as hedge funds—is still limited given the remarkable underlying value of the transactions, although it has been slowly but steadily increasing in recent years.[2] In the textbook definition, a swap transaction is a private contract between two banks to exchange one kind of asset for another at a future date. But there is always a risk—a so-called credit risk—that before the swap date one's counterparty could go bankrupt. In order to guard against this risk, swap counterparties routinely require one another to post collateral until the swap date.[3] It was collateral calls by counterparties in the swaps markets (calls to add to existing collateral because either the value of the collateral or the underlying swap, or the financial stability of the party that posted the collateral, had declined) that brought the insurance giant AIG to its knees in a cycle in which the downgrading of its credit rating led to collateral calls by counterparties, which in turn required AIG to borrow money, which led to further downgrading and more collateral calls (*Financial Times* 2009). A substantial portion of the public funds injected into AIG went to satisfy those counterparties' collateral calls. The global swap industry's core collective reform proposal in response to the financial crisis has been to call for greater collateralization of swap transactions and better accounting for collateral (*Wall Street Journal* 2009). From the industry's point of view, collateral—greater collateralization—is explicitly viewed as the *private market–based alternative to greater governmental regulation* (Counterparty Risk Management Policy Group II 2005, 15, 53–56; ISDA 2010a, 2010b).

And so one might expect that those who favor greater governmental regulation of the financial markets would in turn be suspicious of arguments about the security and stability of collateral. But despite a few lone attempts to reframe the use of AIG bailout funds for collateral calls as an "indirect bailout" to U.S. and foreign counterparties, the issue failed to gain the currency of the bonuses question, for example. Government regulators themselves remain clearly committed to what Larry Summers termed "the rule of law"—enabling the parties to meet their collateral obligations—as a key foundation of financial stability (Andrews and Baker 2009). The U.S. Treasury Department likewise has embraced the increased use of collateral as a key pillar of its "framework for regulatory reform" (U.S. Department of Treasury 2009).

What is interesting about this debate, from a lawyer's point of view, is why such absolute arguments about the enforceability of collateral contracts would be accepted at face value by both the market participants and the public at large—even when some market participants and some segments of the public would have tremendous financial or political interests in generating counterarguments. To begin with market participants: in the AIG case, at least as reported in the press, there were significant negotiations between AIG and its counterparties (such as Goldman Sachs) about the *valuation* of the AIG collateral the counterparties already held and hence the amount of additional collateral that AIG should be required to post (Morgenson and Story 2010; O'Harrow and Dennis 2008). But press reports suggest no debate among AIG and its counterparties about the *legal question*: the question of whether AIG was really obligated to respond to its counterparties' collateral call by posting further collateral in the first place. This was taken as simply a background rule of the game, and one that could not be challenged or opened up for negotiation (as could the *financial questions* of the value of collateral). And the same can be said of the wider public debate: while there was much discussion even of whether employment contracts to pay bonuses to AIG employees could be abrogated or modified, there was surprisingly little public debate about whether AIG could legally renege on its obligations to pay out the much larger sums involved in collateral calls.

In other words, collateral, as a private technology of regulation, has emerged as a quiet nexus of tremendous political and economic *legitimacy*—within the market, the government, and the wider political sphere—at a moment at which both markets and their regulation are facing a dramatic legitimacy deficit internally and externally. And if all other aspects of the financial industry seem to be shrinking, the collateral management industry is enjoying growth rates of around 40% in the past few years (Crosman 2008) as banks add staff, develop new technologies, and pay ever greater attention to collateral.

In legal and economic theory, likewise, writers who have championed collateral as a tool of private legal governance and highlighted the excesses and antinomies of bureaucratic planning have enjoyed rhetorical success. Take, for instance, one of the theorists of markets who has garnered the most attention among legal scholars and policymakers over the last ten years, Friedrich Hayek. Hayek portrays the private sphere as an ethically empowered zone of individual freedom, in which the interests of the general welfare are also maximized: "In a free society the general good consists principally in the facilitation of the pursuit of unknown individual purposes" (Hayek 1976b, 1). Hayek's passionate arguments about the fundamental incapacity of state planning to do as well as the market, and also his belief that "the rule of law excludes state action of the kind variously called 'economic planning,' *'dirigisme,'* or 'interventionism'" (Shenfield 1961, 55) but rather is a set of devices for bolstering private rights (Hayek 1975), has echoed throughout the political culture of the last two decades.

Likewise, in *The Mystery of Capital: Why Capitalism Triumphs in the West and Fails Everywhere Else* (2000), another book that has profoundly shaped legal and policy debates, Hernando De Soto presents an account of the rise of capitalism that has proven to have profound appeal from Sao Paolo to Washington, from the academy to the offices of the IMF. What explains a society's economic ascent from third- to first-world status, De Soto argues, is not colonial history, politics, culture, or the availability of natural resources, but rather property rights:

> The poor inhabitants of [third world and former communist] nations—five-sixths of humanity—do have things, but they lack the process to represent their property and create capital. They have houses but not titles; crops but not deeds; businesses but not statutes of incorporation. It is the unavailability of these essential representations that explains why people who have adapted every other Western invention, from the paper clip to the nuclear reactor, have not been able to produce sufficient capital to make their domestic capitalism work. (6–7)

Specifically, the secret to development lies in the legal unlocking of the transformative power of collateral: When property is registered, it can be easily transferred. And when property can be transferred it can also be posted as collateral in order to secure credit. Credit, in turn, is the precondition of economic growth. De Soto's celebration of the transformative power of collateral has become an important argument for treating the security of property rights as the central element of economic and legal development projects around the world. De Soto echoes here an argument that reverberates through the policy papers of international financial institutions and the academic writings of financial law specialists. In the culmination of a major Asian Development Bank–funded project, for example, Katharina Pistor and Philip Wellons emphasize that

The "invention of credit" has been hailed as a precondition for capitalism. Credit is an essential link between savings and investment. It helps allocate resources to productive use. Substantial evidence justifies our assumption that the level of lending is important for development. (1998, 153)

They quote from the 1989 World Bank Development Report:

The assignment and transferability of property rights promote economic efficiency directly by creating new incentives, but also indirectly by making financial intermediation possible. They do this by allowing borrowers to offer security in the form of mortgages over real estate or other collateral. (154)

Such calls for the establishment of what De Soto terms "Western systems of property registration" around the world, so that title to property will be easily discernible and hence marketable, is only one episode in the most recent drive to "transplant" (Watson 1993) legal technologies from certain first-world states (especially the United States, the United Kingdom, and the European Union) elsewhere. If these seem somewhat far afield from the derivatives markets, note that De Soto has recently once again captured the headlines with the suggestion that financial regulatory reform has much to learn from collateral law reform in the developing world. Financial crises could be avoided, he argues, if there were greater "transparency" in property rights in the derivatives markets—if title were more clearly recorded and collateral rights were more secure (De Soto 2009).

De Soto's claims are hardly new. In fact, for more than a century these arguments have been an active site of encounter between the disciplines of anthropology and law. Take, for example, the work of one John H. Wigmore, American law professor and leading figure in the development of American comparative law. In 1897 Wigmore, just back from several years in Japan where he developed his argument, wrote the first article in comparative law to appear in a major American law journal, "The Pledge Idea: A Study in Comparative Legal Ideas," published in two parts in the *Harvard Law Review*. Drawing on ethnology, ethnography, travelers' chronicles of distant lands, archeology, phonology, and more, the article traces the evolution of modern markets from "primitive" systems of barter to the legal institution of collateral and accompanying creditors' rights. The argument of Wigmore's celebrated text is essentially identical to De Soto's: it is the development of modern legal institutions surrounding collateral that account for economic development and, hence, the growth of civilization. Working from the evolutionary perspective of his day, Wigmore surveys the history of the legal institutions of the world to show how the progressive societies evolved modern sophisticated legal systems for pledging, receiving, and repledging collateral. The point for Wigmore, as for De Soto, is clear: collateral is the foundation of the market, the core of private law, and even the bedrock of the modern way of life. Through Wigmore's own text, of course, collateral also becomes the foundation of the American tradition of comparative law.

As a legal matter, collateral is a complex little doctrinal package. In the United States, it is primarily a matter of the law of secured transactions (U.S. Uniform Commercial Code) although it still bears the imprint of its history as property (chapter 2). In Japan it is a matter of the Civil Code law of obligations and property. Since it so often involves international transactions, Private International Law (or Conflict of Laws, in the United States) is highly relevant. And it is subject to an overlay of a panoply of statutory regimes including bankruptcy law, specialized laws governing derivatives transactions in Japan, and also administrative regulation by agencies, central banks, departments, and ministries responsible for financial supervision.

In the simple technology of *collateral*, this nexus of paper documents, legal theories, legal experts, clerical staff, computer technologies, statutes, and court decisions, then, are encapsulated some very grand hopes. As a transplanted legal technology, collateralization is paradigmatic of global private law solutions. Although collateral is rooted in multiple bodies of national law, it is also a device for running an end-game around certain aspects of national law, such as national bankruptcy codes.[4] It is designed to be in the first instance a tool of self-help. It also is intended to serve as a blueprint for a relationship, what I will call a "private constitution" (chapter 4).

This talk of legal transplants, of development projects aimed at bringing about the rule of law, and the wider concern with the protection of property rights we see in so many places around the world today in turn constitute a larger trend in global governance. Over the last two decades, global governance has increasingly become private governance—regulation through technical legal devices that take power out of the hands of public entities and put it in the hands of private individuals, corporations, armies. Private dispute-resolution regimes, such as arbitration tribunals run by the parties, outside the authority of any state, now adjudicate the bulk of conflicts in certain sectors of the global economy, from oil to finance, and increasingly labor disputes, environmental disputes, and other areas as well.

What is interesting is that these projects most recently tend to trade the language of economics for the language of law: gone in De Soto's account are the buzzwords of neoliberal economics now so tainted by decades of protests by third world nongovernmental organizations against IMF-imposed restructuring programs and discredited quantitative economic analyses purporting to show that all was well inside global financial institutions. In the place of talk of "rational actors" and "incentive systems," or at least in addition to these, one now most often hears talk—on both the right and the left—of "accountability," "transparency," and "the rule of law." Property's positive effects, De Soto tells us, include "transforming people with property interests into accountable individuals" and "networking people" (2000, 54, 58).

With the turn to the private, in other words, we are observing also a turn away from concerns with politics, history, and economy, toward *legal technology*: Property in De Soto's theory of economic development is *a tool* of empowerment, a weapon that can be placed in the hands of the weak as much as the strong, a neutral *instrument* that can be used by anyone, for any purpose. "Law is the instrument that fixes and realizes capital" (2000, 157). The idea that law—private law—can serve as a neutral umpire, a way out of intractable political conflicts between rich and poor, right and left, colonialists and colonized, has succeeded in capturing the fantasies and hopes of a good deal of the world. A marker of the success of the argument is that even arguments against specific legal reforms must now be framed in the language of private property rights, transparency, and accountability. NGOs opposing the expansion of intellectual property rights, or the conversion of indigenous knowledge into titular property, for example, must make arguments in the very same discourse of property rights about the creative possibilities of the "commons" (Flitner 1998).

This resurgence of interest in the private may catch both legal and sociolegal scholars off-guard. It is commonplace to treat the doctrinal distinction between public and private as at once logically incoherent and a mask for various forms of inequality, from gender inequality to the unequal market power of labor and capital.[5] But what is perhaps most intriguing of all is the way the technical legal instruments that accomplish this magic somehow fade into the background of such debates. The enthusiasm for legal transplants among policymakers and development organizations rests on the kind of faith expressed by De Soto that all that is necessary, in order to bring about progress, is a technical tweaking of the legal machinery, a new technocratic system (such as land registration) here, a new law (such as a constitutional provision protecting private property from state encroachment) there. What is often missed is that such claims for privatization are also always claims for technocracy, as in De Soto's advocacy of a state-run property registration system as the solution to the world's development problems (2000).

From this perspective, simple arguments for or against government regulation or private property rights largely miss the mark. There is remarkably little sophisticated critical conversation about the global proliferation and standardization of the technical legal forms themselves that make up an institution such as collateral. That is, if the scope of private property rights ignites broad theoretical debates, the workings of collateral remain in the realm of the "technical"—something somehow outside the conversation, something that does not ignite the passions of academics or NGOs. To make matters even more interesting, the claims of proponents of the private such as De Soto are themselves rife with contradictions of their own: Hayek and his followers championed private law precisely as a respite from technocratic interventionism, an alternative to the inherent limitations of technical reasoning. Yet today it is increasingly argued that it is through the very technical apparatus of the interventionist state that a sphere of private autonomy independent of the same state can be carved out. The new private law is as theoretically and politically confusing for its proponents, it seems, as for its would-be critics and observers.

A Window on Global Financial Governance

Now, these dimensions of collateral alone suggest that it is more normatively laden, more potentially contentious, than its humdrum back-office image would suggest. And indeed, some legal scholars have begun to draw this politics out into the wider debate in important and inspiring ways (Warren and Westbrook 2005, 1197; Edwards and Morrison 2005, 92). My own aim is a bit different: Precisely because collateral is paradigmatic of private regulatory solutions in the financial markets, in this

book I seize on the broad range of concrete legal, institutional, and social practices surrounding the maintenance of collateral relations as a
kind of motif, or lens through which to ask more foundational questions
about the character of governance in the global markets—as an activity that enrolls and implicates a wide range of actors and institutions in
large and small ways, from back-office staff, clerks, executives, lawyers,
government regulators, academics serving as consultants to government
and industry, and international industry organizations. In other words,
I suggest that if one approaches regulatory debates from the standpoint
of the deceptively naïve question, "what is collateral, really, in the derivatives markets?" one begins to grasp a view of regulation as something
very different, neither inherently private nor public, neither inherently
global nor local. Global financial governance is also, I argue, *a set of
routinized but highly compartmentalized knowledge practices, many of
which have a technical legal character.* I explain more fully what I mean
by "technical" and "legal" at the close of chapter 1.

In this book, what I wish to do, therefore, is to take advantage of the
controversies surrounding the private, to exploit the contradictions it
seems to generate in commitments and theoretical positions on all sides,
as a way into the contemporary political condition. I will pursue the nature of legal thought through a study of one concrete case, albeit one that
is already, by its own reckoning, global in scope—the global financial derivatives markets, as they are encountered in Tokyo, and the legal theories, legal techniques, and regulatory practices that sustain those markets
in Japan, but also in the elite law schools of the United States and Japan,
and in the meetings of financial industry groups, bureaucrats, and bankers around the world. As many commentators have pointed out, in addition to the inherent scholarly value of understanding Japanese law and
markets, there are deep similarities between the financial crisis Japan
faced at the time of my field research and the challenges it posed for regulators, and current conditions in the United States (Shirakawa 2009a).

My account focuses both on the high priests and the foot soldiers in
the campaign for the global standardization of collateral rights and practices. From the point of view of the foot soldiers, people referred to in the
financial business simply as the "the back office" or "the documentation
people," "collateral" is a set of practical problems associated with trading, and a set of mechanical, legal, institutional, and documentary technologies for resolving those problems, such as documents, legal opinions,
computer scientists, lawyers, government bureaucrats, and theoretical ac-

ademic work. From the point of view of the high priests—law professors at elite universities around the world, bureaucrats in ministries charged with regulating the financial markets, officials at the central banks and finance ministries of the leading economic powers, legislators, and policymakers—collateral is a matter of high theoretical complexity, a set of problems and puzzles for great minds to solve.

Why an Anthropology of Global Markets Governance?

In order to see new regulatory possibilities, we need new ways of understanding markets alongside and in addition to the dominant approaches of the last twenty years. The starting premise of an anthropological approach is that markets are not abstract machines to be reduced to a few equations or theorems, but messy contexts, full of contradictory forces and elements, actors, languages, institutions, ways of living and knowing. Markets are made up of much more than finance, for example—they are assemblages of many forms of expertise and many kinds of technology. One of these is law, or legal knowledge. And as the example of collateral suggests, legal knowledge turns out to be particularly resilient in times of crisis. It has not suffered the crisis of legitimacy that surrounds, for example, quantitative modeling of financial risk on the one hand or government fiscal policy on the other. Thus, it is particularly important to understand the workings of legal knowledge in the market as a way of grasping what holds together when all else collapses.

My method is ethnographic, the method traditionally deployed by anthropologists to understand socially significant genres of knowledge and action (Geertz 1973, 3–10). The core element of ethnography of course is fieldwork—a sustained and engaged form of study based on relations of trust with one's subjects, often over long periods of time (for my own view of what makes for effective ethnography see Riles 2006b). This kind of research necessarily produces what Clifford Geertz called the "ant's eye view" rather than the "bird's eye view" (1973, 23).

So a question that colleagues trained in other disciplines often have about such research is, how does an ethnographer know she has it right? First, I am beholden to constant feedback and criticisms from my many contacts in the market and the bodies that regulate them. When they think I get it wrong, they are not at all shy about letting me know. Sometimes I accept their criticism and revise my claims, and at other times I understand it as a legitimate reflection of their perspective, from where they stand—further data, and valuable at that. Second, an accurate and insightful ethnographic account will resonate for others with knowledge of comparable communities and institutions elsewhere, and will inspire others to ask similar questions that build toward generalization.

For example, when I read Doug Holmes's ethnographic account of the activities of central bankers in New Zealand (2009), there is much that is *suggestive* to me about what I have learned from Japanese central bankers. The two accounts confirm one another, even if there are (interesting) differences, too. More important, Holmes's account helps me to notice something about my own data I had not noticed before. And this is not all that surprising—Holmes's informants and mine share similar educations and similar training, they attend the same conferences and meetings and read the same journals; they share more with one another, in fact, than they share with many people in their own societies.

Thinking comparatively helps us to realize how events in one place are not nearly as different and disconnected from events elsewhere as one might think. In this book, I will move back and forth frequently between events in the United States and events in Japan. This project did not start out this way. It was initially a project "about Japanese markets." But I quickly confronted the fact that "Japanese" markets, and the people who populate them, are inextricably linked with markets, and theories, and institutions, and people elsewhere. Some examples: to my horror, at a presentation of early research findings in Chicago, an economist with no particular connection to Japan raised his hand and identified one of my key informants by name (thus violating my promise of confidentiality). The two were personal friends dating to the time when my Japanese informant had lived in Chicago, and my description left no doubt in the Chicago economist's mind of whom I was describing. Likewise, an interview with a market participant in Tokyo took a surprising turn when the interviewee suddenly asked detailed questions about a recent vote of the faculty where I was teaching at the time, of interest to him simply as a matter of keeping up with the gossip. Or, regulators and market participants routinely described how they had borrowed models for their activities from the United States. Or again, the latest fashion in regulatory governance studies in the United States borrows its ideas explicitly and directly from practices in the Japanese markets. This is not to say that there are no differences between Japan and the United States, of course. But it is to suggest that markets and societies are not billiard balls—they are already interpenetrating and inter-connected in myriad ways. This means that events in one place—say, debates in American legal theory—can be usefully placed side by side with events somewhere else—say, collateral protocols in Tokyo. Indeed, my informants/colleagues in both worlds were already doing so.

Some readers may still wonder, however, how much the specific cases I describe can tell us about markets generally. I suppose most ethnographers would respond that if they must make a choice, they would choose to say something interesting and surprising about something, to get close enough to let the facts truly shake them of their own assumptions. Another way to put it is that we are aiming here to open up new questions, questions that we hope others with knowledge of markets elsewhere can take up in turn, as much as to nail down ultimate universal answers. Or, as one executive at a large computer company recently said to me, in explaining why her innovation team had moved from hiring quantitative researchers looking at aggregates to hiring ethnographers to study market trends, "I realized that what I needed was not data, but insight."

I believe ethnography is a crucial method for the study of finance where actors are guarded, have particular expertise in subverting the logic of standardized tests and questionnaires, and are quite skilled at producing stylized and glossy accounts of their activities for outside consumption. Ethnography is a useful method for another reason as well. An anthropologist specializes in understanding what is so important, so fundamental, so much a part of the taken-for-granted agreed bases of social life that from the point of view of one's subjects it goes largely unnoticed. If the actors could simply tell you about the symbolic structures underlying their kinship, for example, you wouldn't need ethnography; you could simply conduct a telephone survey. It is the same with legal devices. There are aspects of the lawyer's own instrumentalist knowledge practices that remain woefully misunderstood, underappreciated even, by the lawyer him- or herself. By the end of this inquiry, therefore, I hope to show theorists and practitioners in the law that this given and commonsense dimension of their life work is in fact doing far more work than they could possibly imagine, and that legal expertise is an ensemble of far more nuanced and fine-grained pattern of theories and practices than they acknowledge to themselves.

In the twelve years I have been studying legal reasoning in the global financial markets, I have adapted the ethnographic method as necessary to the particularities of research on global finance. Because my subjects think through the law, for example, I have found it necessary to combine ethnographic description with legal analysis at numerous points. But I have maintained what I believe to be the core elements of the ethnographic method: a long-term commitment to research based on intensive and ongoing relationships with informants, a mix of participant observation and open-ended interviews.[6]

In the last five years, the ethnography of financial markets has blossomed into a serious, rich, and diversified research field. Ethnographers have drawn attention to the practices, rituals, beliefs, and political motivations of the people who self-consciously create and maintain the institutions that engender the market (Ho 2009). They have described the sociology of market institutions that allow markets to come into being (Callon 1998a, 244–69; Callon 1998b, 1–57; Carruthers and Stinchcombe 1999, 353; Leyshon and Thrift 1997). Increasingly, this work engages with a subfield, the anthropology and sociology of knowledge, in order to understand the nature of expert knowledge in the market (Holmes and Marcus 2005; Knorr-Cetina and Bruegger 2002; Maurer 2005b; Miyazaki 2003).

In this tradition, this book will not address the question of whether swaps are good or bad, or how much regulation of the swap markets there should be. In fact, the premise of the book is that the quantitative metric deployed by all sides in the policy debate—how much government regulation is enough, how much is too much—misses what is most interesting and perhaps most important to understand about regulatory governance, that is, its qualitative features. The project of the book is to ask, what are the qualities of particular aspects of legal knowledge that give it resilience, and legitimacy, in particular contexts? The project makes a case for a more careful understanding of the many unnoticed aspects of the rule of law. This book presents a new theory of law and markets, then, but it is purposely "theory close to the ground"—it builds up its analytical categories at close proximity to those of market and regulatory practice and it does so inductively rather than deductively.

Legal Technicalities from a Sociolegal Point of View

My own research started as a project about "regulators"—assuming that regulation was something that happened in government ministries and central banks. But following the actors and focusing on what was important to them eventually led me to see that the boundaries of the "market" and the "regulatory state," as defined in legal studies and accompanying disciplines, are far less clear, that "regulation," better understood as governance,[7] happens in the most unexpected settings: a secretary's cubicle, a law professor's classroom, a meeting of classmates over dinner, the exchange of standardized e-mails over the Internet. My fieldwork focuses not on the traders and fund managers themselves, but on those who self-consciously stand on the legal sidelines, collateral to the financial transaction so to speak—the self-styled architects and sanitation workers of the market. These include the bureaucrats and legal scholars working on financial problems, but also the lawyers within the banks who serve as handmaidens to the traders, "papering the deals," as they say of their work of handling the documentation for swap transactions, and who also collaborate with regulators and academics on "legal reform" projects.

If derivatives may be somewhat far afield from the average reader's experience of law, there is little that is unique about the legal devices and solutions I explore in this book. This is important: I aim to show that when we look at the sites of exotic, new forms of private governance, what we actually find are quotidian, humdrum legal knowledge practices. What we find then is the instantiation of a wider phenomenon, the workings of legal knowledge as a technique of private governance.

My focus on the legal technicalities of private law, as an ethnographic subject in its own right, admittedly runs counter to a powerful trend in sociolegal studies. Sociolegal scholars have long assumed a certain "outsider" perspective on the law (Riles 1994). Until quite recently, sociolegal scholars often self-consciously sought to describe legal institutions from the perspective of the "trenches" rather than the "ivory towers," from the perspective of "law in action" rather than "law in the books" (Pound 1911), to "decenter" law through a focus on norms rather than rules.

On the whole, these scholars have shared a commitment to *critiquing* the hierarchies and inequalities law produced, to describing "how the legitimacy of law is maintained" (Dezalay and Garth 1995, 29), and to drawing attention to social justice issues that they felt were ignored in mainstream legal scholarship. From this perspective, the kind of private law doctrines and practices discussed in this book might hold little inherent interest, as compared to welfare law, labor law, immigration law, and the like—except insofar as one might wish to expose the ideological bias implicit in the notion of a "private" sphere of law in which individuals freely order their affairs unfettered by state action.

As we will see, the legal actors I have studied certainly hold out no fantasy that private law is a sphere free of government intervention; on the contrary, they seek the government's intervention and support at every turn, and they worry about the harm the wrong kinds of governmental interventions might cause them. More important, this critical vision of the sociolegal project has translated into relatively little empirical interest in the character of expert legal knowledge itself. Lawrence Friedman's characterization of the state of the field a generation ago largely still holds today: "Legalism, as a social phenomenon, has been more excoriated than studied. Indeed, neglect has been the destiny of legal reasoning generally, at least from the sociological standpoint" (Friedman 1966, 149).

If social scientists focusing on law have not always given market regulation its due attention, economic sociologists, working from the point of view of an understanding of markets, have repeatedly demonstrated that "markets are not pre-given and exogenous to regulation but rather constituted by regulation, states, and non-state governance" (Schneiberg and Bartley 2010, 285).[8] This has spawned a rich conversation between the subdisciplines of economic sociology and legal sociology about how legal norms shape, but are, in turn, also shaped by market practice (Suchman and Edelman 1996, 905).

From a different disciplinary direction, the behavioral economics of regulation has given us a more complex account of actors' motivations and their implications for regulatory regimes than the standard neoclassical economic model. The suggestion is to supplement economic analysis by filling in the interstices of the rational actor model with accounts of how preferences are created or how cognitive sources of human error explain deviations from the neoclassical model of the rational actor (Jolls, Sunstein, and Thaler 1998; Langevoort 1996; Sunstein 2000, 2003). For example, economists Akerlof and Shiller propose replacing the rational actor model with a view of the economy as populated by "animal spirits":

> Such a world of animal spirits gives the government an opportunity to step in. Its role is to set the conditions in which our animal spirits can be harnessed creatively to serve the greater good. Government must set the rules of the game. . . . Indeed, if we thought that people were totally rational, and that

they acted almost entirely out of economic motives, we too would believe that government should play little role in the regulation of financial markets. . . . But on the contrary, all those animal spirits tend to drive the economy sometimes one way and sometimes another. Without intervention by the government the economy will suffer massive swings in employment. And financial markets will, from time to time, fall into chaos. (2009, 173)

This argument is important, but it is not new. It repeats a longstanding "substantivist" critique of the rational actor model in economic anthropology.[9]

One body of sociolegal work that bridges traditional sociolegal subjects and the kind of phenomena treated in this book concerns the globalization of the legal profession, the effects of globalization on national and local regulatory practices, the disparate social and economic consequences of regulatory structures, and the way transnational or global economic and legal forms are accommodated, resisted, or translated locally. Studies of immigration policies have tracked the legal instantiation of tensions between state interests in excluding migrants from the citizenry and the polity and incorporating migrant labor into the market (Calavita 1998; Coutin 2005). Likewise, sociolegal studies of the disparate effects of free trade regimes such as NAFTA show how reconfigurations of state sovereignty through international agreements, and with these the mundane harmonization of environmental, labor, shipping, packaging and other laws they demand, generate new kinds of difference—new forms of gender inequality, new militarization of borders, new spatial divisions of labor (Buchanan 1994–95).

As more research is done in this area, it is becoming increasingly clear that the old dichotomy between law in the books and law in action, between state-administered rules and society-governed norms, does not do justice to the phenomena at hand. Hence, to define sociolegal studies merely as the critique of rules from the point of view of norms is to seriously limit the discipline's potential (Silbey 2005). As Gunther Teubner (1997) points out, much formal lawmaking takes place without the threat of state-backed coercion, and as Yves Dezalay and Bryant Garth (1996) show, global actors who characterize the world of "law in action" take the indeterminate boundary between state and nonstate mechanisms for granted as a starting assumption (and opportunity) in constructing their own field of action.

Increasingly, therefore, sociolegal studies is no longer confined solely to the "trenches"—it also takes on the "towers." Moreover, there is a marked reflexivity in the work of scholars like Garth and Dezalay: they are quite aware that sociolegal scholars are part of the story, not simply outside critics—that their own work is not just describing the field of international arbitration they write about, for example, but helping to legitimize it. But the sociological hook of these studies—what in their own conception differentiates them from legal scholarship—is that they find something akin to the "social" in the towers of modern law: For Dezalay and Garth (2002), for example, legal knowledge is not so much interesting for its own sake, but as a function of social forces—power politics, competition between different individuals and groups, social hierarchies within legal institutions.

In thinking about how sociolegal studies might take on Lawrence Friedman's challenge of a generation ago and truly study legalism as a cultural phenomenon in its own right, rather than as a mere function of social, political, and economic forces, we can draw inspiration from several analogous projects in related fields. One first source of engagement might be sociologically inspired work in comparative law that has sought to describe legal knowledge as something more, or other, than a function of social forces. Teubner, for example, treats law as a form of self-reflexive communication feedback. Teubner shares with Dezalay and Garth a view of law as what legal actors say it is. However, building on the sociology of Nicholas Luhmann, he treats law as a "discourse" rather than an instrument of individual strategy—a realm of communication and description of a particular form:

> The idiosyncrasies of the profession seem to be a secondary phenomenon. It is the inner logics of the legal discourse itself that builds on normative self-reference and recursivity and thus creates a preference for internal transfer within the global legal system. (Teubner 1998, 16)

Teubner's work brings even greater attention than the sociology of legal experts to the "reflexive" character of legal systems—to their capacity for building their own autonomy by observing and commenting on themselves (as in legal debates about legal process, for example). A second source of inspiration might be recent work in critical legal theory that moves beyond critiquing "the arrested development of legal thought" as a function of "the history of modern politics" (Unger 1996, 34) to carefully describing the experience of the legal actor, and the nature of the acts of judging, drafting contracts, or administering legal projects that characterize her work (Kennedy 2004; Kennedy 1997).

Most recently, a number of scholars seeking to understand the character of legal knowledge have drawn inspiration from debates about the character of scientific and technical knowledge in science and technology studies (STS). Building on his own work on the construction of scientific facts within laboratories, the sociologist of science Bruno Latour has sought to compare scientific fact-making with legal fact-making by engaging in an extensive empirical study of the French Conseil d'État (2002a). Like Teubner, Latour treats the law as a "mode of enunciation" but he is also interested in the material quality of this lawmaking—the mundane chains of documents, of drafts, of reports it takes to produce a judgment. His interest is in how social facts become calculable as a legal dispute through this internal process of producing chains of "inscriptions":

> For both lawyers and scientists, it is possible to speak confidently about the world only once it has been transformed—whether by the word of God, a mathematical code, a play of instruments, a host of predecessors, or by a natural or positive law." (2004, 96)

Likewise, Susan Silbey has explored the interaction between legal and scientific knowledge through a study of how a consent decree between the Environmental Protection Agency and an elite research university concerning environmental practices in the laboratory alters the practice, and even epistemological dimensions, of science. And Mariana Valverde brings paradigms from STS into conversation with a Foucauldian and Nietzschean perspective on the regulation of disorder to understand the relationship between so-called expert and common knowledge in mundane regulatory work such as a police officer's decision, backed by the courts, to close a strip bar or arrest a prostitute (Levi and Valverde 2001; Valverde 2003, 2005). Finally, John Hagan and Ron Levi's ethnographic fieldwork in international criminal law—focusing specifically on the Hague Tribunal for the former Yugoslavia—sheds light on the interaction between different forms of expertise (juridical, journalistic, forensic, and so on) in the formulation of both the authority of transnational law and the ontological "truth" of victimhood (Hagan 2003; Hagan and Levi 2005).

In all of these projects, legal knowledge and the process by which it comes to frame political, social, and epistemological conflicts is a central subject in its own right. Legal knowledge is treated as a phenomenon that is not simply reducible to social pressures and forces, but that has its own epistemological and material autonomy. This focus unhinges subjects such as international human rights, environmental law, and the rights of sexual minorities from an overdrawn and often predictable set of normative debates and allows us to see the questions as the products or effects of the interaction of certain kinds of agency (human and nonhuman), certain kinds of aesthetic practices, certain instruments, certain kinds of expertise. At the same time, it avoids the reification of law and instead allows us to appreciate law as part of a larger pattern of knowledge practices.

And these projects in turn dovetail with a wider interest in anthropology and cognate fields in cultures of expertise. One theme emerging from this work is the articulation, appropriation, and circulation of technical, academic, or artistic knowledge in commercial, bureaucratic, and professional contexts (Born 1995; Brenneis 1988; Holmes and Marcus 2005; Marcus and Myers 1995). It is becoming important to understand how constellations and genres of arguments are replicated and transposed from one domain of knowledge of the next—to understand the borrowings of arguments, doctrines, documents, and critiques that have defined the relationship between theorists and practitioners of different genres of expert knowledge.

In sympathy with this trend, therefore, I want to ask, what kind of knowledge proliferates as collateral becomes the global phenomenon envisaged by proponents of neoliberalism from Wigmore to De Soto? What is the character of this *collateral knowledge*—this knowledge that is self-consciously on the sidelines of market activity, something its practitioners present as of no particular political consequence or worry, and yet as sustaining the market, from the margins? What forms of governance does it bring into being? And what kinds of politics does it set into motion? Through the lens of knowledge practices surrounding collateral relations, I look at the triumph of private law as the self-professed basis of transnational governance, the infrastructure of global markets. That is, I focus on law as a larger practice of collateral knowledge, a sidelined, technical activity, a point of view that is crucial to and yet always self-consciously on the margins—collateral to, yet sustaining, the market itself.

Chapter Overview

Chapter 1, "What Is Collateral?" sets the stage by introducing the lawyers and the documents in the back offices of derivatives units of global
banks to consider what kind of knowledge and forms of subjectivity are
being produced under the guise of "collateral." The function of collateral is to hold back risk, which simply means to place limits on the indeterminacies associated with social, political, economic, and temporal
relations. How does collateral accomplish something so grand as this?
Collateral is sometimes a legal theory, sometimes a material object,
sometimes a person, and sometimes an institution (Latour 1990; Lynch
1993). In each case, however, collateral is what I term a set of routinized
knowledge practices. The chapter explores the role of these routinized
practices in resolving or at least obviating the complex political and epistemological questions that surround derivatives trading. But rather than
a smoothly oiled machine, collateral when seen from up close emerges as
an assembly of glitches, of mistranslations, misunderstandings, and redundancies. The chapter concludes with an explanation of the three core
terms of the book: *legal knowledge, legal technique*, and *technocracy*.

Chapter 2, "The Technocratic State," turns to the public side of legal knowledge practices—and in particular to how legal expertise is deployed within the regulatory state. The chapter builds on two examples
from different times and places—the American legal reforms that radically revised the law of collateral into the law of "secured transactions,"
and the initial stages of Japanese legal reforms aimed at resolving the
question of the legality under Japanese law of the derivatives market
practice known as "netting" (discussed further in chapter 5). On the one
hand, there are important similarities between public and private legal expertise. But there are also differences. Technocrats' concern with
making legal expertise *realistic* leads, on the one hand, to an emphasis
on mixing legal expertise with other forms of expertise, from economics
to ethnography, and on the other hand with a concern with technologies
of *collaboration* with market participants.

Over the last several decades, the knowledge practices described in
chapter 2 have become the target of a pervasive and sophisticated neoliberal critique. If early twentieth-century legal scholars put forward the
technocrat as the model subject—the judge, lawyer, and legal theorist
were to think of themselves as technocratic administrators, nothing less

and nothing more—the neoliberal reforms of the 1990s and 2000s were framed as an attack on the very same character of the technocrat. Chapter 3, "Unwinding Technocracy," gives an ethnographic account of one such episode of neoliberal revolt against the regulatory state and its consequences. Chapter 3 explores how this critique—originating in the academy, but picked up by politicians, journalists, and eventually by bureaucrats themselves—reframed the informal ways Japanese bureaucrats had long regulated the economy as "nontransparent" or even "corrupt," and how the target of such political claims became the person of the bureaucrat and his or her personal ethics. At the same time, parallel "reformist" projects attacked the legal subjectivity of the citizenry, who were described in government reports and the media again and again as having failed to take responsibility (*jiko sekinin*) for their legal rights and responsibilities, and again focused on remaking this subjectivity through an entirely new, American-style legal education system that would produce more professional lawyers who would encourage ordinary people to behave like rational legal actors. The buzzword here is *professionalization*, understood to entail a certain ethical commitment to pragmatic rationality, that is, thinking in terms of relations of means to ends.

In Japan in the 1990s and 2000s, the form the movement for deregulation within and without the bureaucracy took was very much a set of stock arguments borrowed from foreign (and mainly American) public choice analyses of political processes. As devoted students of capitalism, the bureaucrats I worked with saw the point of the critiques of their lack of transparency—but they also suffered the contradictions within capitalist expectations of regulators as able to intervene when necessary but also to leave the market to its own devices. This chapter describes their attempt to reconcile these contradictions in the technical design for a new clearing and settlement system for the Japanese market that would, ostensibly, take bureaucrats' own human agency out of the day-to-day administration of the market.

But we will see that the story is more complicated than it seems. For it was not that bureaucrat converts to public choice theory had accepted their assigned role as agents subservient to the legislature; rather, as a result of their adoption of economic tools of analysis they adopted a different set of *objectives* for their plans. Their newfound objective was to create a world in which people behave more like rational profit-maximizing individuals and less like the negative stereotypes of Japanese corporate employees. So a reform that was explicitly antitechnocratic turned out to enshrine a new, and arguably far more ambitious, role for the technocrat as the architect of new kinds of social relations and the father of new kinds of rational subjects. In the conclusion, I argue that many current proposals to reform the markets and their regulation, despite their cheerful modesty, make very much the same move.

Chapter 4 rounds out the discussion of private and public governance by considering how private legal technique might translate into new public governance methods. Since Friedrich Hayek, debates about the proper relationship between the state and the market, and about the optimal design of regulatory institutions, often turn on assumptions about the workings of legal expertise—and in particular about the difference between public expertise (bureaucratic knowledge) and private expertise (private law). Hayek's central argument, adopted uncritically by a wide array of policymakers and academics across the political spectrum, is a *temporal one*: bureaucratic reasoning is inherently one step *behind* the market, and hence effective market planning is impossible. In contrast, Hayek argues, private ordering is superior because it is of the moment, happening in real time.

Hayek's description of the limitations of bureaucratic planning resonates with the sense of powerlessness and frustration experienced by many government officials as they attempt to manage economic fluctuations. But Hayek's rich (and even empathetic) account of the limits of well-meaning public legal expertise is far less complete when it comes to the strengths of private legal reasoning. Public reasoning has temporal weaknesses, so private reasoning must have equivalent temporal strengths, the argument goes.

This chapter takes on Hayekian arguments against government regulation through a detailed examination of real-world examples of how public and private legal technologies manage the temporal dimensions of risk in the OTC derivatives markets. The specific examples are: the usage of collateral on the private law side, as presented in chapter 1, and the usage of "real-time gross settlement" payment-settlement systems on the public side, as presented in chapter 3. While there is no reason to believe that a public governance method is actually more effective than a private governance method (or vice-versa) as a stop-gap against future uncertainties in the market, there is nevertheless a kind of "Hayekian" perception, by market participants and government officials alike, that the private devices are more *legitimate* and that the experts who deploy these are more knowledgeable.

In order to understand the root of this legitimacy gap, the chapter considers how collateral, as a private legal technology, handles the temporal uncertainties surrounding market risk. At the heart of "collateral" is a deceptively mundane, but actually quite audacious legal trick called the legal fiction. In legal terms, a legal fiction is a statement that is consciously understood to be false, and hence is irrefutable. Collateral is actually just a set of legal fictions, layered one on top of another. I explain how these fictions—which are just as problematically related to market "realities" as government planning technologies—nevertheless come to be much more readily accepted predictors and, indeed, *creators* of market realities.

So does this mean that private regulation is inherently superior to public regulation? The fallacy of the Hayekian argument is the assumption that these "private" technologies can only be deployed by private actors. In fact, there is nothing inherently private or public about the legal fiction or other similar devices of private law. The chapter demonstrates this by showing how financial regulators in Japan redeployed the trick of the legal fiction and hence regained legitimacy in their own eyes and in the eyes of market participants.

Chapter 5 turns to another theme of the book, legal form. The chapter concerns one episode in the construction of the regulatory environment for global OTC derivatives trading in Japan, the drafting of a "netting law" to allow parties to net out all of their obligations to one another in the event of bankruptcy. This fairly obscure technical moment in regulatory reform, ignored almost entirely by academics, labor organizations, and the media, in fact had tremendous economic and political significance. The focus of the chapter is on the move from plans to solve the "netting problem" through a legal interpretation of existing law, to the drafting of an entirely new law with a very peculiar form—what I term a *hollow core*, that is, a law in which all the key terms, from whom it applies to, to what actions are permitted and what are sanctioned, are left to be filled in by bureaucrats at a later date. Although this new law was portrayed by its supporters as a departure from legalism in favor of a more economic approach to law, in line with the public choice approaches outlined in the previous chapter, I argue that in fact it exemplifies the subtle power and efficacy of legal aesthetics. This exemplar of transparency-in-the-making therefore provides a platform for considering understandings of legal form and its uses, including the ways the very embrace of globally transparent legal form may provide a kind of camouflage from the insatiable global demands for transparency itself.

From this point of view, chapter 5 suggests that we rethink the Realist legacy in sociolegal and legal studies and the policy proposals they have spawned—the notion that law should be made to conform to real-world conditions, that empirical research is valuable principally because it brings to the law a dose of the real world, that there is a kind of reality deficit in the law. My ethnography shows how the very point of a legal fiction such as collateral is to place limits on reality or, rather, to draw a line between legal forms of reality and other forms of reality. If one assumption in the post-Realist era is that there is nothing inherently unique about legal knowledge, as compared to bureaucratic managerialism, for example, this chapter, and the book as a whole, shows that what is unique about legal knowledge is its own claims to be unique, set apart, collateral. Projects that seek to debunk such claims (for example by showing that fictions are not unique to law, nor are documentation practices), or that seek to describe law in terms of social or economic realities (norms and practices rather than rules in the sociolegal vocabulary), can never capture the character of legal knowledge because their starting premise, their own faith-like commitment, is precisely the opposite to that of legal knowledge. Perhaps what we need in order to understand the generative power of the law in real-world sites like the financial markets, ironically, is less commitment to the Real. Law is out of touch with reality, as the critics routinely tell us, and that is precisely, if counterintuitively, its promise.

The concluding chapter focuses on the implications of the ethnography for current debates about financial regulatory reform. It pulls the real-world materials presented in the previous chapters together to consider their implications for the limits of existing ways of thinking about regulation and governance, and the possibilities for imagining alternatives. In this chapter I show how the techniques of private regulatory governance provide a little-noticed, less-glamorous, but ultimately highly effective and even potentially transformative alternative to most other current proposals to rebuild the "architecture" of global financial regulation.

Taken as a whole, the book offers a new way of thinking about markets and their regulation—a new set of metaphors for understanding the challenges of market governance and the promise as well as the limitations of law and regulation. My argument is that it is time for an alternative to both the free market mindset *and* the technocratic mindset in regulatory governance, and that the fictional quality of technical legal knowledge provides a model and a set of techniques for getting there.

The ultimate goal of this book is to shift the mood of crisis surrounding the regulation of the global financial system away from simple stories of good and bad apples, of villains and victims, cops and robbers, toward a more sophisticated public understanding of the techniques that make up private and public forms of governance. A greater understanding—among scholars, policymakers, and most of all the general public—of the moves, practices, rituals, aesthetics that constitute global private law is the only path to more sophisticated market governance. Ultimately, this book responds to the current environment of crisis and reform not by proposing an alternative toolbox for policymakers and other high priests of market regulation, but rather by seeking to democratize the understanding of the tools that constitute global public and private governance and to show how ordinary, mundane, day-to-day actions of market participants of all kinds can produce better—that is, more efficient and more just—forms of market regulation.

Notes

1. For a more complete explanation of the mechanics of OTC derivatives transactions tailored to humanists, see LiPuma and Lee 2004. For an introduction to the same material geared to lawyers see Romano 1996.

2. One indicia of the number of institutional participants in the swaps markets is the number of institutional members of ISDA, the International Swaps and Derivatives Association, a trade organization discussed further below. According to a report published in July 2010, there were 207 primary members of ISDA. http://www.isda.org/membership/isdamemberslist.pdf (accessed July 18, 2010).

3. According to ISDA, at the end of 2003, more than US$1 trillion in collateral was in circulation and approximately 50% of all privately negotiated derivatives transactions were collateralized (2005, iv, 9).

4. The rights of the collateral holder are a matter of national property, contract and commercial law. Likewise, the requirements for giving and taking collateral (for creating a security interest in U.S. parlance) are defined by local statutory and common law. In the individual states of the United States, collateral is understood as a species of commercial law enshrined and protected by statute—by the Uniform Commercial Code as adopted in each state.

5. As the introduction to one legal symposium on the subject puts it, "New Private Law reflects a normative regime that both recognizes a distinction between public and private domains and prefers the ordering of the private market to that of public decisionmakers. The preference for the 'private' seems, at a minimum, to tolerate inequality and, perhaps, to reify existing power hierarchies" (Nice 1995–96, 995).

At the same time, the symposium editor recognizes that this new private law does not easily fit into the categories left-leaning critics would roll out in their critiques of such phenomena: "Some of us were struck, however, by differences between New Private Law and these existing schools of thought. For example, New Private Law rejects Formalism's devotion to rules and categories. Unlike Law and Economics, it seems less concerned with efficiency and more concerned with whether an activity is conducted by the private sphere" (995–96).

6. Beginning with a small number of contacts, and using the "snow-ball method," I gradually expanded to a larger network, and also gradually came to become aware of certain key problems or issues in the market. Then, using those issues as case studies, I interviewed a large sample of the actors involved, participated in meetings, conferences, and strategy sessions where possible, socialized with those involved, and supplemented this with archival and legal research.

7. In using the term *governance*, I am purposely appropriating the "lingua franca of the political and business establishments" as analytical terminology of my own, rather than seeking vocabulary from outside as some other critical observers of modern politics have proposed doing (Walters 2004, 43; see also Rose 1999, quoted in Walters 2004). I do so, starting from a point of view that shares many of these criticisms (see the book conclusion). On the theoretical and methodological rationale for such a move, see Riles 2006b.

8. See also Balleisen 2009; Carruthers and Halliday 2000; and Carruthers, Babb, and Halliday 2001.

9. This literature would suggest that there might be a parallel project for anthropologists and other comparativists to analyze the nature of preferences and bounded rationalities in diverse cultural and economic contexts. Indeed, it has been acknowledged by public choice theorists that the public choice model is very much framed with an American political process in mind and that what is needed is further comparative work that would stretch and complexify the models as they are applied in other institutional, legal, and cultural contexts (Bishop 1997, 232). For key texts outlining the substantivist argument, see generally Sahlins 1972; Polanyi 1944, 1968; Bohannan and Bohannan 1968. For key texts outlining the formalist position, see generally Firth 1939; Goodfellow 1939; Herskovits 1952; and LeClair 1962.

CHAPTER ONE

What Is Collateral?

On Legal Technique

In the late 1990s, a visitor to a Japanese derivatives trading floor encountered a large open room full of metal desks and computer screens. At most of these desks, traders hunched over their computers or shouted into their telephones. As the traders entered into a swap with traders at another bank in New York or London, they scribbled the details of the trade onto a form, then tossed it into a basket at the edge of their desk.

But a few desks to one side were stacked high with documents and large quantities of paper. Periodically, the people working behind the stacks of documents collected the forms in the traders' baskets and returned to their desks. Within eyesight of the traders and the manager of the derivatives team, these "documentation people" "papered the trades," as people said. These workers produced confirmation agreements and then sent them to their counterparts at the other bank.

These confirmation documents adhered to a standard format, such that the documentation person's principal task was simply to complete the form, fax it, receive a similar fax from his or her counterpart at the other bank, and file it away. Occasionally, they would discover discrepancies—misunderstandings between the two parties over the terms, for example—and then would refer these back to the traders to resolve or contact their counterparts at the other bank to rectify the error.

Over-the-counter (OTC) derivative markets are intended to be the most private of financial markets. Unlike futures and options, swaps are not designed to be traded over an organized exchange.[1] The parties to a swap make their own rules, tailor their own contracts, and, above all, privately bear the full risk that one or another will not perform its obligations rather than placing their confidence in the exchange as an intermediary. Since securities regulation law was designed to regulate on-exchange activity, much swap trading has fallen between the regulatory cracks.[2] When disputes arise, therefore, often parties' only formal recourse is to bring a lawsuit in a domestic court under ordinary common or civil law claims such as breach of contract or fraud.[3] Since this is often impractical, the number of formal lawsuits arising out of swap transactions is remarkably low, given the notional amount of the transactions at issue. The effect is that the parties have relatively little recourse to state dispute resolution mechanisms to resolve their internal problems and hence as a practical matter their conduct is relatively unregulated by state-derived norms. And this is precisely the appeal of these markets, from participants' point of view.

When the documentation people were not at work completing and dispatching confirmation forms, they huddled behind piles of binders full of printed forms, dictionaries and pencils in hand, talking on the telephone with colleagues at other banks as they worked through the blanks in the forms. The most common printed form was a "Master Agreement" (International Swaps and Derivatives Association 2002)[4] providing the legal framework for all individual swap transactions between any two banks. It defines key practices, rights, and obligations, such as the use of confirmation documents, or the procedures for cashing out obligations in the event of the financial failure of one of the parties.

The form had been produced by representatives of important players in the swap markets, working together under the auspices of the International Swaps and Derivatives Association (ISDA). Founded in 1985, ISDA is a private organization of more than 800 OTC derivatives "dealers"—banks and securities firms that are repeat players ("dealers") in the privately negotiated derivatives industry, the market for derivatives that are not traded through an organized exchange[5] (ISDA 1993; Johnson 2000). The master agreement is one of ISDA's early and lasting achievements and the production of this and other standardized agreements is one of the principal functions of the association (ISDA 1999a, 2).

ISDA's documentation project explicitly seeks to address the particular legal problems emanating from the transnational character of the private derivatives markets such as the ambiguities surrounding choice of law, the differences in national laws governing property rights in collateral, and the complexities of transnational bankruptcy. The ISDA

ISDA®

International Swaps and Derivatives Association, Inc.

2002 MASTER AGREEMENT

dated as of ....

.... and ....

have entered and/or anticipate entering into one or more transactions (each a "Transaction") that are or will be governed by this 2002 Master Agreement, which includes the schedule (the "Schedule"), and the documents and other confirming evidence (each a "Confirmation") exchanged between the parties or otherwise effective for the purpose of confirming or evidencing those Transactions. This 2002 Master Agreement and the Schedule are together referred to as this "Master Agreement".

Accordingly, the parties agree as follows:—

1. Interpretation

(a) ***Definitions.*** The terms defined in Section 14 and elsewhere in this Master Agreement will have the meanings therein specified for the purpose of this Master Agreement.

(b) ***Inconsistency.*** In the event of any inconsistency between the provisions of the Schedule and the other provisions of this Master Agreement, the Schedule will prevail. In the event of any inconsistency between the provisions of any Confirmation and this Master Agreement, such Confirmation will prevail for the purpose of the relevant Transaction.

(c) ***Single Agreement.*** All Transactions are entered into in reliance on the fact that this Master Agreement and all Confirmations form a single agreement between the parties (collectively referred to as this "Agreement"), and the parties would not otherwise enter into any Transactions.

2. Obligations

(a) ***General Conditions.***

(i) Each party will make each payment or delivery specified in each Confirmation to be made by it, subject to the other provisions of this Agreement.

(ii) Payments under this Agreement will be made on the due date for value on that date in the place of the account specified in the relevant Confirmation or otherwise pursuant to this Agreement, in freely transferable funds and in the manner customary for payments in the required currency. Where settlement is by delivery (that is, other than by payment), such delivery will be made for receipt on the due date in the manner customary for the relevant obligation unless otherwise specified in the relevant Confirmation or elsewhere in this Agreement.

Copyright © 2002 by International Swaps and Derivatives Association, Inc.

FIGURE 1. First page of the ISDA Master Agreement. (Reprinted with the permission of the International Swaps and Derivatives Association [IDSA®] © 2002–2010 International Swaps and Derivatives Association.)

Master Agreement also details a set of global industry practices. For example, the ISDA documents contain a series of "definitions" of key terms, written by a committee of representatives of the world's largest swap dealers. These definitions are presented as the unified understanding of the market as a global whole. This project of elaborating sets of rights and obligations through the terms of standardized contracts aims to serve as a basis for global self-regulation.

The ISDA Master Agreement then represents a classic example of what commentators refer to when they speak of a new Lex Mercatoria (Berger 1999), a "private law governing cross-border transactions" "motivated by a strong desire by its proponents to free international transactions from the perceived shackles of national law" (Goode 2005, 539, 545). ISDA's objective in creating documents such as the Master Agreement and the Credit Support Annex (CSA) document (agreements between swap partners concerning the terms under which they would exchange collateral in the course of their swap transactions) is surely to avoid the regulatory authority of some states, at least, and to create binding obligations among its members that do not rely on a state for their authority or legitimacy. ISDA's actions typify what political scientists have in mind when they define a transnational private regime as "an integrated complex of formal and informal institutions that is a source of governance for an economic issue area as a whole" (Cutler, Haufler, and Porter 1999, 13). As Gunther Teubner observes it,

> The focus in law-making is shifting to private regimes, that is, to binding agreements among global players, to private market regulation through multinational enterprises, internal rule-making within international organizations, inter-organizational negotiating systems, and worldwide standardization processes. The dominant sources of law are now to be found at the peripheries of law, at the boundaries with other sectors of world society that are successfully engaging in regional competition with the existing centres of law-making—national parliaments, global legislative institutions and intergovernmental agreements. (2004a, 74)

Such global self-regulation, or global private law as it is known in legal parlance, is now the source of quite a bit of anxiety. Politicians and commentators on the current financial crisis routinely assert that the "unregulated" quality of the derivatives markets (e.g., Bowley 2010; Shiller 2010)—by which they mean unregulated by state law—was a crucial source of the financial crisis.

But if global private law is now often portrayed as largely a bad thing, over the last ten years legal scholars have also seen global private law as a major innovation in the nature of law itself, or at least as a very significant phenomenon in the history of legal development. So-called global private law regimes—private in the sense that they do not rely primarily on the legitimacy or the coercive power of the state for their authority—have fascinated legal theorists for whom the authority, legitimacy, and power of law has long been tethered to the state (Hall and Biersteker 2002). It was once thought that there could be no law without the coercive sanction of the state, and yet such regimes of self-regulation suggest the emergence of a kind of regulatory practice that is nevertheless "beyond the state" (Michaels and Jansen 2006). At the same time, legal theorists have noted that the special character of global private governance renders it particularly difficult for the state to regulate and hence calls for the development of new kinds of regulatory tools (Aman 2004).

But both the defenses and the critiques, both the stories of secrecy and corruption and the stories of innovation and progress, proceed at some distance from the concrete moments, practices, and individuals, like the ones described above, that actually constitute global private governance regimes. More specifically, these arguments for or against global private law stand on a set of anthropological assumptions or claims—assertions about what this private law actually is, from insiders' point of view, about how it is interpreted and experienced "in the real world," and indeed about what motivates the human beings that populate this world—which for the most part go unexamined, untheorized, and undefended empirically. In a nutshell, the pervasive story is this: the derivatives markets are a tribal world of secret customs and close-knit relationships in which actors conspire to develop their own private norms of conduct and to work out their problems among themselves, without appealing to the state, because doing so is in everyone's own best interest. Like all good stories, there is enough truth in this one to stick (Westbrook 2010). But it is also, at the very least, seriously incomplete in ways that have profound implications, both practical and theoretical.

In this chapter, I want to complicate the standard explanation for the authority of global private law that pervades both the utopic and the dystopic accounts—the view that practices of self-regulation work because they enshrine a set of private group *norms* (Hart 1961; Kelsen 1967). I do so by describing ethnographically one arena of global private law, the production of legal documentation for the global swap markets. This will allow us to see global private law as something very different from a body of norms. Global private law is also, I want to suggest, *a routinized but highly compartmentalized set of knowledge practices.*

Why does this matter? First, my alternative description of private law beyond the state has implications for the questions of how and to what extent global private law threatens the legitimacy and regulatory capacity of the state. Up to now, it has been taken for granted by most proponents and critics alike that global private law is something analogous to but ultimately very different from state law.[6] That is, it has been assumed that global private law threatens the legitimacy of the state by taking over the functions of the state through other (ostensibly more efficient, more accepted) means. In contrast, I argue that to the extent that global private law poses a threat to the state, it is not because private law is somehow functionally analogous to but qualitatively different from state law. Rather, if one understands private law beyond the state, as I do, as a set of institutions, actors, doctrines, ideas, material documents—of knowledge practices—one begins to see remarkable similarities between the technical workings of global private law and the nature of "state work." Later chapters will explore the nature of legal knowledge inside the state in detail. But here suffice it to say that a better understanding of what is "outside the state" will also help move us toward a better understanding of what is state global regulatory practice, and hence of how private and public can and do work together to address global problems. Let's begin with some background about the particular artifact through which we will embark on this exploration, collateral.

Collateral Practices

One of the principal tasks facing Tokyo bank documentation staff in the 1990s and early 2000s was the completion, execution, and filing of ISDA CSA documents.[7] For reasons related to questions of choice of law (legal questions about what law should apply to the collateral, discussed further below), the CSA initially existed in four versions—a New York law version, two UK law versions, and a Japanese law version.[8] Subsequently ISDA pulled these alternative forms together into one new document, the 2001 ISDA Margin Provisions, which asks parties to choose what law should apply to collateral transactions involving different kinds of collateral (2001).

The core terms of the CSAs resemble those of a standard collateral agreement in each jurisdiction: one party agrees, according to whatever legal theory is prevalent in that jurisdiction, that its obligations will be secured by some form of asset—usually cash or treasury bonds. It further outlines the conditions under which the party receiving the collateral can use it to satisfy the obligation. The CSAs follow the same format as the Master Agreement. The pre-printed form provides a set of basic terms, but allows the parties to customize some aspects of the agreement by filling in the blanks, choosing among given alternatives, and completing a schedule at the end.[9] During the period of my fieldwork (1998–2001), the CSA was widely used in the United States and Europe whenever swap partners exchanged collateral.[10] It was just starting to be used in Japan, however, largely at the urging of foreign counterparties. Exchanging collateral was increasingly a standard part of derivatives trading worldwide.

The most common forms of collateral globally were cash denominated in U.S. dollars and U.S. government bonds (ISDA 2000, 2). Japanese bank employees explained this in two ways. First, American counterparties were more familiar with Treasury bonds and liked to work with what was familiar to them (rather than Japanese government bonds). Second, American counterparties felt relatively confident that rights in "American" forms of collateral such as Treasury bonds were likely to be governed by U.S. law. Japanese banks most commonly posted either U.S. Treasury Bills, Japanese government bonds, or cash denominated in Japanese yen. The standard ISDA credit agreements provided for the daily valuation of each side's portfolio and mandated that either side post additional collateral if the value of its portfolio fell below certain thresholds, or if certain events such as a downgrading of the firm's bond rating occurred. ISDA estimates that at the end of 2006, US$1.335 trillion in collateral was in circulation (fig. 2) and approximately 59% of all privately negotiated derivatives transactions were collateralized (ISDA 2007, 4).

Parties posted collateral by depositing it in computerized book entry accounts maintained by intermediaries who specialized in holding collateral such as Euroclear or Cedel Bank, known as international central securities depositories (ICSDs) (Hval 1997). How much collateral a party was required to post depended on the party's credit rating and the amount of exposure or credit risk at stake in the particular transaction.[11] Because Japanese banks' credit ratings had plummeted in the aftermath of the Asian financial crisis on concerns about these banks' practice of keeping bad loans on the books, posting collateral, on the terms demanded by foreign counterparties, became a precondition to derivatives trading.[12]

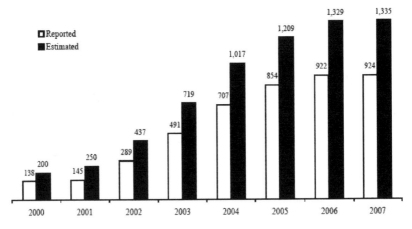

FIGURE 2. Collateral in circulation (ISDA 2007, 5)

Legal Experts

In Japan, this paper regime is managed by an army of "back office" or "documentation" people. Like the vast majority of law graduates, these are generally individuals who have graduated from prestigious law faculties but have either declined to take the bar examination or failed it and hence are not qualified to appear in court. Unlike those who pass the bar exam,[13] these other legal experts—described somewhat disparagingly in the English-language literature as "quasi-lawyers" or "scriveners"—staff the legal office of Japanese companies doing work that, in many other countries, is done by professional lawyers, as well as a mix of other work that might in the United States be done by paralegals in some cases and by company managers in others (Riles and Uchida 2009). In contrast to the more glamorous front office, where well-paid traders revered for their financial genius or their wizard-like intuition about markets work their computer screens and telephones (Miyazaki 2003),[14] the back office and its employees existed to supply the legal infrastructure for the trades. Before traders from two banks could enter into a swap, it fell upon the documentation people to fill in the forms.

Although separated by a few meters, the traders and documentation people I knew inhabited different universes. Documentation people, men and a handful of women aged twenty-three to forty-six, were not mathematicians, but legal technicians. They earned less money than others involved in derivatives trading. They worked long hours, with little chance of advancement, since their expertise in legal documentation had little use beyond the back office. And if time is the core disciplining metric of labor in the modern markets (de Goede 2005, 110–14), the labor of the legal expert was disciplined in a very specific way: the plodding work of documentation, with its before-the-fact work of negotiating the terms, and its after-the-fact work of "papering the trades" with confirmation documents, differed entirely from the up-to-the-minute excitement of trading. In other words, these collateral managers and their work were tethered to but ultimately quite collateral to trading, and to the accompanying heroic agency and real-time temporality of the trader. Collateral and collateral managers were documentary and human afterthoughts.

For example, one of my closest informants, a man I will call Sato, was a quiet, portly, balding man in his early forties. When we met, he was usually dressed in the blue polyester suit that for many years had been the standard uniform of Japanese salary men, but which many employees had by then already scornfully abandoned in favor of more stylish and personalized forms of dress. His rumpled tie betrayed the long hours he spent slumped at his desk. A native of rural Shikoku, Sato had passed the stringent examination for admission to the University of Tokyo faculty of law, an impressive feat for a student from a rural community without an elite secondary school educational background. But by his own account he ultimately had graduated in the bottom third of his law school class. This rendered him ineligible for the prestigious government positions reserved for the best University of Tokyo law graduates. He had also declined to sit for the national bar examination and hence could not work as a *bengoshi* or lawyer licensed to work in a law firm and appear at court. And so he had sought the next best thing, a position in the back office of a prestigious financial institution.

Sato's true passion was traveling the world. On his two-week yearly vacation he had already managed to visit over 100 countries, including Afghanistan, Uzbekistan, Kazakhstan, and Bulgaria, and he confided in me that he planned to visit every country in the world before he retired. His "dream," as he called it, was to become a board member of ISDA, the International Swaps and Derivatives Association. ISDA had only two Japanese board members, both of whom were prominent back-office employees—particularly "famous" (as Sato put it) persons who held positions at important banks. He often recounted to me, in extensive and envious detail, the stories he had heard from them about wine-tasting trips in Napa Valley and golf outings in Europe. For this, however, he would have to learn to speak fluent English, and he was working hard at his English on train rides to and from work, although his knowledge of English came primarily from his reading of legal documents, which gave it a particularly legalese character.

But documentation was not the only form of legal expertise at stake in collateral. Before a document like the ISDA collateral annex could come into existence, legal academics, and qualified lawyers working closely with them inside the most prestigious law firms, read and wrote academic articles about the meaning of the sections of the Civil Code governing collateral relations, drafted legal opinions about collateral issues on behalf of their clients (domestic and foreign banks), and held extensive meetings with government officials and with ISDA lawyers overseas to devise "solutions to problems." Collateral, then, was the constellation of both theoretical and doctrinal maneuvers and material documents.

Why Collateralize?

It is worth taking a step back to appreciate why collateral would emerge as so important to the global derivatives markets. Because a swap transaction is a private contract between two banks to exchange one kind of asset for another at a future date, there is always a risk—a so-called credit risk—that before the swap date one's counterparty could go bankrupt (Hval 1997). If that occurs, under the bankruptcy laws of most countries, the solvent party is still liable to uphold its side of the bargain, while the bankrupt party is excused from performance. In order to guard against this risk, swap counterparties routinely require one another to post collateral until the swap date.

In ISDA's own terms,

> The word "collateral" comes from the Latin collateralis, which means something that is to the side, or not direct. In the case of a privately negotiated derivatives transaction, the essential mechanism by which collateralization works is to provide an asset of value that is to the side of the primary transaction; in the event of default on the primary transaction, the collateral receiver has recourse to the collateral asset and can thus indirectly make good any loss suffered. (ISDA 2005, 7)

Simply put, collateral is important because it puts the counterparty ahead of other creditors in the queue to recover what one is owed, in the event one's counterparty defaults on its obligations. Consider, for example, a simple garden variety transaction in the global derivatives markets: Suppose Bank A in Tokyo and Bank B in London enter into a swap transaction—a contractual agreement to exchange 100 million yen for Euros at today's exchange rate at a date one year into the future. This "swap" is simply a contract, a promise, made now (in T1) to exchange something at a future date (T2). Or rather, it is two separate promises: Bank A promises to transfer 100 million yen at T2, and at the same time, Bank B promises to transfer the equivalent in euros.

But suppose that several months after entering into the swap transaction, Bank A files for bankruptcy. This means that Bank A seeks the protection of the national courts from its creditors: Bank A receives from the court permission not to pay its creditors what it owes, while the court sorts through the debtor's assets, and prioritizes the claims of all the creditors. In practice, once Bank A has initiated bankruptcy proceedings, Bank B can expect to recuperate only pennies on the dollar owed. In effect, Bank A's bankruptcy means that Bank A need not fulfill its half of the bargain with Bank B. However, under the bankruptcy law of Japan, the United Kingdom, the United States, and most other countries, bankruptcy usually does not excuse those who owe the bankrupt party from meeting their obligations. The reason is simple: the objective of bankruptcy is to get the bankrupt party back on its feet or, if that is not possible, at least to liquidate the bankrupt party and share its assets as fairly as possible among its creditors, and this requires that resources continue to flow in. Hence because a swap is two separate promises to deliver in T2—one from Bank A to Bank B, and one from Bank B to Bank A—Bank A's excuse from fulfilling its promise does not excuse Bank B from meeting its side of the bargain.

But now suppose that in T1 when the parties enter into the swap, Bank B insists that Bank A post collateral—perhaps 100 million yen worth of Japanese government bonds—to cover the transaction. The arrangement would provide that Bank B would return the collateral in T2 if Bank A meets its obligations under the swap. If, within the coming year, Bank A should prove unable to meet its obligations, however, Bank B will simply keep the collateral. In some jurisdictions, Bank B can do this before Bank A even declares bankruptcy, as long as certain conditions are met, and it need not even do anything complicated, controversial, or expensive such as going before a judge or filing special papers. It simply keeps the collateral (meaning, in practical terms, that the intermediary holding the collateral records it as belonging to Bank B).

Or perhaps before Bank B manages to claim the collateral, Bank A declares bankruptcy. In that case, under the local bankruptcy law of many jurisdictions, Bank B is a "secured creditor" entitled to full recovery up to the amount of the value of the collateral. Assuming the transaction is fully collateralized, meaning that the amount of collateral Bank B received from Bank A is equal to what Bank A had promised to deliver on T2, Bank B has lost nothing.

With the increasing volatility of the financial markets and the spectacular losses of some notorious derivatives markets participants in the 1990s, parties had become increasingly concerned about such problems of "credit risk"—the possibility that their counterparties might not fulfill the obligations to make the periodic payments the swap provided for.[15] Hence it had become commonplace for either party, or both, to demand that the other post collateral to back up its obligations. In the late 1990s and early 2000s, when Japanese banks found themselves saddled with bad debt and hence with low bond ratings, the ability to post collateral, and collateral of the nature and quantity demanded by their predominantly American and European counterparties, became the precondition to swap trading. Hence from the point of view of market participants there is a practical sense in which Hernando De Soto and John Wigmore are right when they assert that collateral is the foundation of the financial markets (see the introduction): one cannot trade without posting collateral, and posting collateral increasingly becomes a kind of trading of its own, as participants in the market jockey over what kind of collateral to post and how to calculate its fluctuating value.

But collateralization has one major disadvantage, from market participants' point of view: it requires having large amounts of liquid assets on hand. Posting collateral ties up those assets for the duration of the swap, and hence costs the party posting collateral the opportunity to invest those assets in other, more lucrative ways. The practice of posting collateral and making margin calls also requires each individual market participant to put in place elaborate procedures for tracking and valuing collateral on a global basis and also requires the services of intermediary custodians. This in turn costs money, but it also demands that each participant in the swap markets (including end users) implement internal procedures for handling collateral, train specialized staff to handle collateral, and delineate the relative authority of management, back office, and trading staff regarding these matters. At the time of my fieldwork, many Japanese participants in the swap markets did not have the institutional capacity to adequately manage collateral.

Collateralization is not the only means available to swap partners to protect themselves against credit risk. They can engage in further swap transactions with the same or other parties that have the effect of canceling out (or hedging) the credit risk of a particular swap, although this is often difficult to do in practice because of the unique, tailored quality of many swaps. They can choose to deal only with parties with a particularly good bond rating. Or they can trade through an intermediary clearinghouse, such as SwapClear, that functions much like an exchange (Scott 2006, 610, 617). However, such clearing houses usually only clear so-called plain vanilla or ordinary swaps. As the ISDA documentation explains,

> Generally, each party is prepared to leave a portion of its exposure to the opposite number uncollateralized. How much risk the parties will take increases if the counterparty's credit rating is strong. Lawyers write a sliding scale of uncollateralized exposure into the collateral document so the uncollateralized exposure that will be allowed goes down if the counterparty's rating drops. (2003)

Collateral as Global Private Law

All this activity is relevant to the nature of global private law and to the question of the extent to which it operates outside or beyond the state in two senses. First, the ISDA Master Agreement is the work of a powerful global private organization, just the kind of organization that is now at the center of many debates about global private law (Davis 2006, 1075).

Second, collateralization is a legal technology that is paradigmatic of global private law solutions. Although collateral is an artifact of multiple kinds of national law, it is also a device for running an end-game around certain aspects of national law. In the event of bankruptcy, collateral gives swap counterparties a more favorable mechanism through which to resolve disputes than the priority system of national bankruptcy law—a system designed to protect the interest of third parties.[16] Collateral is a self-help mechanism: in many jurisdictions the collateral holder may simply keep the collateral to satisfy the debtor's obligations, without going to court.[17] Collateral therefore emerges as a solution to a practical problem of transnational governance. The problem is that the terms of the national bankruptcy laws of many of the countries in which derivatives trading occurs, and the way these are interpreted and enforced by national bankruptcy judges, do not suit the global derivatives industry because they do not prioritize their claims ahead of all others (Bebchuk and Fried 1996, 857).[18]

But collateral has many other advantages other than protection against bankruptcy. For example, it becomes a vehicle for the parties to privately steer their relationship through other turbulent waters: the ISDA Master Agreement lists a number of "events" short of bankruptcy that trigger the collateral holder's right to close out its positions and use the collateral to satisfy any residual debts.[19] In this respect, collateral shares certain functional features with the uses of barter in international trade (Marin and Schnitzer 2002) or the rules commercial banks have developed for letter of credit practices (Levit 2005, 125). We might say that collateral becomes, in a practical sense, a kind of private constitution for the parties' relationship (Mann 1997). I will expand on this point in chapter 4.

Now, the official statements of ISDA notwithstanding, it is obvious that the "merely technical protocols" surrounding collateral relations are in fact highly political, and that these ostensibly "entirely private" regulatory practices are intertwined with state law in myriad ways.[20] Generations of legal theorists have definitively established that the distinction between private conduct and regulation and state action is ultimately something of a fiction because at some point private rules are always dependent upon state legal institutions for enforcement. For this reason, private law—rules of conduct independently agreed upon by the parties rather than dictated by the state—is in fact an artifact of state power (Cohen 1927, 8) in the sense that it only exists by virtue of the state's delegation of legal authority to the private industry or group in the form of its willingness to enforce the parties' bargain if necessary.

A number of commentators have demonstrated that this point is as true for global private law as it is for garden-variety domestic private law. They point out that the architecture of the transnational global private law regime is founded on the national private law of property and contract in particular. Caroline Bradley emphasizes, for example, that contracts rely upon the mechanisms of the state and transform these in turn, such that the "apparent sharp distinction between governmental and self-regulation soon breaks down" (2005, 127–28).

It is certainly true that collateral is an artifact of multiple kinds of publicly created law. Collateral transactions in the privately traded derivatives markets raise particular problems of interface between multiple national legal systems, including problems of determining what law applies to any particular collateral transaction (Guynn 1996; Guynn and Tahyar 1996, 170).[21]

The transnational nature of collateral goes beyond the mere (but important) fact that the parties to a swap are often incorporated in different jurisdictions. Collateral may be posted in different currencies, or in the form of government bonds issued by different governments. The collateral is held with intermediaries often incorporated in yet other jurisdictions, with places of business in still other locales. These intermediaries book the collateral in computerized ledgers maintained on servers that may be located yet elsewhere in the world. And if, as is permitted under the law of some countries, the pledgee (the party that receives the collateral) "repledges" the collateral to yet another party to satisfy its own obligations, which then repledges it again, then lawyers are left to make sense of a constant global movement of collateral in and out of accounts in many jurisdictions in terms of legal rules created to address a far more stationary and localized conception of property and contract rights.

Given the significant differences in national laws concerning collateral, one threshold legal question is, what law applies to any given problem (Guynn 1996; Guynn and Tahyar 1996)? This issue is the province of "private international law" (or conflict of laws as it is known in the United States)—the law that determines which local jurisdiction's law of collateral governs. The answers to these questions are murky, doctrinally arcane, and just as variable from jurisdiction to jurisdiction as is the law of collateral itself (Borchers 1998, 165).[22] Robert Wai (2002) terms these thorny doctrinal problems "touchdown points" in the relationship between global private governance and national law—points at which the efforts of private organizations such as ISDA to achieve "liftoff" from national regimes comes to rest on national law itself.[23]

Collateral is also intertwined with state law where it is the foundation for *coordination* between some market participants and regulators. The Bank for International Settlements' capitalization requirements for banks—the amount of liquid capital banks must keep on hand to ensure that their activities do not endanger the stability of the financial markets as a whole—credit counterparties for collateralization in calculating capital adequacy requirements. Hence banks that collateralize their swap transactions can lower their capital adequacy requirements and this makes trading cheaper (Basel Committee on Banking Supervision 1999). For bankers I knew, this was a major reason to collateralize swap transactions. In this sense, collateral is a form of compliance with an important policy objective of state regulators—ensuring that the parties are protected against levels of risk that could cause systemic harm—albeit one framed as voluntary compliance in exchange for exemption from certain state regulations concerning capital adequacy requirements. Viewed from another perspective, it represents a delegation of state authority to monitor systemic risk to private parties. Either way, what is at stake is that "private firms are made partners in regulation, implicitly and explicitly enlisted to fill out the substance of public legal norms" (Bamberger 2010, 683–84).

The legal experts with whom I worked would embrace all of these points. They understood full well that the private law of collateral is always only a partial global solution to their local legal problems.[24] They were intimately aware, for example, that the terms of any collateral agreement must satisfy national requirements for creating a valid and enforceable security interest in order for the lender to be able to use the collateral, or again, that national bankruptcy law must recognize the primacy of the interest of "secured creditors" over other creditors if the collateral agreement is to have force once the debtor has declared bankruptcy. In fact, it was at these junctures that the legal actors I studied labored—these constraints created legal work for them to do.

For example, where the terms in ISDA's standardized documents conflict with the norms enshrined in national statutory or judge-made law, ISDA actively works to supplant or change the latter so that it conforms to the former. ISDA hires local lawyers to investigate discrepancies between the terms of ISDA documents and national law and, where necessary, to lobby governments to change national law to either conform to the terms of the Master Agreement or explicitly declare the ISDA documents enforceable.[25] At the urging of ISDA and other industry groups, and with active input from these organizations, several transnational bodies are busy creating substantive legal rules concerning collateral that would apply in multiple jurisdictions and supersede national law. ISDA has pressed for the creation of a treaty—perhaps the ultimate example of global state law—that would mandate that national judges respect private parties' right to choose whatever law they wish to have applied to their collateral agreements.[26] In response to lobbying from ISDA (Coiley 2001, 119), the European Union has adopted a Directive on Financial Collateral Arrangements, which defines how security interests are to be created in EU member states, and what rights the holder of collateral obtains.[27] And ISDA has also worked with UNIDROIT, the international body devoted to unifying private law globally,[28] on a Convention on Harmonised Substantive Rules regarding Intermediated Securities to be adopted by individual nations as international law.[29] ISDA members aim not only to create substantive legal rights through private contracts, then, but also to influence the shape of those rights as they find expression in state law.

Moreover, the argument that private law is ultimately a pass through to state power overlooks the role of the materiality of ISDA documents in the global private governance regime. The rhetorical force of the argument that judges, regulators, and other outsiders will wreak chaos on the markets if they fail to honor market practices is perhaps different because of the sheer physical ubiquity of these documents. For example, in the early 1990s, the ISDA Master Agreement's procedures for closing out the agreement in the case of the bankruptcy of one party, and its delineation of the rights of the other party in such a scenario, arguably conflicted with the substantive rules and procedures of many national bankruptcy regimes. However, the widespread use of the Master Agreement—the physical existence of thousands of such signed documents—transformed the feel of the question of what to do about substantive legal rules that industry members found unfavorable, a policy question, into a far more general and *technical* question of the enforceability of a contract in each national jurisdiction.

The sociological fact that material documents matter admittedly contradicts the longstanding Legal Realist assertion that the paper of the contract means little, and that it is the ongoing relationship between the parties, and not the document, that matters (Macaulay 1976–77, 507; Macaulay, Kidwell, Withford, and Galanter 1995). But for legal experts in the global derivatives markets, material documents are crucial technologies of private transnational legal infrastructure—devices through which particular technical, institutional, political, legal, and economic arrangements gain solidity and durability (Latour 2002a). This is not to say that judges do not understand that a privately created document is legally meaningful only to the extent that a court holds it to be enforceable. But in order for the transaction to "work," all sides (parties and judges alike) must be *both* aware of the "truth" that state power lies behind all private legal regimes and able to momentarily forget this fact to immerse themselves in the practical and material day-to-day experience of doing private law.

So here is what I want to emphasize: What Wai describes as "touchdown points"—the points at which global private law comes to rest on state law—were for my informants, also, *projects*—problems that demanded creative work, political mobilization, technical skill, and considerable devotion. And what legal scholars would view as private bargains made in the shadow of state law were for my informants, also, material objects. What is most interesting about artifacts of private global governance such as collateral, when viewed in practice, therefore, is not the more academic question of whether they are private and outside the purview of the state, or public and within state control, but rather how the impulse, the fantasy of a privately regulated global market, engenders particular kinds of practical projects, particular material artifacts, particular registers of engagement between lawyers working under the umbrella of organizations such as ISDA and national and international lawmakers, judges, and regulators.

Rethinking Global Private Law as a World of Norms

Proponents and critics of global derivatives markets alike tend to have a singular view of how these markets hold together. In this view, the global derivatives markets "work" in the absence of state regulation (until, of course, they don't) because the derivatives markets are a kind of world unto themselves where everyone knows each other and insiders view it as in their own selfish interest to play by the customary rules. The story here is of a kind of subculture, or tribe, or network, governed by its own cultural norms and values of reciprocity—you scratch my back and I scratch yours. This vision of the world not as a system of states but as a system of private networks, and of global private law as an artifact of global social networks of various kinds (Appelbaum, Felstiner, and Gessner 2001; Picciotto 1996–97, 1014) is an intuitively attractive argument for why the private regulation of certain "arcane" markets has been so successful and why these markets pose such a challenge to nation-states that seek to regulate them.

This view that private norms are the true source of authority and functionality in markets dominates legal debates about global private governance regimes more generally. In this view, global private law takes on the force and legitimacy of "law" for members of a given global industry or group by virtue of the fact that it embodies a set of *norms* particular to that industry or group. Klaus Peter Berger, for example, writes that business people "create their own law through the drafting, use and refinement of general conditions of trade, standardized contracts and other clauses as well as the development of practices and usages, elevating them from regional to world-wide customs" (1999, 27–28). Appelbaum, Felstiner, and Gessner (2001) argue that relations of trust and reciprocity, engendered by cultural and social bonds, often are the true guarantors of cross-border business relationships.[30]

For many observers, the rise of private norm-making organizations like ISDA is a cause for celebration because of the efficiencies and creative regulatory solutions that such private organizations are deemed to provide. For example, writing about the use of self-regulation standards in the securities industry, Karmel and Kelly assert that "[s]ince SRO standards and other soft law are based on a consensus by participants in the markets, soft law is frequently more informed and more effective than statutory law, although it may eventually be translated into statutes or rules for enforcement purposes" (2009, 885). A longstanding insight of the law and society literature likewise is that the mundane activity of "repeat players"–such as insiders in the global private derivatives markets—produces legal regimes (Galanter 1974, 95). Edelman, Uggen, and Erlanger for example argue in the context of the regulation of organizations that "the meaning of law . . . unfolds dynamically across organizational, professional, and legal fields" (1999, 406). Global legal norms and institutions are created through the efforts of individual legal actors, working on particular projects in the service of their very locally defined interests based upon their social networks—their personal career interests, the interests of their families or class, or of their firms and organizations—to forge alliances with others (Dezalay and Garth 1996). There is even an aura of democratization in phrases like "bottom-up lawmaking" used to describe this evolution global of private law norms (Levit 2005, 125). Implicit in or running alongside this view is often a mild materialist claim that a revolution in information technologies and in the character of capitalism has occurred, resulting in a largely inevitable trend toward the demise of state lawmaking authority (Cerny 2000, 59; Westbrook 2004a).

But the view of global private law as a regime of norms is equally pervasive among those who decry such delegation of state power to global private authorities. The theorist of globalization Saskia Sassen, for example, laments that we now face "a normative transformation in the [sense] of a privatizing of certain capacities for making norms" (2004, 61) with negative consequences for the legitimacy of nation-states. And of course, when it comes to the derivatives markets, the dominant story is now a profoundly negative tale of insiders' abuses of their connections.

For these observers, these norms are *analogous*, both in their coercive power and their legitimacy, to the authority of the state, within the purview of the particular community or market sector where they apply. In some versions of this dogma, social networks serve the same purposes as state coercion in regulating behavior and enforcing compliance, and social norms are the products of social networks. Barach Richman (2006) offers the classic example of diamond merchants for whom close cultural and social connections make threats of ostracism or public shaming for those who violate customary norms very real.[31] These systems of private norms ultimately appear as self-evidently more real, more legitimate, more innovative, more complex, closer to the ground, than the state itself.[32]

In other versions, the spontaneous quality of group norms makes them both more efficient and more just (Ellickson 1991). Ethnographers of the financial markets, for example, have argued that social relations often substitute for the impossibly high information costs associated with effectively policing one's agreements in the global marketplace. The argument is that small "clubs" of actors come to know and trust one another intimately, and to develop a rich network of norms governing their transactions, and that very locally defined social relations of trust and informal norms come to substitute for both financial knowledge and legal norms (Abolafia 1996; Zaloom 2006).

On its face, it is a convincing story. But does this description of global private law as a collection of norms, and of organizations such as ISDA as norm creators, accurately capture the knowledge work at issue in the day-to-day activity of derivatives markets governance, or does it obscure as much as it reveals? From an ethnographic perspective, there is something amiss in the descriptions of global private governance as cozy normative communities busy codifying their norms in standardized documents.

From Norms to Techniques

In legal terms, collateral is a body of doctrines and theories, a specialized set of property rights. As such, it is the object of a great deal of expert attention and care: In Tokyo, legal academics, and qualified lawyers working closely with them inside the most prestigious law firms, read and wrote academic articles about the meaning of the sections of the Civil Code governing collateral relations, and they applied these to collateral in the derivatives markets in legal opinions drafted on behalf of their clients (in particular the foreign banks). Government bureaucrats studied foreign laws, debated law reform projects, drafted new laws, and implemented existing ones. These aspects of the knowledge work entailed in financial markets governance are explored in subsequent chapters.

But in the financial markets, one also encounters "collateral" as a mountain of specific preprinted forms that must be completed and filed before trading can begin, and of confirmation documents that must be exchanged after each trade. Although the document standardizes many aspects of the practice of swap trading, it also allows for a certain amount of flexibility and adaptation by its users through a "schedule" at the end in which the parties can specify some of the details to their particular relationship, such as how payments are to be made. Hence the task of the documentation people was to tailor the agreement to the needs of the bank and its counterparties by filling in the blanks in the form. What ISDA members, through their battalions of documentation people working around the globe, were busy making were not rules, not norms, not sources of law, but documents.

At first blush, it may seem odd to focus on this kind of routine legal work as a paradigmatic example of global private lawmaking. It has become commonplace in sociolegal studies to comment on the "creative capacities of lawyers" (Cain and Harrington 1994, 1)—in bringing clients together, inventing innovative solutions to business problems, pushing the development of law, and hence shaping the character of society. It is these creative capacities that distinguish lawyers from other workers in the economy. But the rote and repetitive work of the documentation people, defined by its precision and attention to detail rather than its creativity, and by its distance from legal theory, points to another, too little acknowledged modality of legal knowledge. In the remainder of this chapter I want to focus more attention on this particular slice of financial governance practice.

The standard way of approaching a contract such as the ISDA master agreement is to ask what it *means*—that is, to treat it as a text that entextualizes (Silverstein and Urban 1996) a particular set of group norms, the kind of norms that, as I already mentioned, are assumed to dominate in the world of private markets.[33]

But there is something fundamentally wrong with this approach: forms are often not meant to be read, but to be *completed*. That is, ISDA documents are technologies that channel a very specific kind of activity, form-filling (Brenneis 2006, 41; Miyazaki 2006a, 206). As ISDA puts it in the User's Guide to the 1992 ISDA Master Agreements,

> The advantage to market participants using the printed forms is to reduce the time and expense involved in reviewing documentation prepared by another party. . . . It is also advantageous to use the printed forms even if market participants wish to make additions or deletions, for this enables them to focus on the actual changes being made to a 1992 Agreement. (1993, 2)

In other words, the ISDA form is a script for a particular kind of collaboration between two parties—the documentation person at Bank A and the documentation person at Bank B.

A point of exception with the legal literature on standardized contracts may help to explain what I mean. A central focus of the debate about standardized contracts concerns the worry that so-called boilerplate contracts unduly favor the party with the greater bargaining power and hence are socially undesirable. The standard law and economics response is that among insiders in an industry such as the global private derivatives markets, power imbalances are not such a large problem since standardized contracts in these industries are the result of negotiations among a close-knit group of mutually reliant players (Choi and Gulati 2006).[34] The argument in other words is that the text of standardized contracts in such contacts enshrines the group norms of a unique and tightly-defined community.

The documentation experts I worked with would have agreed that concerns about the negative effect of boilerplate on power imbalances in contracting were misplaced, although not for the reason asserted in the standardized contracts literature. In Japan the form was used primarily by insiders in their dealings with one another.[35] Among these insiders, power imbalances most certainly existed: a bank with a poor credit rating had to accept more unfavorable terms and post far more collateral in order to trade. In the wake of the banking scandals of the 1990s, Japanese banks' credit ratings put them at a significant disadvantage relative to their foreign counterparts. Moreover, there was a perception among traders at Japanese banks that Japanese traders lacked the experience and skill necessary to succeed against foreign traders in the global derivatives markets (Miyazaki 2006b). On the legal front, likewise, ISDA's center of gravity was in London and New York, not in Tokyo. The lawyers who set ISDA policy were trained in American or British law, and although they came to Tokyo regularly and worked with committees of industry representatives that usually included Japanese representation, they interacted far less with Japanese bankers than they did with bankers at the top swap houses in London and New York, and understood considerably less about the legal problems of Japanese banks than about the problems in New York or London. Hence the ISDA documents emerged as responses to problems framed first in New York and London, and only imperfectly accommodated, to the extent possible, the specific concerns of Japanese banks. From this point of view it would seem that the standardized portions of the document enshrined the interests of the more powerful—the market participants in London and New York—against the less powerful, in places like Tokyo.

But the people who handled documentation in Tokyo insisted to me that the weak position of Japanese banks did not find expression in the *standardized portions* of the form, per se. Rather, what interested them were the way such inequities and power imbalances played out in the *negotiated* portions of the form, that is, the parts that got their daily attention. In practice, the customized aspects of these agreements were often determined by the party in the strongest position—whether it was the party with the best credit rating, or the "dealer" in relationship to an "end user" such as a manufacturing company seeking to hedge against fluctuations in the price of a particular raw material. People in charge of documentation explained that in practice there was little room for "negotiation" of the nonstandardized terms. In most cases, counterparties abroad dictated the terms and they largely accepted them.

Of course this is participants' own idiosyncratic view, but it is interesting as such: what it does reveal is how these particular legal actors experienced the standardized contract on a practical daily basis. That is, I surmise that these insiders most likely paid less attention to the inequities in the standardized portions of the form than they did to the inequities in the nonstandardized portions because they *hardly ever looked at the printed portions of the form.*

This, of course, does not mean the printed text is irrelevant; indeed, the printed text can become a subject of controversy, subject to interpretation by a court or by some other dispute resolution body somewhere down the line.[36] But as Stuart Macaulay long ago explained (1963), the contract here is important, but not simply in the straightforward sense of providing a potential future judge with guidance about the nature of the bargain between the parties, should a dispute occur. The reality is that formal or informal disputes about the meaning of the standardized language of ISDA master agreements are remarkably rare given the number of transactions made on the basis of these agreements and the notional amounts at stake. The rest of the time, the focus is on the blanks in the form. The ISDA case then forces us to query the assumption that standardized documents are nothing but texts, texts that memorialize group norms.

Unlike lawyers, organizational sociologists since Max Weber (1968) have looked to documents as crucial technologies of bureaucratic organization. Sociologists have shown how documentary practices shape behavior within organizations (Ouchi and Wilkins 1985): they play a "coordinating function" within organizations (Smith 1990, 213), they serve as a management tool, and they enable the routinization of innovation (Hargadon and Sutton 1997; Heimer 2006).[37] From this perspective, we can see how ISDA documents work as tools for engaging in a communicative routine. The routine consists of a set of material practices of document production, filing, and exchange—practices that in turn call for further routines, and further documents (Riles 2006a, 71).[38] In this sense, the document makes possible a set of exchanges defined by a particular kind of technical legal expertise.[39] I would like to claim these mundane exchanges as an element of global private governance.

Let me give one concrete example of what I mean. Sometimes filling in the collateral forms presented what my informants described as "difficult problems." Swap trading partners—foreign swap partners—wished to have extensive rights concerning the collateral of Japanese banks they held (ISDA 2000; Avanzato 1998, 2). They wanted to be able to sell the collateral to a third party or to use it as collateral of their own in future swap transactions (Johnson 1997, 949; Mapother 1998, 74). And these "difficult problems" raised further questions of theory and doctrine. American and UK law allowed for this so-called rehypothecation, but the law of Japan provided that the holder of collateral had certain duties of care, and hence could not alienate the collateral without the permission of the party that had initially posted it. One threshold legal question, therefore, was what country's law would govern the rights over collateral posted by a Japanese bank with an American bank, for example—Japanese or American law (Guynn 1996).

The full answer to this legal question involves complex and murky jurisprudential and even epistemological issues (what law should govern a transaction between a Japanese and UK bank, posted to their subsidiaries in the Cayman Islands, involving a swap of Chinese currency for Singaporean currency? And given that in most legal systems the law traditionally attempts to answer such questions in territorial terms, where did the transaction take place? Where is the collateral, some numbers in some accounts, "held"?) But the lawyers at ISDA headquarters in New York had prescribed a simple solution grounded not in legal theory but in concrete practices of documentation. These lawyers had produced a "collateral annex" (ISDA 1999a, 1999b; Suetens 1995, 15) to the ISDA Master Agreement which included, among other things, a clause specifying that the parties agreed in advance that all disputes over collateral should be governed by either UK or New York law. The form simply required documentation people to circle "law of New York" or "law of the United Kingdom," to initial the document signaling their assent, and to file it.[40] The difference between a legal document and a legal theory—even if all would agree at another level of argument that the document is just an instantiation of the theory—"cut the network" (Strathern 1996, 517) of legal theorizing. Sometimes naïve commonsense distinctions between the ontological status of theories and objects have their practical uses. In this case, it provided a way out of doctrinal debates which ISDA lawyers understood to be endless.

Crucially, the ISDA form does not presume that documentation people are members of a tight-knit "club," people who know and trust one another (Levit 2005, 131). The documentation people I worked with did not belong to any such "club"—their counterparties were often anonymous voices on the other end of a telephone, or people on the other end of the fax or e-mail. Rather, this routine is made possible not by a set of shared norms, but by a given set of *aesthetic criteria*[41] that these people would claim as their technical expertise and that captivated their attention and energy: printed forms are distinguished from other genres of communication such as letters, legal opinions, or e-mail messages by their very rigid aesthetic standards (Riles 2006b, 1). These aesthetic criteria in turn demand that the users of the forms engage in very specific forms of behavior: One chooses the law that applies to the ISDA master agreement by circling the proper word; one delineates who is the responsible contact person for the agreement by completing the relevant box. The form is not set out to be read; it is presumed that the "users" (the term is significant) will jump to the blanks and complete them, most likely in the order they appear. One could, of course, say that the users of ISDA forms I knew represented a community of a kind in the sense that they shared a set of institutional practices, codes of behavior, a kind of technical expertise, by virtue of the fact of their employment in particular kinds of institutions (e.g., banks and securities firms). But this would simply restate the argument: ISDA forms are one important material impetus for as well as instantiation of this institutional affinity. The collaboration made possible by the printed form is certainly consequential, in other words, but it is also normatively and socially thin (Luhmann 1985).

I realize that many readers will resist the claim that a body of law could derive its authority from aesthetic criteria rather than from social norms. If this is difficult to accept from a point of view in which law is imagined as a (less legitimate) artifact of (more authentic) social relations, it is, I think, very much part of the lawyer's common sense understanding of the law.[42] If one asks lawyers or regulators in the financial markets why collateral is important, one hears a simple, standard story about the obviation of norms. It goes something like this:

Suppose you are a risk assessment officer at a New York bank engaged in derivatives transactions with counterparties in Tokyo, and you are charged with evaluating the risk that those counterparties might fail. In order to succeed at your task you would need to know a great many things. You would need to understand the finances of your counterparties very well, which would mean penetrating the world of Japanese bookkeeping and understanding how bad loans have been hidden on the books over the last decades. You would need to know something about the internal politics within the firms at issue, and their consequences for current investment decisions that might not be reflected on last year's books. You would need to have a series of mathematical models, and computers for running those models, in order to try to understand the way, taken as a whole, your firm's and your counterparty's portfolios might complement one another in ways that created hidden kinds of risk. You would need to know a great deal about the regulatory and economic environment both in Japan and globally in order to predict how events beyond the firm would shape its financial outlook. Finally, you would need to understand the cultural environment of the market and its regulators in order to make sense of all of these. This kind of detailed "local knowledge" and valuation technology is a tall order. Although the advertising campaigns of certain consulting firms confidently profess their access to this kind of knowledge, none of my informants would have been so bold or so foolish as to claim such knowledge for themselves.

But if you are a risk assessment officer, you have at your disposal a far simpler, far more efficient, far less messy tool than social relations, norms, and trust in people and institutions. You have collateral. Assume now that the transactions you are evaluating are collateralized. Now you do not need to know anything about the culture, economics, or politics. You do not need to know the intricate details of your counterparties' balance sheets. You simply need to know that the transaction is collateralized. Assuming you are satisfied with the amount and quality of the collateral, your analysis is finished; you can check it off your list and move on to your next transaction.[43] Instead of trusting social relations, you trust collateral.

In practitioners' own ideology, therefore, collateral, emerges as a way of *setting limits* on the messy complexities of a global market, a way of *obviating the need for* knowledge and trust, an alternative to developing shared private norms. One could say that in fact collateral is the precise opposite of social norms, what makes norms superfluous. That is, collateral makes it possible for global actors to deal with one another without trust, without shared norms, without a thick web of personal relations or an elaborate alternative system of dispute resolution. I intend this as a larger point about the capacity of law which has been largely ignored by legal theorists: the capacity to simplify, to place limits on social, political, and analytical relations alike. One argument of this book is that this is a distinctive feature and achievement of legal knowledge, and one that is far more consequential than meets the eye.

My own first entrée into the larger significance of collateral for a theory of legal knowledge came from what I took to be just such obfuscation: my informants' manifest lack of interest in the subject of disputes. As a legal anthropologist, I am predisposed to take an interest in disputes and cultures of disputing, and so I naturally peppered my informants with questions about how disputes among counterparties over the terms of a swap get resolved. Given the notional amounts at stake, I reasoned that these disputes must occupy considerable effort and energy. To my dismay, however, these questions elicited little interest on the part of the documentation people I knew. "We just work these things out," I was told again and again, with a standard shrug, before people turned the conversation back to subjects of greater concern to them. When, confident that people were hiding something, I pointed out that the ISDA CSA documents provide for a set of procedures to be followed in the event of a dispute, people laughed. No one actually followed those procedures, I was told. Rather, they tended to have in mind a range within which, should a dispute arise, they would simply go along and not contest. If the disputed amount was outside that range, they would come to some agreement, usually by splitting the difference. At one point, one informant told me, it was suggested that a more formal dispute resolution mechanism should be set up, but the idea was abandoned because "nobody wanted to serve on it."

To grasp the significance of this fact, contrast collateral with a favorite subject in the theory of global private law, international commercial arbitration. Arbitration is interesting because we can see in it private actors banding together, elaborating their own dispute resolution system, developing over time their own body of adjudicative norms and, eventually, garnering state approval for these norms. That is, arbitration is interesting because it is quite explicitly an analog to state law, an *alternative* to state law with all of state law's functional elements—a regime of norms, a set of procedures, a set of problems (disputes). But collateral works according to a quite different logic. For, in its ambition at least, if a transaction is collateralized, there is *no need* for dispute resolution in the first place. The dispute is (in theory) already resolved, already collateralized, so to speak, before it ever comes into existence. Collateral arrangements are a form of law that aims to be the *obviation* of dispute resolution, as well as its apotheosis. Indeed, collateral is difficult to see as a "topic" of legal theory precisely because its *modus operandi* is not at all alternative and analogous to standard law, with its disputes resolved according to norms enshrined in legal processes. And just because things often do not turn out so neatly in practice does not mean that we should ignore the fantasy, the ambition, the hope of collateral.

To be clear, this is not to say that there are no reasons for disputes. On the contrary, as we will see in later chapters, there are endless sources of conflict in the swap markets, from the valuation of collateral and of the underlying swap transactions to the nature of the rights and duties of the parties, to the question of what conditions—such as a breach of the agreement by one party—would excuse the parties from fulfilling their contractual obligations. My point, however, is that the concrete and mundane practices surrounding collateral administration shift those disputes onto a different terrain—onto the terrain of ISDA protocols and procedures.

I do not want to overstate the point. Surely norms and trust and social relations have their place. My aim is simply to point out that legal arrangements and legal knowledge (here, the doctrine of collateral) do more than simply enshrine group norms (Valverde 2005). The chapters that follow explore a number of other legal devices that obviate complexity, social relations, and norms of all that we could shorthand as the social meaning of legal rules.

Standardization

One way of getting at what I am trying to describe here is the vocabulary of standards and standardization. Standardization is without a doubt an important element of what ISDA members call the "document's architecture." In fact, ISDA's own standardizing work is itself a kind of standardized trade organization project. Many different trade groups produce preprinted contracts of this kind (Davis 2006). There is little in the architecture of the ISDA agreement itself that is, in fact, all that unique.

The legal literature on standardized contracts emphasizes that standardized contracts facilitate "coordination" among the parties by focusing attention on certain "focal points" and allowing the parties to treat others as settled (Ahdieh 2006, 1033; Choi and Gulati 2006). There are "network benefits" to standardized contracts whereby the more parties use the contracts, the more standard they become and hence more valuable they become to all users (Kahan and Klausner 1997, 72). Here law and economics scholars amplify an argument industry organizations make for themselves: the ISDA guidelines for collateral practitioners booklet states, "[I]t can be valuable to use industry standard forms because they can offer objectivity, consistency and a body of judicial and operational experience and can shorten negotiation because they are more readily accepted" (ISDA 1999b, 27).

A core insight of the law and economics literature on standardized contracts is that standardization serves the important function of reducing the transaction costs associated with producing new contracts, such as researching the law and drafting the terms of the contract ("learning benefits"). For example, Kahan and Klausner point out that standardized contracts also reduce litigation costs because they deploy terms that have already been vetted in court (1997, 719–20).

This becomes particularly crucial in a global trading environment, where the cost of ensuring that one's practices are not open to challenge in the diverse jurisdictions in which the swap dealer operates can be prohibitively high.[44] Savings on litigation and other legal costs is certainly an objective of ISDA members in using these forms. ISDA advertises access to legal opinions concerning the enforceability of its collateral agreements and its netting agreements (see chapter 5) as a core benefit of membership in the association.[45]

Where law and economics scholars focus on cost savings, sociolegal scholars have emphasized how standardization produces new legal regimes through the routinization of work and professional roles. For example, Mark Suchman, working in the context of the development of intellectual property law in Silicon Valley, draws attention to mundane practices of contract production as one source, among others, of the creation of new legal norms. Suchman points to "a significant but often overlooked aspect of industrial governance: the routinization of transactional practices within a developing organizational community" (2007, 2).[46]

Standardization is also a central concern in the field of science and technology studies (STS). Research in this field has shown how standards produce so-called epistemic networks—collections of projects, associated ideas and technologies for working on them, and ultimately, the "truths" that emerge as self-evident and incontrovertible from these.[47] In an argument remarkably evocative of the legal ideology of collateral's role in placing limits on market complexities I have already described, the economic sociologist Michel Callon (1998b) has shown how the very existence of a market, as a field of knowledge and exchange, depends upon the possibility of certain forms of equivalence, and hence upon a wide range of techniques for cutting off, excluding, or purifying complexity so as to render values universally calculable. One cannot trade until the picture is simplified enough that everyone can calculate the relative value of goods in the same way. One of the tasks of legal and economic knowledge, then, is to draw "a clear and precise boundary . . . between the relations which the agents will take into account and which will serve in their calculations and those which will be thrown out of the calculation as such." As he puts it, "economics, in the broad sense of the term, performs, shapes and formats the economy, rather than observing how it functions" (2, 16).[48]

Documents are crucial technologies of this kind of standardization, or formatting.[49] Documents are "immutable, presentable, readable and combinable" artifacts that can mobilize networks of ideas, persons, and technologies (Latour and Woolgar 1986 (1979), 26). In other words, documents help to format or standardize the market because of their unique ability to travel across boundaries—cultural boundaries, forms of expertise, institutions, physical distances by virtue of their material and aesthetic form.

Note that standardization, in this understanding, is both a conceptual project and a material project. Theories (like legal doctrines surrounding collateral) generate material objects (like collateral documents), and material objects in turn make theorization possible (Miller 2005). Behind and within objects are theories (Henare, Holbraad, Wastell 2006; Thrift 2005) and behind theories are objects. To extend the point to law, legal theories have concrete effects in the world in part because of the kind of material practices of lawmaking they put into motion.

In very much this sense, "collateral" is not just one thing. It takes several different forms—material documents, legal reform projects, legal theories, legal doctrines, mathematical calculations, and more. Moreover, the fact that this complex constellation of practices can be concretized in a standard document matters for the stability and legitimacy of ISDA's regulatory regime. The document can travel across national borders, from one trading environment and one regulatory system to another, and the preprinted form allows documentation staff in a bank in one country to engage in a routine of completion that involves collaboration with someone else they have never seen, in a different jurisdiction, thousands of miles away.

Collateral, then, is an achievement of standardization—standardization across different jurisdictions, but also standardization across different kinds of expertise. The management of collateral depends not only on law but also on complex questions of portfolio valuation: In order to determine how much collateral must be posted for a given swap transaction, the parties must agree on the value of the "exposure" (the amount of risk) at issue in the underlying transaction as well as on the value of the collateral itself. This valuation process is by definition an impossible exercise since, by the very terms of the efficient market hypothesis, if the parties agreed upon the value of a swap they would have no reason to enter into the transaction in the first place (Miyazaki 2003). In fact, by the time of my fieldwork, the difficulties inherent in collateral valuation had caught the eye of traders who had begun to see that there was little difference, in economic terms, between the kind of speculation that characterized the swap transaction, and the risks and bets parties had to take in evaluating and accepting the collateral that they posted to guarantee those transactions. That is, they entered into swap transactions in order to engage in parallel collateral transactions, which allowed them to take certain kinds of risks in the market. For these traders, collateral had become part of the action, something inseparable in economic terms from the logic of the underlying transaction, even if it was legally imagined as something entirely distinct from and collateral to the transaction itself.

However, despite the limitations of the computer models, indeed despite the fact that there were no ultimate answers to the question, "what is the value of this portfolio, at this moment," the mathematicians and computer experts, not the legal experts, had emerged as the masters of these impossibilities.[50] Valuation was performed with complex computer systems and programs run by experts in advanced mathematics and computer science.

This meant that the administration of collateral required translation across different forms of expertise—computer science, accounting, law, finance, management, regulatory compliance, and more. For example, one of the central organizational problems that preoccupied documentation people was the problem of "booking collateral globally"—of accounting for all the collateral transactions of a bank's various offices around the world in one "book." This further standardization project—a project of coordinating among documentation people in various offices—depended on having standard ways of valuing collateral in each office. Legal standardization required computational standardization, which in turn required institutional standardization.

In science studies terms, then, collateral is what the anthropologist of science Joan Fujimura terms a "standardized package . . . a theory and a standardized set of technologies" that together make it possible "to *locally concretize the abstraction in different practices* to construct new problems" (1992, 169, 179). This constellation of theoretical, material and aesthetic features, and the forms of expertise that go with them—what I will call the technical quality of global private law—generates its own durability, its own commitment, quite apart from any set of shared norms among users on the one hand, or any threat of state enforcement of these agreements on the other.

Glitches in the System

Of course recent events have dramatically demonstrated the limits of these techniques. In 2008, as the value of certain swaps went into dramatic free fall, disputes over the valuation of collateral engaged increasingly higher echelons of managers in discussions that no longer partook of the ISDA protocol. Some of these negotiations ended in serious conflict; some led to the downfall of venerable financial institutions; and the Federal Reserve's own position in these negotiations remains politically controversial to this day (Guerrera, Bullock, and MacIntosh 2008; Morgenson and Story 2010; O'Harrow and Dennis 2008). The private turns out to be not so private after all. The ultimate involvement of the state in these transactions—not as a site of dispute resolution of last resort, but as a facilitator and guarantor of deals—is not in fact as unusual a development as one might think. In chapter 5 we will explore an example from the Asian financial crisis of the Japanese state's informal involvement in private parties' disputes over collateral. Contrary to industry executives' descriptions of the conditions that precipitated a need for government intervention as a "perfect storm," an "act of god," a "tsunami," and so on, such conditions are not at all unpredictable. As Katsunori Mikuniya, the commissioner of Japan's Financial Services Agency, wryly put it in a recent speech, "While the current financial crisis has been described as a once-in-a-century credit tsunami, Tokyo, as a financial center, has experienced two tsunamis over the past decade" (2009). In fact, much of the ethnography in the chapters that follow is, in one way or another, an exploration of what happens when collateral *fails* to work as a simple backstop and technical protocol for private governance beyond the state in this way.

To begin with, not only is global private law not private, it is also not global. Contrary to the technical fantasy, the preprinted material form of ISDA documents, drafted by American and British lawyers, written in English, and laden with assumptions about market practices in the American and British markets, was literally nonsensical in the Japanese market. For example, the New York document prescribed that collateral should be transferred within three days, as was the practice in New York. But at the time, neither the Japanese banks, nor the clearing system for Japanese government bonds maintained by the Bank of Japan, could manage a transfer within this time period. Hence to sign on to this document was to commit to an impossibility. From documentation people's point of view, the discontinuities among technologies were as apparent and salient as the connections.

Making this supposedly global document "workable" in Japan, then, was hard work of its own.[51] The institutional venue for the transplantation of this foreign legal regime to the Japanese market were the meetings of a "documentation committee" of back-office staff from various Japanese and foreign banks sponsored by ISDA Tokyo. They discussed how to adapt forms to what they saw as the technological, legal, and institutional limits of the Japanese market relative to foreign markets. They sought to supplement the standardized forms with a set of locally defined standardized practices. At these meetings, back-office staff discussed the details of form filling with an aim to "standardize" and "create protocols" for the completion of these forms in Japan, where the terms of the forms raised problems or made assumptions inappropriate to the context of the Japanese market (for a discussion of the significance of the work of back-office people see Basel Committee on Banking Supervision 2003, 7). Standardization then became for these lawyers a further technical project, the framework for their documentation work.

We could say much of the same about the relationship between law and other forms of expertise in the financial markets. The STS literature emphasizes the way documents and technical standards allow disparate forms of expertise (such as law and finance) to come together. But this picture of smooth translatability and collaboration, while something of a fantasy, did not sit well with the actual experience of the documentation people I knew. Once, for example, Sato told me about the emergence of a new kind of figure within American banks—a collateral manager. This person, he said with admiration, understood both systems and law, and hence could operate "globally." Collateral managers commanded enormous salaries and led glamorous existences as they moved between global offices of a bank, following the flow of collateral from one office to the next. I asked Sato whether becoming such a character might not be a "dream" for him, alongside becoming an ISDA board member. But he refused the suggestion: "I am not good at math. It would be too much for me. Such a big person does not exist in Japan." One of the features of the work of the documentation people was that it locked them into a relationship with a set of concepts, machines, and persons that they were acutely aware they did not understand—into a relationship premised on a lack of knowledge. As lawyers, they were intensely aware that they did not understand the mathematical details of collateral valuation, for example, nor did they understand the humans and machines that performed these calculations. And yet the work of documentation depended in concrete and ubiquitous ways on valuation.

From an institutional point of view, these legal experts' lack of knowledge of the financial details had many advantages. First, they remained at arms' length from certain details banks might want to keep under wraps—from proprietary information about trading technologies to problematic trading strategies—and hence posed relatively less threat to their firms as they went about interacting with regulators, academics, and other outsiders. But equally important, the resolution of certain kinds of problems resulting from the failure of other financial technologies— coming to an agreement about whether more collateral should in fact be posted on a given transaction, for example, when two banks' valuation models produced vastly different analyses—required an ability to step back and see the transaction from another point of view. To see something from a different point of view (a legal point of view) is much easier if one does not already inhabit the dominant trader's frame of analysis. In a global market in which complexity is the taken for granted starting point (Strathern 1991), a practice that steps back, that makes the picture simple by shutting off the flow of information (Stinchcombe 2001) is value for money indeed. Part of what rendered the documentation people experts was their lack of knowledge of certain aspects of the financial markets. And, in fact, this disconnect between traders and lawyers was later encouraged by financial regulators who insisted, as part of market reforms, that lawyers be physically moved to a different space, the "back office," in hopes that this physical divide would render them more institutionally, conceptually, and socially independent from traders.

So in place of networks of people, institutions, objects, experts, and ideas that create coherent standards, new forms of transparency, communities of expertise, and truths, a coherent doctrinal or sociological whole, then, I suggest that we understand the ensemble of legal techniques that make up the private governance of the global derivatives markets as an assemblage of glitches—pockets of lack of knowledge, breaks between theory and practice, genres of opacity, differences in ontological status, lack of understanding of the agency and expertise of others. We have a flurry of activity that creates distinctions, sets limits, cuts one genre of thought and one line of analysis from another, activity that is not building anything in particular, that does not "add up" to a new legal regime, or a new market sphere, or a new source of epistemological or juridical authority.

What Makes Legal Knowledge Technical?
A Preliminary Overview

In this chapter, I have proposed that we shift our thinking about governance in the global financial markets in a significant way. Rather than viewing these markets as governed by arcane group norms (good or bad), we can see governance as mediated through the technical legal knowledge that is both literally and figuratively collateral to the market. The chapters that follow explore the surprising empirical complexities of this insight. But before going further, I want to summarize what I mean by technical legal knowledge, and to flag some of the puzzles and indeterminacies inherent to the subject. I intend this summary as a preview of and guide to what is to come and so I expect that in this initial form this outline will raise a good deal of questions and even provoke some skepticism. Nevertheless, here, in a nutshell, is what I mean when I suggest that we focus on the technical quality of law:

A Constellation of Elements

The first thing that needs to be said is that legal technicality is a package. The technical character of law, as I will use the term, encompasses diverse and even at times contradictory subjects and practices. These include, (1) certain ideologies—legal instrumentalism and managerialism (more on this below); (2) certain categories of experts—especially scholars, bureaucrats and practitioners who treat the law as a kind of tool or machine and who see themselves as modest but expertly devoted technicians; (3) a problem-solving paradigm—an orientation toward defining concrete, practical problems and toward crafting solutions; (4) a form of reasoning and argumentation, from eight-part tests to reasoning by analogy, to the production of stock types of policy arguments to practices of statutory interpretation or citation to case law.

Not all of these elements are present everywhere, and some (such as the skill of deploying policy arguments) are more important in some legal traditions, while others (such as the skill of interpreting the sections of a legal code) will be more significant elsewhere. What these reference collectively, however, is a way of doing legal knowledge, and the cast of experts and tools and artifacts of such doing. That is, "technical legal knowledge" is actually a constellation of material and aesthetic features, and forms of expertise that go with them.

This constellation or package is important to the durability and legitimacy of global markets governance. As we saw, collateral is a set of material and procedural knowledge practices, a set of documentary and institutional tools and outputs that encourages certain forms of collaboration according to carefully scripted routines. Just as in science, where scientific truths emerge as universally accepted and legitimate by virtue of the way available scientific instruments, scientific theories, and institutional and social relations work together and reinforce one another,[52] in the financial markets legitimacy emerges from these interlocking technical practices of communication (Luhmann 1985, 200).

Neither Public nor Private

I have suggested in this chapter how significant the technical quality of law is for global private governance. But as the allusion to bureaucrats in the previous paragraph suggests, there is nothing inherently public or private about legal technicalities. As we will see in chapters 2, 3, and 4, these technicalities pervade regulatory practice within and without the state.

The state also is not just the expression of a set of political norms, nor is it just the institutionalization of a set of communities, or economic interests. It is also a set of knowledge practices engaged in by state actors of all kinds—of making distinctions, compartmentalizing, cutting off, and setting limits. It is through these practices that political legitimacy—the kind of legitimacy that is the hallmark of the liberal state—is created and manipulated. These practices have also long been defining acts of statehood even though they are by no means the province of state actors alone. Think, for example, of what we mean by proceduralism, or by the mechanics of jurisdiction, as practiced by state judicial authorities—like the mechanisms for creating limits described in this chapter, these too are scripts or routines for cutting off, compartmentalizing, and hence channeling politics. Viewed from this perspective, global private law (understood, as I have here, as technical knowledge) is not a radical departure from state law, but really more of the same.

In the next chapter, we will see that there is however a difference between how these devices are deployed within the state and without. I will call this the difference between "technocracy" and "technique" (see below). The chapters that follow describe this difference and demonstrate its implications in detail.

Invisible at Best, and Suspect at Worst

Legal technique is not something that gets much attention among social critics, policymakers, even lawyers (Valverde 2009). Indeed, part of what this package of diverse actions, artifacts, and instruments share is the simple fact that most people are liable to find them profoundly uninteresting at best, and offensive at worst. The Oxford English Dictionary's definition of a legal technicality betrays the derogatory view in which this aspect of legal thought is commonly held: "A point or a detail of a set of rules; spec. a minor legal point, esp. when considered as trivial or when used to evade the intention of the law." One reason for the discomfort, I think, is that, as we saw in this chapter, legal technicality can't simply be understood as the embodiment of legitimate political principles, group customs, or norms. In fact, as we saw, legal technicality is a (highly imperfect) device for privately making the very need for norms go away: global actors seek to take their disputes out of the hands of national regulation and dispose of them, before they ever come to be.

The Defining Feature of Law

Nevertheless, the technical dimension of law is, empirically speaking, the core of law as a practice. It is what distinguishes law from politics, or philosophy, or for that matter art or literature. As Jeremy Waldron points out in his response to calls for eliminating technical language from the law, "an ability and a willingness to locate particular issues within the framework of legal concepts and doctrine remain essential parts of the modern lawyer's craft" (2000, 17). Like Waldron, I want to suggest that if we wish to think about law or regulation in markets or society at large we cannot do without an appreciation of legal technicality because law without legal technique is not law at all.

Purported Political Neutrality

The self-conscious image of legal technique is that it is neutral and agnostic as to its purposes and applications. It is only a tool, nothing more, and can be used by anyone anywhere for any purpose. A technical legal question is by definition not a political matter; it is just a question of how to make the wheels turn better. This view of technical law as neutral and removed from the rough and tumble of fights over how to allocate scarce resources in society itself has political consequences. As we have seen in this chapter, technical regulatory regimes accord special power to insiders and professionals and magically obscure their own politics as, for example, legal rules with profound distributive consequences get framed as merely technical matters. As Carruthers and Halliday (2000) comment for the analogous case of bankruptcy law:

> We find that the ability of professions to exercise lawmaking power in an area such as bankruptcy law increases significantly when agenda setting, inventing and drafting new laws, and legislative politicking takes place underneath the wider horizon of political debate. Politics take place at two levels: when it is above the political horizon, it activates all the forces and counterforces of the political system and thus imports into technical or financial law reform a much wider set of issues than pertain to the substantive and administrative core of the reform itself; this also activates classic patterns of oppositionalism. When it is below the political horizon, it is not widely debated; it does not stir public controversy; it does not activate usual interest group polarities and conflicts; and it does not trigger instinctive party political opposition. Below the horizon, professions can exert much more influence, and they do so characteristically by insisting that their contributions are technical, expert, and neutral and thus do not warrant the scrutiny that might otherwise focus upon them. (74)

Relationship of Means to Ends

Now, as I have defined it, technical thinking need not inherently constitute a technology, that is, a "means to fulfill a human purpose." A way of thinking could simply be technical, in all the senses described here, for its own sake, as a way of life or being, without any larger ambitions about its implications in the world. And yet one of the hallmarks of twentieth-century American legal thought, exported purposely to Japan in the form of corporate and securities laws modeled directly on American law, is that legal technicality is a tool, a technology for doing something, a *means to an end*. That is, technical law ultimately is, and properly should be, an instrument of political interests (e.g., Cohen 1927; Hale 1923).

This understanding of law has a modern aesthetic dimension: it is a call for form to follow function. As the American Legal Realist Roscoe Pound put it,

> Being scientific as a means towards an end, [the law] should be judged by the result it achieves, not by the niceties of its internal structure; it should most be valued by the extent to which it meets its end, not by the beauty of its logical processes or the strictness with which its rules proceed from the dogma it takes for its foundation. (1908, 605)

It also borrows heaving from the American Pragmatist view of all knowledge as a tool with practical uses and consequences (Grey 1991).[53]

This idea is not solely an early twentieth-century American invention, of course, nor is it incompatible with civilian legal thought. The German legal philosopher Hans Kelsen, very much a product and proponent of the Civilian notion of law as a systematic and coherent whole, also vigorously asserted that "Law is a means, a specific social means, not an end" (Kelsen 1941, 80). Of course in this formulation of the relation of means to ends, there is no question about which is most important: Kelsen emphasizes here the primacy of the ends, of the social, over the legal means. The point is that legal tools are *only* tools, to remind lawyers of what their tools are *for*. In chapter 5 we will see an example from Japan of how these claims get deployed and redeployed in battles over regulatory reform.

A Routinized, Compartmentalized Form of Knowledge

What makes legal thought technical is that it entails a set of communicative and conceptual routines (Weber 1968). It is a special skill set as well as the tools needed to deploy those skills and the artifacts they put into motion, skills largely learned through apprenticeship to other master craftspeople rather than through formal legal education. This is what I mean by law as a culture of expertise. As we saw in this chapter, these routines also set legal thought and legal thinkers apart from the rest of market activity; they render legal thought collateral. This in turn raises problems of translatability and empathy across different domains of market activity (Teixeira 2004, 305, 311). But it also enables communication and collaboration across different social, cultural, or political milieu, as long as the same routines hold: A back-office staff member in the Bahamas can resolve an error in a swap transaction with a counterpart in Tokyo or Shanghai in much the same way as she would do with a counterpart across the street.

Practical, That Is, Antitheoretical

Another defining aspect of legal technique is that it is self-consciously practitioner-oriented—in the tradition of the "technical school" as opposed to the university, technical thought is the modus operandi of those who self-consciously eschew "high theory" in favor of an interest in what they view as real-world problems (Kramer 1991; Posnak 1988, 681–682; Sedler 1983; Seidelson 1981, 207). It is a series of problem-solving methods, as opposed to theories, a way of disposing of actual regulatory problems, or disputes, or legal puzzles (e.g., Rabel 1945). Technical law is the "Black hole of legal theory."[54] It is self-consciously low-brow.

Note that there is a kind of paradox to this identity: technical thought exists to facilitate the market, to solve problems as they come up, in the moment (more on this in chapter 3). Yet it does so by virtue of being just one step removed from, collateral to, those day-to-day market problems—technical law is technical, and is law, and hence is most definitely not corporate managerialism or financial trading, in the eyes of its practitioners. Being intimately involved by being just a little distant is the move here. Legal technique is what keeps a committed problem-solver from lapsing into the (slightly vulgar, in lawyers' eyes) role of an actual market participant.

Designed to Travel

All of this means also that technicalities are designed to travel globally. As in the case of ISDA master agreements, they are seen as, among other things, a response to the special problems of the globalization of markets. They can circulate globally but also be translated locally, and indeed it is the job of the legal expert to manage this translation.

Private Regulation: The Technical as Technique

In the chapters that follow, we will see that the elements of technical legal knowledge I have outlined so far can be experienced, deployed, and performed in two different modalities. The first of these is particularly (though as we will see in chapter 4, not exclusively) prevalent in private regulatory regimes. The ethnographic experience of observing legal experts working in financial practice, and also of training lawyers in the uses of their tools, has taught me that lawyers value their tools in a particular way. Legal knowledge is certainly not an end in itself—it always has a larger purpose. But at the same time, it is also not simply a pass-through to an economic or social end. Rather, the day-to-day focus— what garners lawyers' attention, what engages their passion and demands focus, are the means themselves, the technical instruments, their manipulation and use. An ethnography of technical legal expertise, then, must acknowledge the centrality of technique—of the skill and the art, the aesthetics and the bricolage, the satisfaction of rehearsing and perhaps innovating upon or adding to a set of moves and postures one has observed, apprenticed, debated with other initiates. The crucial complexity here is that lawyers are not naive aesthetes: they will always insist that they ultimately value these technical moves only as practical problem-solving tools, defined by practitioners as a question of ends, that is to say, a question of what doctrines are ultimately for. In the long run, it is the ends that matter. But as Keynes famously said, "we leave the long run to the undergraduates" (Guyer 2007, 412). In the meantime, expert technicians focus on the means.

What is at issue here, ultimately, is the experience and larger consequences of legal form. A body of new research in sociolegal studies has demonstrated that the particular legal form regulation takes has wide-ranging social consequences. For example, against the popular view that the law simply expresses popular antipathy toward immigrants found in the wider "society," Calavita's sociological research among Spanish immigration officials and immigrants shows how the doctrines of immigration law actually construct migrants as outlaws and hence produce popular antipathy toward them (1998). Susan Coutin, Bill Maurer, and Barbara Yngvesson (2002) have compared the regulatory practices in the global financial markets, global adoption markets, and immigration regimes to focus on the "legitimation work of globalization"—that is, the work of delineating acceptable cross-border flows (of money, laborers, or babies, for example) from unacceptable ones. Their project points to the large jurisprudential and political questions at stake in such seemingly mundane regulatory practices as "issuing and denying documents, sealing and opening records, regulating and criminalizing transactions, and repudiating and claiming countries and persons" (804).

For anyone educated in American law in this century, this may come as a surprise: Formalism—the view that legal form constrains politics—has long been the foil against which generations of legal theories, from realism to legal process to critical legal studies and law and economics, have defined themselves. What Roscoe Pound disparaged as "mechanical jurisprudence" has been caricatured as a deductive method of reasoning that proceeds according to artificially discrete legal categories and levels of analysis (from the abstract to the concrete, or from broad jurisprudential principles to the facts of the particular case). In the United States, formalism is also associated disparagingly with *Lochner*, that is, with the judge's refusal to implicate the act of judging in the political and social contests of the time. Finally, formalism has been associated with statutes and rule-based decisionmaking, and with theories of judicial interpretation that naively mistake language as a constraint on decisionmaking. In this view, formalism is opposed to contextual methods of interpretation that anchor the meaning of legal doctrines in functions and purposes and in historically contingent and socially constructed understandings, and to judicial decisionmaking that emphasizes standards, policies, and pragmatic institutional solutions to political problems rather than distinctively legal ones.

But an ethnography of lawyers in practice suggests that such arguments are deficient in two crucial aspects. First, they take too simplistic a view of practitioners' commitments to their tools. A lawyer may assert that the language of a statute constrains and also, at another moment, assert that it does not. Far from being a naive formalist, she is actually a most sophisticated epistemologist: she can take both positions at once. This is what I will term, following Hans Vaihinger, the *As If* approach to legal form (chapter 4). Second, such arguments fail to account for the appreciation for the craft of legal form, the pleasure and satisfaction and power and also humility of skating a perfect figure eight, knowing that it has been skated countless times before (chapter 5).

It is in this complicated sense that I will speak of legal technique as having a certain degree of agency of its own. Now, to be clear, our tools do not turn us into automatons; technology can always be resisted, or broken, or abandoned, or tinkered with, or replaced altogether, or ignored. But as anyone who has ever used a word processor, or picked up a tennis racquet, or ridden on a subway surely knows, our tools also shape how we think, what we aspire to achieve, where we choose to go. On this point, STS is particularly helpful where it deals specifically with the character of scientific and technical *instruments* as epistemological and material objects but also as agents of a kind. This work has also shown how once created, instruments partially condition/constrain social analysis *and* social relations, as well as enabling them (Pickering 1997; Winner 1977).

In a recent article, the philosopher and sociologist of science Bruno Latour has suggested that we think of technologies "in the mode of the detour":

> Technology is the art of the curve, or what, following Serres, I have called "translation." . . . When we say there is a technical problem to resolve, we precisely wish to introduce the addressee to the detour, to the labyrinth that he will have to confront before pursuing his initial objectives. When we admire the technique of a specialist, we rightly recognize in it the passage that no one can master, except him, and specifically him, who besides does not know what he is doing (all the specialists in systems of expertise recognize this to their cost). How far we are from the function, from domination, from instrumentality! We find ourselves unexpectedly placed in front of what permits us (without understanding why) or what prevents us (without understanding that either) to have direct access to the goals. (Latour 2002b, 251)

Here Latour restates a point made by Dewey, who famously suggested that unless one is a utopian, the means available must redefine the ends one seeks to achieve (Dewey 1998):

> If we fail to recognize how much the use of a technique, however simple, has displaced, translated, modified, or inflected the initial intention, it is simply because we have changed the end in changing the means, and because,

through a slipping of the will, we have begun to wish something quite else from what we at first desired. If you want to keep your intentions straight, your plans inflexible, your programmes of action rigid, then do not pass through any form of technological life. The detour will translate, will betray, your most imperious desires (Latour 2002b, 252).

What I want to suggest here is that the defining characteristic of technical legal knowledge, in its predominantly private law instantiation as an affinity toward technique, is a deep intuitive appreciation of this point, and hence a profound, but always practical subtlety—perhaps even two-mindedness—about the relationship between one's work and the wider world. We will explore this point further in chapters 4 and 5.

Public Regulation: The Technical as Technocratic

All of the elements of technical legal knowledge I have described can also be experienced and deployed in another modality, however. This modality is predominantly (though not exclusively) associated with public regulation. It is explored further in chapters 2, 3, and 4. For now, suffice it to say that the principal difference between technocratic knowledge and technique inheres in the way the technocrat relates to his tools, and hence what he or she imagines to be his impact in the world. That is, technocracy entails a much more straightforward, much less subtle, conception of technical expertise as a means to an end. Here, the emphasis is much more firmly on the ends to be achieved, and there is less time to get caught up in the wonder of the means. In consequence, the technocrat has less respect for his tools; the thought of mixing them with economics, or policy science, or even ethnography (Holmes 2009) does not offend his sensibilities in the least. The technocrat's sense of "being in charge" can lead to arrogance. But it can also translate into a sense of profound responsibility and self-blame when things go wrong, something that private lawyers rarely experience in quite the same way.

My point, then, will be that all the ideological rhetoric to the contrary, the differences between public and private regulation are far more subtle than usually assumed. Both are working the same machine, but they have become accustomed to working it in different ways, to placing the emphasis at different points. The larger claim will be that there is nothing that inherently impedes private legal technicians from behaving like technocrats or public servants from embracing legal technique, and here lie real nonutopian possibilities for rethinking market regulation.

Notes

1. A core element of financial markets regulation reform in many countries, however, will involve moving at least a portion of swaps trading onto something like an exchange.

2. In the absence of sufficient case law or regulatory actions by the U.S. Securities and Exchange Commission or the Commodity Futures Trading Commission, there has long been uncertainty about the implications of American securities laws for the derivatives markets. The statutory language (concerning such issues as fraud and insider trading) of the American securities laws is very broadly drafted, and designed with the kinds of fraud that would apply to manipulation of on-exchange trading in mind. The case law, likewise, is closely linked to on-exchange transactions. Although doctrinal arguments for the application of portions of the securities laws to certain entities in the swap markets could be made, until 2010, neither the SEC nor the CFTC has shown a strong inclination to develop those arguments.

Nevertheless, the trading activities of swap partners are subject to various forms of regulation, by virtue of these players' nature as regulated institutions. As Hal Scott points out, however, this can lead to irregular levels of regulation in a market that includes a variety of parties, including banks, securities firms, corporations, hedge funds, governments and individuals:

> As a formal matter, the derivatives activities of banks in the United States are highly regulated by bank supervisors. This regulation involves detailed examination of their activities as well as the capital requirements discussed below. . . . However, there is no regulatory framework for supervision of the derivatives activities of securities firms by the SEC or the Commodity Futures Trading Corporation (CFTC). Securities firms are not generally regulated for safety and soundness except through capital requirements, and unregistered affiliates of such firms dealing in swaps have not even been subject to capital requirements, until the SEC's proposal in 2003 in response to the EU's Conglomerates Directive. (Scott 2006, 640)

Banks are subject to capitalization requirements under the terms of the Bank for International Settlements (BIS), an international organization of bank regulators. There are also disclosure and accounting rules that apply to public companies.

3. Most lawsuits by end users of derivatives against dealers have been brought

on common law and statutory grounds such as fraud and failure to disclose material information, or on arguments that the end user plaintiff was prohibited from engaging in derivatives trading (Partnoy 2001, 421; Scott 2006, 663). Lawsuits by dealers in contrast usually seek to enforce the terms of the ISDA agreement, and hence involve the interpretation of the terms of that agreement.

4. ISDA produced the first version of its master agreement in 1987. ISDA revised it in 1992 and again in 2002 to account for new kinds of derivatives products developed in the intervening years (ISDA 1987; 1992; 2002a).

5. See ISDA membership, http://www.isda.org/membership/.

6. For an account of how global private law might be analogous to state law, see Snyder 2003, 371. As Ralf Michaels and Nils Jansen argue, this assumption is more prevalent in the common law literature on private law. In the civil law tradition, in contrast, a different conception of both private law and of the state would hold that private law is in fact a part of state law (Michaels and Jansen 2006, 843).

7. ISDA published the first credit support document in 1994 (ISDA 1994).

8. The 1994 ISDA Credit Support Annex (CSA) presumes that the parties select New York law. In 2000, an ISDA survey found that 61% of CSA users used the New York law form, "reflecting the fact that most collateralized counterparties are in the United States and Canada" (ISDA 2000, 2).

The ISDA Credit Support Annex (Transfer) and ISDA Credit Support Deed (Security Interest), both published in 1995, are two separate documents that work from the point of view of different legal theories of the collateral transaction (ISDA 1995). Under UK law, structuring the collateral transaction as an outright transfer coupled with an obligation to return comparable securities at the close of the transaction provides more rights to the collateral holder (such as the right of rehypothecation) and involves fewer filing requirements. But because some debtors will not accept these terms, ISDA also provides the credit support deed, under which there are filing requirements and the collateral holder has more limited rights vis-à-vis the collateral.

The Credit Support Annex subject to Japanese law was published in 1995.

9. For example the parties can determine such things as whether or not a merger counts as a "credit event," which triggers a party's right to demand further collateral.

10. ISDA estimates that as of 2001 there were somewhere between 1500 and 2500 counterparties using the form, and a total of 12,000 signed bilateral collateral agreements (ISDA 2000, 1) and that by 2003 there were more than 54,000 such signed agreements (ISDA 2005, iv).

11. ISDA's collateral guidelines for practitioners urged the parties to consider the counterparty type (dealer, fund manager, or end user), the public debt rating of the counterparty, the "size, tenor and volatility of the portfolio" of swaps open between the two parties, as well as issues such as the jurisdiction in which

the counterparty is located, in deciding how much and what kind of collateral to demand (ISDA 1999b, 11–12).

12. On the credit rating agency as its own form of global private power which in turn derives much of its power from delegation of authority to it by national governments, see Partnoy 1999; Schwarcz 2002.

13. The pass rate for the bar exam in recent years has been between 2% and 5%. The vast majority of law graduates never even attempt the examination (Riles and Uchida 2009).

14. The contrast is from the point of view of back-office legal staff. From the point of view of the front office, of course, there is much internal differentiation. On the difference between "quants" and "traders" in the front office in a French bank, for example, see Lepinay 2007, 91.

15. In its influential report, the Counterparty Risk Management Policy Group, a committee of market leaders led by E. Gerald Corrigan, then chairman of Goldman Sachs, asserts that "counterparty risk, and in particular counterparty credit risk, is probably the single most important variable in determining whether and with what speed financial *disturbances* become financial *shocks* with potential systemic traits" (Counterparty Risk Management Policy Group II 2005, 7).

16. This fact is generally celebrated in the writings of derivatives lawyers and by some scholars of derivatives law and decried by some scholars of bankruptcy law (Summe 2001, 186). For criticisms from bankruptcy law scholars, see Mann 1995, 993; Mann 1997, 625; Warren and Westbrook 2005, 1197; and Edwards and Morrison 2005, 92.

17. Perhaps this is why a recent study of creditor rights in twelve transition economies found that the protections afforded creditors by collateral law correlate better than the protections afforded creditors by bankruptcy law with increased levels of lending (Haselmann, Pistor, and Vig 2006).

18. As Carruthers, Babb, and Halliday show, bankruptcy law reform is part of the standard package of neoliberal reforms instituted by countries around the world since the early 1990s (2001, 94, 105). These reforms in most cases actually run counter to other neoliberal reforms because by favoring reorganization over liquidation they continue to protect debtors from creditors and to preserve a sphere of national regulation from the reach of global capital (116–18).

19. 1992 ISDA Master Agreement, sec. 6.

20. "Transnational merchant law, which is generally and mistakenly regarded in purely technical, functional, and 'apolitical' terms, is . . . a central and crucial mediator of domestic and global political/legal orders in that it enables the extraterritorial application of national laws as well as the domestic application of transnational commercial law" (Cutler 2003, 4).

21. Conflict of laws issues occupied the attention of ISDA legal staff as much

as any other area of law. Foreign holders of collateral feared that in the event of the bankruptcy of a counterparty in Tokyo, for example, Japanese bankruptcy courts might choose to apply Japanese law and they might not recognize the priority of the collateral transaction over other creditors' claims. According to Hattori and Henderson, Japanese bankruptcy law takes a strongly territorialist position whereby Japanese courts can adjudicate only those assets within Japanese territory (Hattori and Henderson 1983 § 11–27, § 11–28, § 11–29). However, case law diverges from this "to the point where Japanese bankruptcy proceedings affect foreign assets, and foreign bankruptcy proceedings affect assets in Japan" (§ 11–28).

22. On questions relating to the validity of the collateral, some jurisdictions, following classical private international law rules, look to the law of the place where the securities are held. But doctrine in this area developed to deal with tangible forms of property, such as paper securities, where collateral is now but numbers in a computerized account, or in multiple accounts, maintained by multiple intermediaries, such that the question of where it "is" for the purpose of this analysis is almost metaphysically unanswerable. One resolution adopted by some jurisdictions (including the United States in the wake of recent revisions to the UCC, as concerns certain issues) is to look to the law of the place where the intermediary whose account the collateral is held with is located (Potok 1999, 12). Recent revisions to articles 8 and 9 specifically take the UCC global by addressing questions of choice of law and tailoring the terms to the character of cross-border transactions according to UCC § 8–110 (b):

The local law of the securities intermediary's jurisdiction, as specified in subsection (e), governs:

(1) acquisition of a security entitlement from the securities intermediary;
(2) the rights and duties of the securities intermediary and entitlement holder arising out of a security entitlement;
(3) whether the securities intermediary owes any duties to an adverse claimant to a security entitlement; and
(4) whether an adverse claim can be asserted against a person who acquires a security entitlement from the securities intermediary or a person who purchases a security entitlement or interest therein from an entitlement holder.

Another approach (adopted in the United States by UCC Article 9 with respect to certain issues relating to the validity of the security interest) is to look to the law of the location of the debtor. See UCC Article 9 (1999); 3 U.L.A. 9, 9 (Supp. 1999) (effective July 1, 2001) (Bull 2000, 679).

For many (but not all) legal issues surrounding validity, Japanese courts will look to the law of the place where the securities were issued (Kanda 2002, 366). But this says nothing about what law would govern the question of the priority of the collateral holder's claim in the event of bankruptcy. The question of how different national courts with jurisdiction over the assets of a bankrupt company with transnational contacts should coordinate, and when they should defer to the law of another jurisdiction, remains very much unresolved (Buxbaum 2000, 23).

23. Wai adapts the Legal Realist and critical legal studies insight that technical legal issues (such as which law should apply) are always already forms of political compromise and hence open for reopening as tools of political change (Unger 2001) to suggest that Private International Law is uniquely suited to address the particular problems posed by the global private such as overlapping legal regimes, or "regulatory gaps" where no particular state regulates a certain practice (Wai 2002, 209).

24. As one such lawyer writes, "The ISDA Agreement should not be perceived as a law unto itself. The fundamental legal principles of contract law, company law, trust law, the law of torts and the law of insolvency, etc., still apply, as appropriate, in circumstances where an ISDA Agreement becomes the subject-matter of litigation. From a business standpoint, the significance of national boundaries has decreased considerably in the last decade. However, it remains the case that, from a legal standpoint, national boundaries continue to be very important, not least in the context of insolvency" (Foy 1999, 104).

25. In the United States, intensive lobbying on the part of ISDA has resulted in important revisions of New York state law, the UCC, and the national bankruptcy law, and has averted other proposed regulation opposed by ISDA. The European Union likewise has responded to ISDA lobbying by producing a directive on collateral supported by ISDA. In Japan, ISDA has an elaborate system of committees in place to address legal reforms as well as high-level contacts in all relevant branches of the Japanese bureaucracy. The representatives of even the foreign banks at ISDA Tokyo meetings are almost exclusively Japanese employees of these foreign banks, typically graduates of top universities who have former professors with respected credentials and former classmates in the bureaucracy and on the bench.

26. On December 13, 2002, the Hague Conference on Private International Law adopted a Convention on the Law Applicable to Certain Rights in Respect of Securities Held with an Intermediary. This convention, a product of intensive lobbying by ISDA and other global commercial groups, affirms that if the agreement between the intermediary and the custodian of the security specifies which law should apply, that law applies as long as it bears a reasonable relationship to the transaction. The first order principle of the convention is the freedom of the account holder and intermediary (but not the pledgor and pledgee) to choose the applicable law by contract. Groups such as ISDA participated actively in the drafting of the convention. In an article in support of the convention, the Hague Conference official with primary responsibility for its drafting defends this freedom of contract principle on grounds that states have an interest in economic development, and in supporting "certainty in the marketplace promoted

by the Convention" (Sigman and Bernasconi 2005, 35). The convention was concluded July 5, 2006. However, the convention has not yet come into force. And in any case, even if which law governs the collateral agreement is settled, this does not resolve the question of the relationship between the law of collateral and the law of bankruptcy: it does not preclude a Japanese bankruptcy court, for example, from recognizing the collateral as valid under New York law as specified by the CSA, but then applying Japanese bankruptcy law to the question of whether the collateral holder should be able to keep the collateral after a bankruptcy filing.

27. Parliament and Council Directive 2002/47 on financial collateral arrangements, O.J. (L 168) 43. On the reasons for EU regulation, see Summe 2001.

28. UNIDROIT, the International Institute for the Unification of Private Law, is "a global legal organization with 59 Member States whose laws include all the key systems of financial law around the world" (UNIDROIT 2003, 5).

29. The UNIDROIT Secretariat submitted a preliminary draft on December 23, 2004, which was further negotiated by a committee of experts in May 2005 (UNIDROIT 2005). See also ISDA 2002c.

30. In contrast, the fact that these global norms are "spontaneously generated" and not the product of purposeful law-making activity has led one commentator to doubt whether they are coherent enough to constitute a source of law (Goode 2005, 547).

31. Many political scientists and lawyers describe private norms as more "complex" and "heterodox" than state law because each industry makes its own norms. The result is a pluralistic legal order with no clear hierarchies of norms (Cerny 2000, 60). In this view, the single unitary state is an obsolete idea, and we should instead understand law as many coexisting, fragmented, sometimes integrated, sometimes conflicting normative orders with different degrees of access to coercive authority—the coercive authority of the state and of other forces in society (Santos 2002, 85).

32. The notion that communities—in this case communities of global market players—solve their problems and order their behavior independently of the state by creating their own unique norms is an idea that anthropologists bear some responsibility for introducing to law and policy debates early in the last century. This assumption traces its genealogy back to early anthropological arguments. Bronislaw Malinowski, one of the founding fathers of modern social anthropology, for example, remained deeply suspicious of the political consequences of early twentieth-century progressive legal scholars' love of the regulatory state:

> If you try to make this mechanism [law] penetrate where it does not belong, you either make law ineffective or else when you try to make it effective you destroy the very institutions which you wish to build up. The school opened to espionage, the home opened to the police, the churches surveyed by a band of orga-

> nized hooligans . . . these are the results of the complete disorga-
> nization of law in modern society. . . .
>
> [I]n modern jurisprudence we must demand a wider vision
> from the theoretician, a vision which will give him the capac-
> ity to help us practically. Law is being used nowadays as a pana-
> cea. Politics is running riot. Every thing is to be settled by some
> grand council or committee of commissars. That way lies real
> savagery, such as is not to be found in primitive societies. Such
> artificial rules either do not work or work at such cost to the most
> fundamental institutions of mankind: family, religious commu-
> nity, school, and the communion of people for recreation, sport
> and pleasure, that all the substance of social life and culture are
> destroyed. (Malinowski 1961, lxix–lxxi)

Ironically, Malinowski the anthropologist voices here the same suspicions of
state interventionism as does the libertarian F. A. Hayek, writing at approximately the same time (Hayek 1948a, 1948b, 1952). The sociolegal literature repeats the same refrain where it emphasizes that the real source of security of
contract in the global marketplace is not legal institutions but private networks
built on relations of trust among global elites. This notion of the primacy of
group norms has become the basis for new borrowings from anthropology in legal scholarship as well. The legal scholar Paul Schiff Berman for example calls
for borrowing from the insights of anthropology and cognate fields in the study
of globalization to afford "a more nuanced idea of how people actually form affiliations, construct communities, and receive and develop legal norms" (Berman 2005, 485, 489).

33. A recent empirical paper hints at trouble for the view of standardized contracts as mere vessels of textual meaning. Choi and Gulati make the interesting
claim that some terms of boilerplate often have no clear meaning even among industry members (2006, 1129). They do not enshrine clearly accepted norms, in
other words.

34. Concerns about boilerplate contracts first arose in the context of contracts
between industry and consumers. Hillman and Rachlinski (2002) query whether
these concerns are valid even in this limited context. What the law and economics literature on standardize contracts so far fails to address fully is the effect of
such contracts on third parties who are not insiders—parties such as potential
creditors in bankruptcy in the case of ISDA agreements. Unsurprisingly, my informants also did not show a great deal of concern about the wider consequences
of their contracts for the interests of third parties and other outsiders.

35. It is certainly the case that the ISDA forms aim to present terms favorable
to industry insiders—to dealers rather than end users of derivatives. As Prof.
Christian Johnson puts it,

> Dealers place strong pressure on end users to sign the dealer's
> draft of Schedule and other documents without making any
> changes. . . . [T]he preprinted form of ISDA Master Agree-
> ment was drafted through ISDA by dealers to serve the needs
> and requirements of dealers. Often the Schedule presented by
> the dealer is particularly one-sided and should be reviewed care-
> fully. . . . Industry practice is to make no changes directly on any
> of the pre-printed ISDA forms. The only information that is typ-
> ically added to the preprinted form is the date of the agreement,
> the parties' names and possibly their jurisdiction of organization
> and their respective signature blocks. (Johnson 2000, 18)

36. Anna Gelpern (personal communication) makes the important observation that what is boilerplate and what is negotiated can shift over time in such
agreements, such that what is "mere" boilerplate at one moment can become
highly significant negotiated text at another.

37. For example, Raffel (1979) describes how hospital medical records create alliances, and Smith (1990, 216) shows how social relations are "mediated"
through items such as passports, birth certificates, application forms, and bills.
Henderson (1999) considers how changes in the instruments of design technology in turn lead to other changes in organizational structure. Wheeler analyzes
recordkeeping as a tool of social control made potent by a number of special
characteristics of the file—its legitimacy or authority, its permanence, its transferability, its facelessness, and the fact that files can be combined and organized
in a number of different ways (Wheeler and Russell Sage Foundation 1969, 5).

38. In his analysis of recommendation forms, for example, anthropologist
Don Brenneis (2006) shows how these forms anticipate and call forth certain disciplined responses from evaluators that nevertheless sometimes leave room for
unanticipated surprises. Likewise, Hirokazu Miyazaki (2006a) has shown how
a tabular record prepared in advance of a mortuary gift-giving ritual anticipates
certain kinds of form-filling practices and also formats a particular kind of experience of the ritual at the moment of its completion. In a somewhat analogous way, Karen Knorr-Cetina and Urs Bruegger describe traders' visual experience of the market through the formatting of a computer screen such as the
Bloomberg terminal as a kind of "postsocial" form of relationality (2002, 161).
As Mariana Valverde puts it, documentation demands that we ask "not about
the content of claims but about *process* and *flow*—about how actors pick through
documents or discourses and cobble together new governing machines that recy-
cle old bits in new ways" (2005, 419).

39. "How are . . . deals legally accomplished in the absence of a fully developed framework of global law? The key to this lies in *legal work*, and the role
of legal work in transnational transactions. The term *legal work* is used here to

mean technical work, with and on the law, undertaken usually but not necessarily by lawyers, in specific transactions for specific clients" (McBarnet 2002, 98–99).

40. In addressing the private international law issues surrounding collateral by creating versions of its collateral agreement that are specifically tailored to the laws of the United Kingdom, New York, and Japan, ISDA relies upon a doctrine of private international law that in matters of contract the parties should be able to choose which law applies to their transaction so long as it bears a reasonable relationship to the transaction (Scoles 2004, 947). In Japanese law, this principle is codified in a statute (Law Concerning the Applications of Laws in General 1898). Article 7 (1) reads: "As regards the formation and effect of a juristic act, the question as to the law of which country is to govern shall be determined by the intention of the parties."

41. By "aesthetic," I do not mean beautiful or even pleasing. Rather drawing on the anthropologist Gregory Bateson's definition of an aesthetic sensibility as "empathy towards pattern" (1980, 8), I use the term to signal the power of form to define the limits and possibilities of thought and social life (Riles 2000; Strathern 1988, 1991).

42. Susan Silbey has produced a detailed critical retrospective on the traditional law and society view that law is simply an artifact of social context (2005, 323).

43. Observers point to the "disintermediation" (Cerny 2000, 62) of finance through techniques of securitization as a "qualitative change in the global markets" (Ronit and Schneider 2000).

44. The existing debate on standardized contracts is curiously domestic in its theoretical focus. This is all the more surprising because some of the work includes excellent case studies of contracts tailored for paradigmatically transnational legal problems (Choi and Gulati 2006; Gelpern and Gulati 2007).

45. ISDA's Web site states,

> Only ISDA members are entitled to receive the Association's legal opinions on the enforceability of the netting provisions of the 1992 and 2002 ISDA Master Agreements, which enable institutions to reduce credit risk and consequently capital requirements in jurisdictions subject to BIS capital regulations. ISDA has obtained netting opinions for 50 jurisdictions. Each year, ISDA commissions additional netting opinions for its members. In addition, ISDA obtains collateral opinions for its members. At present, ISDA has obtained 43 collateral opinions and these opinions are updated annually for members. (http://www.isda .org/membership, accessed July 20, 2010)

Choi and Gulati recount a case of the emergence of an ambiguity with respect to a term in the ISDA Master Agreement and argue that, in that case as in others, "the response was immediate. . . . The presence of ISDA ensured a mechanism for coordination and prompt response" (2006, 1144).

46. Likewise, Doreen McBarnet and Michael Powell argue, for the case of international tax lawyers and corporate takeover law respectively, that law is the artifact of the accumulation of individual legal projects and of solutions developed by lawyers operating separately in the service of their clients (McBarnet 1994, 73; 2002; Powell 1993, 423).

47. Science studies scholars have argued that scientific truths and economic markets are artifacts of networks of theories, ideas, people, institutions, machines, and other "actants"—nodes of animate and inanimate agency (Latour 1987, 1996).

48. Callon's argument departs from the legal ideology, however, where it emphasizes how such "framing" devices also inevitably lead to "overflowing," that is, the frame cannot hold back the floods of complexity and calculation breaks down.

49. Working first in scientific contexts, Bruno Latour and Steve Woolgar have described scientific documents as "inscriptions" (Hevia 1968; Latour and Woolgar 1986) and scientific work as the practice of producing, circulating, and evaluating these inscriptions. Latour and Woolgar describe scientists as "compulsive and almost manic writers" who spend their days making lists, filling in forms, writing numbers on samples, and drafting and redrafting articles (48). They draw attention to "transcription devices" that "transform pieces of matter into written documents" such as graphs or diagrams that in turn are manipulated into documents of yet other kinds (51). More recently, Latour has extended the analysis to law in his study of the French Conseil d'État (Latour 2002a).

50. Dezalay and Garth (2002) describe a parallel case: in the conflict between economists and lawyers over who would emerge as master of the ambiguities of development in mid-twentieth century Latin America, the economists emerged as the victors in many (but not all) cases.

51. Carruthers and Stinchcombe (1999) show how the abstraction and standardization required in order to have market liquidity is always "a social and cognitive achievement."

52. STS scholars have repeatedly shown how scientific instruments such as the microscope are material encasements of scientific theories, and they have emphasized the way the tenacity and even object qualities of instruments are shaped by theoretical arguments as well as by social or political relations. The authority and contestability of theories, likewise, is defined by the instrument's epistemological, political, and physical durability (Gooding, Pinch, and Shaffer 1989; Latour 1987).

53. On the influence of pragmatism on Legal Realism, see Horwitz 1977. As Cornel West has put it, the core of pragmatism consists in "a future-oriented instrumentalism that tries to deploy thought as a weapon to enable more effective

action" (1989, 5). In William James's words, "The pragmatic method . . . is to try to interpret each notion by tracing its respective practical consequences. What difference would it practically make to anyone if this notion rather than that notion were true?" (2000, 194).

54. As Duncan Kennedy once put it, in reference to the technicalities of the field of Conflict of Laws. Personal communication with author, 1999.

CHAPTER TWO

The Technocratic State

In the introduction, I alluded to the contradictions, changes of heart, and uneasy alliances that pervade the ideological debates about state intervention in markets, and markets' intervention in states. One recurring theme in these conversations is a marked anxiety about the encroachment of the realm of the private on the realm of the public (so-called special interests) and of the realm of the public on the private (so-called socialism). What all this anxiety suggests is that for better or worse, public and private are inexorably entangled. So if we want to understand the workings of private law, we need to understand something about public law as well.

The aim of this chapter, then, is to explore the public side of technical legal knowledge. What does technical legal knowledge look like? How is it different when it is practiced by agents of the state? We will see that state knowledge—what I will call "technocratic knowledge," with absolutely no normative valence, positive or negative, intended—is indeed different from the private technical expertise discussed in the last chapter. But ideological claims for or against the encroachment of the state on the market or the market on the state notwithstanding, we will see that there are also many important similarities. To put it simply, both public and private actors face uncertainty of all kinds in their work in the market. And both confront these uncertainties using their own bounded rationality—their own conceptual tools. We will see how these tools, moreover, are often legal tools—technical legal expertise and its outputs.

In focusing on the conceptual tools and moves of regulators, what Frank Upham has termed "regulatory style" (1996), I paint a complementary but different picture of the behavior of regulators than the dominant account in academic, journalistic, and policy circles. The main-

stream account focuses on the "interests" and "incentives" of regulators—
how pressures from within the political process or "capture" by certain
special interests lead to a lack of regulatory confidence, courage, and
stamina or, worse, lead regulators to sacrifice the interests of the many
in favor of the interests of the few. The image here is of the regulator as a
rational actor responding, selfishly but nevertheless rationally, to the institutional setting in which she finds herself. In chapter 3 we will see how
this story served as the driving narrative for massive neoliberal reforms
in Japan in the 1990s. But more recently the story has also been picked
up by progressives who seek to explain why regulators failed to prevent
the recent economic crisis (Carnell 2010).

I don't want to suggest that interests and incentives are irrelevant. But
surely if each of us simply reflects for a moment on our own lives we can
also understand that interests and incentives are never the whole story.
To begin with, people's motivations are more complicated than the rational actor model suggests. But even where motivations do work as suggested in these accounts, surely *how* regulators do their work—how they
think, what tools they use, and hence what possibilities they can or cannot imagine—is as important as *why* they do what they do.[1]

Thinking in ethnographic detail about technocratic legal knowledge—
about how regulators think—also helps us to see new possibilities in
the stale old debates about the legitimacy of state intervention in markets. For some, the dismantling of the state over the last twenty years has
been a cause for celebration. In this view, public solutions are almost always coercive, inefficient, unresponsive, and even degrading to ordinary
people. These arguments may have been quieted just a touch by the recent dramatic debacles in the financial markets but they have not disap-
peared. In the United States recently, they resurface in populist activism
against state-sponsored health insurance (populism often underwritten
by private insurance companies), in ominous threats from the financial
industry to move its operations offshore if it becomes subject to excessive regulation, and in the handwringing of politicians who suggest that
we go slow on reform and take cognizance of the possible unintended
consequences of any new regulatory program.

Meanwhile, throughout the last twenty years of dismantling the state,
progressive legal scholars have produced normative defenses of state
power, while social scientists have documented the social consequences
of its dismantling. Now, of course, progressives are once again advocating hard for rebuilding a new regulatory state. What is surprising, how-

ever, is how quickly those of us on this side of things have settled into a "back to the future" mindset. Policy proposals on the table, from the re-creation of the Glass-Steagall Act to the creation of a new consumer credit agency are explicitly modeled on the initiatives of the early, energetic years of the regulatory state. An important new progressive foundation on markets reform issues has adopted as its name the Roosevelt Institute, and the title of its blog says it all: "New Deal 2.0."

Now a return to the New Deal might be the right way to go. I certainly support efforts to rein in large financial interests and to democratize finance. But if we are to make headway in these political debates for and against the withering state and, more important, if we are to imagine all the best, possible alternatives for market regulation, it becomes important to understand exactly what kind of state is being defended or attacked, or mimicked by private regulatory solutions, or incorporated into new transnational regulatory initiatives. It becomes important to understand how certain perennial anxieties about the legitimacy of the regulatory state, and certain perennial solutions and responses to those anxieties, are intimately bound up with how "state work" is done through technical legal devices.

Finally, understanding how much is shared between public and private knowledge work—understanding how technical legal knowledge can take the form of either private technique or public technocracy—helps to break down the knee-jerk view that public and private are always at loggerheads. It opens us up to new possibilities for collaboration between the two regulatory spheres. We often say that private regulation ultimately depends upon the state, and hence is not fully private. But how exactly is this the case, at the level of daily practice? What are the mechanisms for this partnership, what are the actors, the institutions, the moves, the artifacts that come into line to make this a reality? We lack a clear picture of the knowledge practices that constitute the abstract notion of state and market relations.

I propose to look closely at two examples of the technocratic state in action. Since the early twentieth century American regulatory state is now increasingly the model for the new progressive agenda, I turn first to technocratic legal knowledge in this period. Legal historians have clearly demonstrated that one cannot understand the success of the early twentieth-century regulatory state independently of the rise of a theoretical movement in the law known as Legal Realism. It should be no surprise, given the calls to recreate this regulatory state, that in the legal academy a New Legal Realism movement has blossomed and is gaining speed. Given all this, understanding the *how* of Realism, and its elaboration in state regulatory projects, may give us a richer and more complex picture of what we are advocating for, when we call for the return to the old regulatory state. The episode of Realist reform I will focus on concerns the legal reimagination of the central motif of this book, collateral.

This example serves another purpose in this book. Japan's post–World War II occupation was administered by American New Dealers who laid in place the legal foundations for its regulatory state. Although Japan's underlying civil law is largely of German and French origin, Japan's constitutional provisions governing property rights, and its laws governing corporations, banking, and securities were drafted by American occupation-era technocrats and bear a strong resemblance to the American laws of that time (in some cases they actually go beyond the U.S. progressive standard, as New Dealers posted to Japan took advantage of their authority to push through regulatory agendas that would have met with conservative opposition in the United States). Lawyers involved in the corporate and securities law fields in Japan frequently insist to me that this area of Japanese law is "American," and most of the experts in these fields choose to study abroad in the United States if they study abroad, and read and engage American scholarship and policy debates when they turn to foreign materials. In this field, in other words, understanding Japan demands understanding something about the American New Deal regulatory experience.

My second example concerns an episode in the Japanese financial bureaucracy's involvement in the market at the time of my fieldwork. Japan is known for its system of "administrative guidance"—what some term "informal lawmaking." I will describe one episode in administrative guidance I observed in the field—the effort to accommodate the desire of global swap industry participants to ensure that the industry practice of "netting out" transactions in the case of counterparty default was protected under Japanese law.

These two examples, from different jurisdictions, different regulatory cultures, and different periods in the historical development of the regulatory state hint at the diversity of forms technocracy can take. But thinking comparatively across these two examples also brings to light certain similarities in the uses of legal technique.

One final thought before we begin: I imagine that some readers will find this focus on regulatory practice as knowledge practice a bit odd, perhaps beside the point, too much fluff, something of a detour from the serious issues of the day. Perhaps some may even feel that by talking of the state as a set of knowledge practices I am trivializing it. What I hope to convince the reader of, however, is that knowledge is not a flourish or a detour; it is a very serious thing. The legal techniques at work in doing state work are real. They are consequential. And thinking of the state as the practice and effects of knowledge work does not trivialize it, but specify it. As we will see in chapter 3, precisely because it is so important, technocratic knowledge has been the site of tremendous ideological and legal conflict. Critics of state regulation have repeatedly managed to delegitimize state involvement in the market by trivializing the knowledge practices of technocrats. So readers who believe there is a legitimate role for the state to play in markets, but who do not have time for a serious inquiry into the nature of technocratic knowledge, might ask themselves if they have not unwittingly taken on board the neoliberal critique.

From Pledge to Secured Transaction

"Have you heard the phrase, 'sunlight is the best disinfectant?'" writes a progressive blogger on the financial reforms. "Do you know where it comes from? It's from the progressive Supreme Court Justice Louis Brandeis . . . from a book he wrote in 1914 called Other People's Money" (Konczal 2010). The blogger goes on to claim current reforms as heirs to New Deal progressivism:

> These arguments from Brandeis formed the core of the New Deal financial reforms. . . . Resolution authority is just an updated FDIC. . . . The CFPA [Consumer Finance Protection Act] is just an updated Securities Act. . . . I think history is on our side. And we have the ideas needed for this battle. So let's fight.

Louis Brandeis is, of course, an inspiration not just for progressive bloggers but for generations of legal scholars and practicing lawyers. He is generally regarded as one of the most skilled practitioners of the legal craft, and also as someone whose opinions and writings *modernized* American lawyers' way of thinking about what the law is and what it should accomplish in society and the markets. And so it is interesting that Brandeis's book on finance mentioned by this blogger contains almost no law at all. In this book, Brandeis proposes rather a series of institutional reforms: requiring greater transparency about how investment banks set their rates; establishing cooperative credit associations that could compete with the interests of Wall Street on behalf of producers and consumers, and so on. He is proposing new forms of institutional design, new kinds of market arrangements.

If lawyers may be somewhat disappointed to find that Brandeis has little to say about the role of law in market reform, it may disappoint this blogger also to know that Brandeis's tradition of legal thought has inspired present-day market reform projects across the political spectrum, and not just on the left. The predominantly conservative law and economics movement for example, which played a pivotal role in market deregulation over the last twenty years (chapter 3), is very much heir to this larger project of replacing legal frameworks of reasoning with frameworks that are closer to the market. The example of Legal Realist market reform that follows, likewise, does not fit squarely into an agenda of progressive market regulation.

In its contemporary doctrinal form, the American law of collateral, governed by Article 9 of the Uniform Commercial Code, is the artifact of one of the most ambitious legal reform projects of the twentieth century. In 1951 the Uniform Commercial Code (UCC) drafting committee, led by the renowned Realist legal theorist Karl Llewellyn, set out to propose a new set of rules governing the taking of collateral among merchants. The drafters of Article 9 were Karl Llewellyn, Soia Mentschikoff, Grant Gilmore, and Allison Dunham (Gilmore 1951, 27).

Earlier parts of the code already constituted a radical rethinking of the law of merchants according to Llewellyn's own version of Legal Realism. And yet, according to a drafter, "No other area of the code proposes such a radical departure from prior law" (Gilmore 1951, 27). The objective was an overthrow of the old legal regime of outdated and technical legal syllogisms in favor of something modern and new. Specifically, the drafters of the UCC envisioned a change from the legal categories such as chattel mortgage, or pledge, to a new, and singular device with an invented name, "security," defined purely by its economic function and hence by the community of its users—merchants (1951, 27). As Llewellyn explained, the idea was to abandon legal categories in favor of categories that rationalized existing market practice:

> In regard to secured commercial transactions, there is a wealth of recognized legal devices, traditional, established, familiar at least to the rather small selection of lawyers who have specialized in the field. . . . What more is needed? The answer runs in terms of seven ideas: clarity; simplicity, convenience, and fairness . . . ; completeness, accessibility, and uniformity. (1948, 687)

As Garrard put it in the context of the earlier American Law Institute project of restatement of the law of security,

> pledge is simple enough if we accept the thing for what it really is, and quit discussing it from the standpoint of common law actions. In other words, the pledge is really a security device. . . . It is, in truth, a method of dealing in property for the purpose of securing payment of a debt. (1938, 355–56)

Because the functions of these various doctrines were the same, the rational thing to do was to abolish them and replace them with one singular instrument, the security interest.

Up to that point, collateral had been treated as a species of property law—a special category of property right. But for Llewellyn, property law was abstract and out of touch with merchant realities. Title was a "static concept" whereas "the essence of the Sales transaction is dynamic" (1938, 166–67). Llewellyn's project of harmonizing, simplifying, and unifying, then, was a project of displacing the categories of property law with a new kind of law altogether—a law of what was really at stake, with a modern, technical name, "secured transactions," not beholden to existing legal categories but rather defined by the needs of the market. As one of the drafters wrote, "It cuts across what have been regarded as separate fields of law, introduces a completely new terminology, incidentally repeals much older law, and in the process creates, and attempts to solve, new problems of its own" (Gilmore 1951, 28).

As was Llewellyn's ambition throughout the UCC, the drafters drew directly on "technical information supplied by financing agencies" about the uses of security arrangements and sought to fashion legal rules that "more accurately reflect operating methods" (Gilmore 1951, 34). The objective was an "examination of the fact-situations to which the concepts are applied" followed by their transformation "into standard tools for systematic use" (Llewellyn 1938, 161). The drafters of Article 9 took pains to insist that their project was not a project of reform of the Left or

the Right, and in fact was likely to make enemies on both sides of the political spectrum (Gilmore 1951, 47). Rather it was a purely instrumentalist, technocratic project of rendering the law more efficient, systematic,
and coordinated.

As mentioned above, Llewellyn's radical reforms of the law of collateral grew directly out of a movement in legal thought known as Legal Realism, which held above all that the law should be brought into
line with reality (Horwitz 1992). In this view, the formal qualities of
law—what made law different from, say, engineering or policy science—
were a problem, an embarrassment even, because they did not reflect reality. Rather than tinker with the abstractions of legal title (property
law), Llewellyn proposed to rethink property interests in terms of market participants' understandings of how risk should be allocated (Wiseman 1987, 493). Eliminating such formalities or technicalities in this Realist view made the law more transparent, and hence more efficient. For
Llewellyn, moreover, judging should be an open-ended empirical inves-
tigation into the nature of realities—more akin to ethnography than to
traditional legal analysis (Danzig 1975, 625), something he knew quite
a bit about as a longtime scholarly collaborator with the anthropologist
E. Adamson Hoebel. In this view, the technical stuff of law—most of
what I focus on in this book—was just "law in the books." It was not a
useful resource for regulatory practice because it was all entirely ma-
nipulable by experts anyway. Rather, it was the social and economic
realities that always drove the law; it was in the real world that better solutions could be found—credit cooperatives for Brandeis or the market
practice of securing transactions for Llewellyn.

Like Brandeis, Karl Llewellyn was, in fact, no outsider to legal
thought—on the contrary, he was one of its greatest practitioners and
promoters. But as a law reform project, the UCC radically mixed law
with other forms of technical market expertise—finance, merchant relations, ethnography. Law in this view was just a part of a wider project of sophisticated institutional and market design. State regulation of
markets involved designing institutions that reflect and work with market realities to channel them in better (more efficient, or more progressive) directions.

The modernization of collateral law into the law of secured transactions depended upon one basic jurisprudential conception: law should
be a means to an (economic) end. This was the key dogma of the Realist movement. Law was, in Roscoe Pound's words, "a means to an end,

that end ultimately being the determination of what rules of decision are to be applied to given factual situations" (1959, 285). For Benjamin Cardozo, likewise, "Few rules in our time are so well established that they may not be called upon any day to justify their existence as means adapted to an end" (1921, 98). Karl Llewellyn insisted that Realism demanded a "conception of law as means to social ends and not as an end in itself; so that any part needs constantly to be examined for its purpose, and for its effect, and to be judged in the light of both and their relation to each other" (1931, 1236). As Walter Cook put it,

> This view [his own view of legal knowledge] does not lead to the discarding of all principles and rules, but quite the contrary. It demands them as tools with which to work; as tools without which we cannot work effectively. It does, however, make sure that they are used as tools and are not perverted to an apparently mechanical use. (1924, 487)

As we saw in the last chapter, this idea of law as a means to an end is an important element of legal technique. It is as important to private law as to public regulatory thinking. On this point, moreover, Cook and others were borrowing from a wider philosophical tradition of thinking of knowledge as a tool or an instrument with practical uses and consequences. This tradition, American Pragmatism, as expressed in particular in the philosophy of John Dewey, sought to replace philosophical questions of cause and effect with practical questions of instrumentalities, and of means and ends.[2] In particular, the emphasis on the workings of judicial knowledge borrowed from antifoundationalist and antirationalist approaches to truth as the outcome of purposeful social practice rather than logic (Clark 2002). In thinking of law as a means to an end, therefore, the Realists found common ground with early twentieth-century politicians, philosophers, and social scientists concerned with countering the threat of socialism, developing scientific justifications for capitalist democracy, and promoting social reform (Ross 1991, 143). Pragmatism also provided the rationale for moving away from pure legal thought and mixing legal expertise with market expertise, as in the UCC project. As Henry James pointed out, pragmatism's success lay in its ability to "harmonize" many kinds of knowledge:

> *Theories thus become instruments, not answers to enigmas, in which we can rest.* We don't lie back upon them, we move forward, and, on occasion, make

nature over again by their aid. Pragmatism unstiffens all our theories, limbers them up and sets each one at work. (James 2000, 196)

The idea here was that the chaotic, continually changing nature of social and economic problems could be accommodated and even embraced by a highly rationalized, technical means/ends framework that would calibrate the law according to changing conditions.

Now it will be clear that this project demands a certain state of mind, a certain attitude toward one's tools on the part of the technocratic reformer. There is a confidence, an energy, a creativity, a hopefulness and enthusiasm about the UCC project and parallel New Deal era reforms that understandably inspires present-day progressives. There is also a curiosity about the world—a fascination with actual real-world practices and a confidence that incorporating these into the law would represent a positive innovation. But it also takes considerable confidence in one's intellect—perhaps even a certain degree of arrogance—to believe that one can just muddle through pragmatically, borrowing at will, from one kind of expertise here and another kind there. The attitude was one of confidence that on balance, the legal expert—recast now as a state manager, planner—could muddle through. As Landis put it in a statement intended as a celebration of the administrative state:

> This breadth of jurisdiction and freedom of disposition tends somewhat to make judges jacks-of-all-trades and masters of none. Modern jurisprudence with its pragmatic approach is only too conscious of this problem. To its solution it brings little more than a method of analysis, a method that calls upon the other sciences to provide the norms. It thus expands rather than contracts areas of inquiry. If the issues for decision are sociological in nature, the answers must be on that plane. If the problem is a business problem, the answer must be derived from that source. But incredible areas of fact may be involved in the disposition of a business problem that calls not only for legal intelligence but also for wisdom in the ways of industrial operation. (Landis 1938, 31)

Gone is the humility toward the tradition of legal form that defined legal technique. Legal technique now is just a tool, just one tool among others, in the hands of some very smart technocrats.

Implicit here also is a view of what the proper role for the state in the market should be. The state, through its master planners and their sophisticated cross-disciplinary knowledge work, should be involved. Far from the view that such involvement is politically problematic, the view here is that it is the very emblem of the state's legitimacy: legitimacy depends on effectiveness in solving real world problems.

But, of course, as anyone who has ever attempted to study the UCC knows, it is about as technical as it gets. It is surely not the case, therefore, that the Realist reforms erased legal technicalities from the law. On the contrary. And like the old technicalities of private law, this new technicality was imagined by its proponents as essentially nonpolitical. The UCC, from its drafters' point of view, was a neutral tool, politically speaking. It simply made commercial relations more efficient. Before thinking about this further, let us now turn to our second example of technocracy in action.

Bureaucratic Bargaining

As Steven Vogel has put it, the wave of very radical neoliberal reforms in Japan in the 1990s and 2000s known as the Big Bang were a "bureaucratic-led bargain" (2005, 220). In the postwar era, the Japanese bureaucracy has been a powerful institution. For several centuries it has attracted Japan's best and brightest. A son's (and more recently a daughter's) passage of the stringent examinations systems that stand between a graduate of an elite university and a position in the bureaucracy has been the key to social mobility. In the postwar period, the prewar ideology of technocracy in the service of militarism was quite smoothly converted into technocracy in the service of anti-imperialism, democracy, and economic growth, and in this conversion the technocratic dimension of U.S. politics described in the last section held particular appeal (Hein 2004; Morris-Suzuki 1994, 163; cf. Harootunian 2000, 101). Bureaucrats are well compensated, in comparison to government employees in many other countries and to many of their peers in the private sector. But their greatest reward comes in the form of prestige—the respect that they garner from their classmates, family, friends, and of course their clients in the industries they regulate (Koh 1989; McVeigh 1998).

The average Japanese bureaucrat is the kind of person who has the intelligence, drive, and self-discipline necessary to master the large quantities of information tested on the stringent entrance examinations to top universities and to the bureaucracy itself. Most of the bureaucrats

I knew were ardently, if sometimes somewhat paternalistically, devoted to the mission of improving welfare by carefully managing the economy. They believed in their own intellectual capacities and technical skills, and they also shared a sense of responsibility for the consequences of their mistakes. Even at what was the height of neoliberalism, most confessed a Keynesian ambivalence about the market's tendency toward self-destabilization and, hence, a belief in the need for intervention, at the margins, through planning. They also were painfully aware of the limits of their actual authority over market participants (Haley 1987).

Among all the branches of the Japanese bureaucracy, the financial bureaucracy has traditionally held the highest status. The Bank of Japan (BOJ) is responsible for the payments system, interest rate policy, and banking supervision (Bank of Japan Act 1997; Patrick 1962). It is staffed almost exclusively by graduates of Japan's top three universities, although in recent years, its ability to recruit the most desirable candidates has suffered as graduates increasingly choose careers in private practice (Milhaupt and West 2003, 451).[3] In the last two decades, the Bank has sent many of its young staff to obtain higher degrees in economics, law, or policy studies at top American universities.

In general, in the postwar era, the bureaucracy has led the policy agenda and the legislature has followed (Niskanen 1971). The bureaucracy's power is heightened within a parliamentary system in which there has historically been no credible opposition and hence elections were not so much referenda on national policy issues as opportunities for local politicians to debate their achievements in securing national resources for local concerns. As one political scientist puts it, "Diet members have served primarily as intermediaries or 'pipes' (*paipu*) between these particularistic constituencies and the national government" (Schwartz 1998, 20). The power of the Japanese bureaucracy to set the policy agenda has certainly been enabled by its intellectual resources and high social prestige. Until recently, at least, it has also been facilitated by its reputation as a more competent, educated, dedicated, and objective policymaker than the political branch. If this is difficult for an American audience to imagine, one might think of the American press's extremely deferential treatment of the Federal Reserve and its chairman in the 1990s as an American analog.

Despite these sources of bureaucratic power and authority, the legal authority of bureaucrats to enforce their policies is surprisingly weak (Haley 1987, 1995). Moreover, the authority of the Japanese bureaucracy is profoundly shaped by struggles between bureaucratic units (Calder 1993; Schwartz 1998).[4] In the field of financial regulation, the longstanding struggle between the Ministry of Finance (MOF) and the BOJ has been especially important (Miller 1996; Pempel 1987). Both institutions have had often overlapping regulatory authority over Japanese financial institution, and since 2000, a new Financial Services Agency (FSA) reporting to the prime minister's office rather than to the Ministry of Finance, has assumed many of the former planning, supervisory and regulatory duties of the Ministry of Finance. Until its revision in 1997, the Bank of Japan Law gave the Ministry of Finance supervisory and budgetary authority over the BOJ.[5]

The conflict between ministries was a central element of the political landscape, and one keenly navigated by market participants themselves. BOJ bureaucrats repeatedly alluded to the differences in institutional culture between MOF and BOJ in explaining, with a certain institutional pride, the role they played in supporting the economy. One person described MOF as "almost militaristic" in its adherence to hierarchies and its controls on the activities and positions taken by junior bureaucrats, and contrasted these to the toleration of dissent within the BOJ.

In this environment of high prestige, intensive factionalism, relative autonomy from elected politicians, and weak legal authority, the political science literature focuses on two policymaking practices. The first of these is what is known as administrative guidance (*gyosei shido*), or ex ante regulation—nonbinding and private dialogues between the regulator and the client in which both sides make requests of one another (cf. Johnson 1982, 242–72; Ramseyer and Nakazato 1998, 205–11; Rosenbluth 1989). These activities range from efforts to resolve disputes among market participants, to negotiations over the penalties and terms for future compliance with violations of law, to the identification and coordinated resolution of market problems not covered by any explicit statutory mandate.

One of the striking elements of the policy process is the bureaucracy's extensive use of private parties to assist with its work. Japanese bureaucrats call on the staff of private sector entities they regulate to conduct research on particular questions, they summon them to explain particular transactions, products, or economic problems they seek to understand, and they even involve them, as in the case described below, in the process of drafting laws and ordinances. The small numbers of bureaucrats relative to the size and complexity of the problems (Calder 1993,

98; Schwartz 1998, 26; Upham 1996, 441) and a self-consciousness about their personnel's lack of technical training (many of MOF's bureaucrats are graduates of undergraduate programs in law, and therefore have next to no formal knowledge of financial products) is the explanation for the practice I was most often given by industry participants called upon to play this role.

In a sense, Japan's administrative guidance system is a well-developed, longstanding, real-world example of the now-fashionable "new governance" or "democratic experimentalism" advocated by John Braithwaite, Charles Sabel, and others, in which regulators collaborate actively with market participants in both the rule-making and implementation process (Braithwaite 1999, 2002; Dorf and Sabel 1998; Fung, Graham, Weil, and Fagotto 2004; Nickel 2006). Frank Upham has argued that Japan's system of "administrative guidance" is better understood as a system of "privatized regulation" in which

> Japanese bureaucrats delegate their public power to private parties and function not as direct implementers of regulatory policy, but, at most, as overseers of its private implementation. This pattern frequently extends to the formation of policy as well as its implementation, and the bureaucratic role diminishes to intervention at moments of political crisis. (1996, 399)

The BOJ's dealings with market participants have been classic examples of this "informal" regulatory system.[6] The bureaucrats I knew maintained elaborate "networks of contacts" with their classmates working in industry (Calder 1989, 279; Schaede 1995, 293).[7] These relations were actively promoted by both industry and bureaucracy, for example, through the availability of research fellowships for employees of major banks at the BOJ's research unit. Senior Bank staff told me that one of the purposes of sending young bureaucrats to pursue master's degrees at elite American universities, for example, was to give them time to develop close friendships with Japanese of their own age working in the private sector, whom they would be able to get to know under less constrained circumstances overseas. The bureaucrats I knew regularly made use of these contacts in their work and expected their subordinates to do the same.

The second and equally important practice is the extensive use of committees of high-profile academics and journalists (*shingikai*) to set and publicize regulatory policy (Schwartz 1998). Here, bureaucrats trade on their pasts as star students and hence their connections to their former professors to engage in personal collaboration with academics working together with younger graduates of top law faculties now in private practice at elite law firms (Dore 1999, 86; Vogel 1994, 220).

I now turn to how bureaucrats deployed these two approaches to policymaking in one concrete case I observed, the project of creating a "netting law" for the derivatives industry.

The Making of a Problem

Americans had clear regulations. European countries started working on rules. Foreigners expressed to Japanese banks that this was a problem. —*Sato*

The financial instability of the late 1990s had introduced a new kind of risk to swap trading—the risk that a party to a swap transaction might go bankrupt before the completion of the transaction and hence prove unable to fulfill its side of the swap bargain. Market participants talked of a potential "domino effect" in which one bank's failure to meet its obligations to other banks in turn would leave others without the assets to meet their own.

As we have seen, one way of addressing this problem was to collateralize each transaction. But collateral is an expensive solution if, for every swap transaction, a bank must tie up an amount of collateral equal to the entire value of the transaction. Market participants had come to address this issue through a scheme known as "netting" (Hendricks 1994). It was likely, given the small number of players in the market, that at any given moment a financial institution had a number of swap contracts outstanding with another institution, and hence market participants reasoned that it was possible to theorize a debt owed on one swap transaction as counterbalanced by a credit on another. If they could "net out" all their transactions they would only need to collateralize the remaining outstanding debt. For example, if Bank A must post $1 million in collateral with Bank B but on the same day Bank B must post $2 million in collateral with Bank A, and if at the moment of Bank B's bankruptcy the parties could "net out" their obligations, it would only be necessary for Bank B to post $1 million in collateral with Bank A and both sides could free up $1 million in cash now.

For market participants, therefore, netting is yet another technical practice, like collateral, that manages the risks associated with economic interdependency in the market by creating a new form of technical interdependency. Like collateral, netting has been absorbed into global state regulatory practice through Bank of International Settlement capital adequacy requirements that radically reduce the amount of capital banks must have on hand, if they net out their obligations (Bank for International Settlements 2002).

As with collateral, this practice took a documentary form. The ISDA Master Agreement described in chapter 1 stipulated that in the event of bankruptcy, the parties would "net out" all of their outstanding swaps in this way (ISDA 1992). In other words, by signing the Master Agreement, the parties agreed that in the event of a bank failure they would treat all their transactions *as if* they had, from the beginning, constituted one singular metatransaction. Hence they would calculate the balance of all debts and credits as a lump sum one side owed the other and give that debt priority above other debts.

The parties were well aware that this was only one way to understand the transaction, of course. From another point of view, swaps were just so many individual exchanges. Moreover, from the point of view of wider social and economic interests, this practice could look like a giveaway to industry insiders: As described in chapter 1, bankruptcy by definition means that there are not enough funds to go around, that some of the creditors will not get paid. At the time of the bankruptcy of Bank B, the employees of Bank B, for example, or its landlord, or the cleaning service it hires to clean the building at night, might ask why a Japanese court should honor this private arrangement between swap partners to put their own debts at the head of the queue, before all other claims. The politics of this become even more stark when one considers that, on the whole, the class of swap counterparties is likely to be a largely foreign class—big banks in New York and London—while the class of other creditors (employees, cleaning companies, and so on) is likely to be a far more domestic, local set of interests. The "netting problem," as it was known among lawyers in the market, concerned whether such netting agreements actually would be enforceable if challenged in a Japanese bankruptcy court (Kanda 1994; Shindo et al. 1994; Shindo 1996a, 1996b; Yamana 1998)—whether a judge was likely to be enlisted in market participants' theory of the event (Latour and Woolgar 1986).[8] In the United States, as a result of the industry's extensive lobbying of Congress, the Bankruptcy Code explicitly mandates the enforcement of such netting agreements.[9] Yet in Japan, as in the United Kingdom and many other countries, the Bankruptcy Code was silent on this question.[10]

How did netting emerge as a market problem that demanded a legal solution? My interviews with numerous figures involved suggest that the story begins in the mid-1980s when netting became a central concern at the epicenters of the swap markets in New York and London, and the global swap industry began to ask questions about the enforceability of netting in other markets such as Japan. Over a period of several years, most likely at the urging of foreign bank employees, numerous commentaries on the issue appeared in the foreign press. As one banker told me of MOF's awakening to the netting issue, "Every once in a while another story would appear in the Financial Times and after a while they realized the issue was not going to disappear."

The first step here was a classic of traditional administrative guidance. The Tokyo foreign bankers' association raised the issue with MOF officials intermittently. MOF responded first with a letter by Vice Minister of Finance Eisuke Sakakibara, one of the most respected government economists among foreign bankers, to the foreign banks stating that netting agreements were enforceable in Japan.

This was quite common practice. When an unsettled legal question emerged, the common procedure was for the industry, through the Zenginkyo, or Federation of Bankers Association of Japan, to approach the Ministry of Finance and ask for advice.[11] A Ministry official would then inform the industry association of its view. Although there certainly were cases suggesting caution, the bankers I knew claimed that until foreigners had come along and muddied the waters, this usually settled the matter. If MOF said X or Y practice was okay, it was okay. In fact, in this particular case, MOF took the unusually accommodating step of putting its opinion in writing—something rarely done in its dealings with Japanese market participants.

Since our topic is legal expertise, let us pause the story for just a moment to notice where legal expertise is located in this kind of system. In this technocracy, it is the bureaucracy that provides legal advice to the market as a whole, and market participants largely rely on this advice, as untested in the courts as it may be, just as in the United States (as increasingly in today's Japan, after the relative decline of administrative guidance in the wake of neoliberal reforms) market participants usually rely on the untested opinions of legal experts they have privately hired (Milhaupt and West 2004).

Much has been made of the small numbers of practicing lawyers in Japan. What has sometimes been lost in this conversation is an appreciation that under the administrative guidance system, legal expertise was largely *public*, not private. It was a public good provided by the state to the market. This, of course, has changed radically with neoliberal reforms. Law has increasingly become a technique for mediating the relationship between state and market, not an artifact of public technocratic expertise. This shift is at the heart of arguments for the need for a dramatic increase in the number of practicing lawyers in Japan today (Riles and Uchida 2009).

To return to our story, the response of the foreign banks to the MOF letter was lukewarm. They took a formal view of bureaucratic authority. In the case of bankruptcy, it would be up to the courts to uphold netting contracts, foreign bankers insisted, and MOF had no formal authority to predict what the courts would do. The only result one could rely on, they insisted, was either a significant court decision (something they themselves were unwilling to risk going to court to obtain) or a new statute explicitly protecting netting, as in the United States. In practice, foreign banks' position was more subtle than this high-minded legal formalism would suggest, however. The enforceability of close-out netting agreements was not raised in trade negotiations between the U.S. and Japanese governments because ISDA's official position was that Japanese law already protected close-out netting agreements.

So in the mid-1980s, foreign banks tried a second approach. They began raising the issue of netting in negotiations over swap transactions with their Japanese counterparts. Foreign banks insisted on calculating their Japanese counterparties' credit limits for swaps transactions based on a gross rather than a net exposure basis, explaining that as long as netting was not enforceable in Japan they had no choice but to do so. At first, this made little difference to Japanese swap dealers since Japanese financial institutions had more than enough capital to sustain their trading activities. Yet when Japan's economic bubble finally burst in the early 1990s, Japanese banks began to feel more constrained. The response of the foreign banking community was simply that it was up to Japanese banks to lobby their government for regulatory change.

For the Japanese banks themselves, netting was at that stage more of a hypothetical concept than an actual market tool. Until early 1995, most Japanese banks did not have the technological capacity to calculate their exposure on a net basis, and so they were not in a position to take advantage of the benefits of netting. At one of the middle-tier city banks where I conducted fieldwork, for example, close-out netting had only been in use internally since 1997.[12] As the head of one of the most technologically sophisticated trading divisions among Japanese banks told me,

> In the mid-'80s we had no system to calculate all the transactions. In calculating exposure, we just set the potential exposure [arbitrarily]. We ignored current exposure completely. . . . If it's a simple swap, cash flow is easy. You set cash flow, discount it using the discount rate using market price—there are several ways of doing this but the basic idea is very simple. But if you include options, then you have to calculate exposure for each of the components one by one; it can't be done by machine. Maybe at that time U.S. banks were doing it but maybe not. In any case, they coped with the problems. They knew the importance of this but we didn't.

The conditions that made netting an impossibility were not just matters of computing, but matters of institutional politics:

> We had to explain to the credit department "what is current exposure." The first thing we have to do was to convince them, "why can't we do this transaction?" Derivatives themselves were new for old-fashioned bankers. So in the late '80s we [derivatives unit managers] educated board members. Even at that time, the credit people said, if exposure is like that [something flexible, constantly changing] how can I set a credit line? You can't go over that line. It's a line. It exists. It's not a moving limit.

In sum, the impetus for clarifying the status of netting agreements came primarily from foreign banks. Yet, for the most part, foreign actors left the task of lobbying the Japanese government to their Japanese counterparts. From 1995 to 1997, each year the lead bank of the Zenginkyo raised the issue of netting with MOF officials, but got little response. Then, in June 1997, MOF officials contacted Sanwa Bank, which at that time chaired the Zenginkyo, and informed them that an American bond rating agency had expressed doubt about the enforceability of netting agreements. This had evidently given MOF officials pause: could the netting issue have consequences for the bond rating of Japanese banks?

Or is this story correct? I first learned of the netting problem from the staff of the research unit of the BOJ, known as the Institute for Monetary and Economic Studies.[13] In an introductory interview, a senior staff-

member enthusiastically suggested that the netting law might be a fruit-
ful subject for my research—he clearly wanted me to write this story.
In response to my question about how the legality of close-out netting
first appeared on the policy agenda, this staff-member was vague: "it
was generally agreed within the community of legal scholars and lawyers that close-out netting agreements in ISDA master agreements were
enforceable in Japan but some people felt some uncertainty as to how
courts would rule," he said. I would later hear two suggestively different accounts of how the legal community came to see the promulgation
of a new statute as the proper solution to the netting problem. As already mentioned, some claimed that Moody's, the American bond rating
agency, had first raised the issue with the MOF bureaucrats charged with
oversight of the derivatives markets. This first account, then, was an account of foreign intervention. Yet many others dated the original formulation of a "problem" several years earlier and assigned responsibility for
the issue to the staff of the BOJ. Officially, the BOJ has no authority in
matters of financial regulatory reform. Yet, through its "study groups,"
the BOJ often played a most important role in the reforms (cf. Schwartz
1998). Through an unofficial study group involving young lawyers, academics, and Bank staff members, the Institute for Monetary and Economic Studies (the research unit of the BOJ) initiated a conversation
about the enforceability of netting contracts which later blossomed into
the formulation of the arguments for the legality of close-out netting ar-
ticulated in the legal opinions solicited by ISDA on the enforceability of
netting agreements under Japanese law (the so-called Shindo opinions
discussed further in chapter 5). The study group's report was circulated
quietly within the industry, the academic community, and government,
and its members included at least one of the associates of the law firm
that ultimately drafted the Shindo legal opinions.

The conflict between ministries was a central element of the story as
well. One of the earliest public statements from the government on the
enforceability of netting contracts was the outcome of such a conflict.
In a private communication with ISDA representatives, Ministry of Justice officials had confirmed that the close-out netting clause in another
ISDA contract tailored to foreign exchange swaps, the International Foreign Exchange Master Agreement, was enforceable. ISDA then printed
a statement in the booklet accompanying the Japanese language version
of that agreement to the effect that the clause had been approved by the
government. When Ministry of Justice staff members learned that this

assurance was to appear publicly in print, they phoned officials at the Ministry of Finance and asked them to ensure that the statement would be removed from the ISDA booklet. MOF officials sided with ISDA, however, and refused to force them to remove the comment, and the statement became part of the public record.

In sum, the early stages of the government's handling of the netting issue were classic examples of the so-called informal system of administrative guidance so often discussed in the political science literature.[14] This effort to address the netting problem was characterized by a high degree of personal collaboration between academics and bureaucrats working together with younger graduates of elite law faculties now in private law practice. The legislative branch, and elected politicians more broadly, did not play a major role in the events chronicled here.[15] In this respect, this case conforms with other accounts of regulation in the Japanese financial sector (Rosenbluth 1989, 26–38; Schwartz 1998, 170–71).[16]

Collaboration

So what can these two very different examples of technocracy in action teach us about public and private forms of market governance—about the way legal knowledge is routinely deployed within the state? First, note that the expert lawyers in charge of these state-based reform projects shared some affinities with the private lawyers we encountered in the last chapter. In both cases, regulation is conceived as a means to an end. In both cases, skill at manipulating legal technique matters.

In both cases, likewise, bureaucratic reasoning resulted in highly technical legal solutions to pressing market problems. And in fact the bureaucrat's technical legal skills are the basis for the bureaucrat's confidence, prestige, and even political status. Japanese lawyers I knew in private practice could often tell me the precise law school ranking of a particular classmate now working in the financial bureaucracy, and they would usually follow by pointing out how much higher this ranking was than their own. Being perceived as "smart" at legal technicalities was a powerful lever of its own in market intervention.

So then what is the difference between *technocracy* on the one hand and legal *technique* as practiced in private financial governance (as discussed in chapter 1) on the other? There was a slight difference of emphasis or affect in the way regulators deployed their legal tools. It is a subtle thing: for technocrats, we saw, the focus was more squarely on the ends, not the means. Tools mattered, but only so much. What mattered more were market *realities*. For the reformers in the UCC project, for example, legal tools could be combined with any other kind of tool in the service of making the law more realistic and solving real problems in the world. For Japanese bureaucrats, likewise, skill at legal technique facilitated complex interactions with market participants. Legal technicalities were tools for achieving something specific in the social world of the market. In contrast, as we began to see in chapter 1, and we will see further in chapters 4 and 5, the masters of private legal technique show much less concern about its groundedness in reality. As a skill, legal technique assumes a more epistemologically subtle approach.

So regulators are not different from market participants by virtue of their tools. That is, they, like market participants, govern through a set of technical legal devices and instruments. What is different about the technocratic regulatory framework for legal expertise, rather, is regulators' perspective when they deploy these tools.[17]

But technocrats' commitment to—perhaps even anxiety about—keeping their intellectual projects grounded in the real world is complicated. Because just as legal experts in the financial markets understand their work as somewhat collateral to trading, technocrats understand their work as somewhat collateral to the market as a whole—on the outside, fixing the system, looking in. Their job is to deploy legal technologies upon the market, from a distance, in light of the problems and solutions they see by virtue of the fact that they are at a step removed from the market. It is a perspective at a distance.

Anthropologists and historians who have studied bureaucracy (often from the perspective of bureaucracy's clients) have described technocratic thought as a kind of thinking that is abstracted from local details, and that easily spills into arrogance, aloofness, and an inability to appreciate technocratic error or the negative consequences of policies (Ferguson 1990; Mitchell 2002). They have further shown how this kind of thought often breeds distrust and disillusion among its clients. A Japanese expert in administrative law puts the point powerfully when he writes of "Japanese ambivalent feelings" toward technocratic knowledge:

A positive value of substantive informality in governance is considered to be that the government may be able to provide a quick and flexible way of pursuing public purposes, although fear of erosion of the rule of law and accompanying vagueness can never be denied. Such vagueness not only raises a question of legitimacy, but also can lead to inefficiency and unfairness, rather than flexibility and satisfaction. These ambivalent feelings do exist among Japanese lawyers. As a result, the utility of informality is praised, while informality is argued against as a deviation from the path of the rule of law. (Nakagawa 2000, 211)

To look at the problem from the point of view of the bureaucrats themselves, as I encountered them, however, technocratic arrogance, aloofness and paternalism can belie an awareness of the tremendous intellectual and political burden that rests on the shoulders of the bureaucrat to come up with solutions. The cult of technocratic "smartness" demands that the bureaucrat deliver, or else be exposed to (sometimes quite harsh and unrelenting) public criticism. To make matters worse, few of the bureaucrats I knew ultimately put tremendous faith in their technical tools (Holmes 2009). This lack of faith was built into the project: the very premise of the Realist revolution for example was that legal technique was indeterminate. As we will see in chapter 3, these bureaucrats faced a crisis of confidence in their own intellect and their tools.

Sometimes, moreover, there is more variation in the motives and perspectives, as well as the knowledge practices of bureaucrats, than the clients of bureaucracies may recognize. Consider, for example, the very different approaches to regulation of BOJ and MOF, as described by market participants I knew. Industry participants reported that meetings at MOF always occurred within earshot of superiors rather than in closed rooms to insure that junior bureaucrats would not reveal confidential information, and that they complained that they often were even required to discuss their problems within earshot of competitors who had also come to meet with officials on a particular day. Although MOF also had a research unit, that unit did not play the same kind of role in the activities of the industry participants I interviewed. None of my informants had spent time in residence there, nor had they participated in study groups associated with the Ministry. But while the BOJ staff I knew also maintained some distance from market participants, at the same time they viewed it as part of their mandate to be involved actively—even socially—in the market. Day-to-day informal contact with market participants was, in their view, the instrument of their intervention (Holmes 2009).[18] Some people working in the market summed the issue up for me by saying that "the Bank of Japan is our mother, but the Ministry of Finance is our father," a Japanese reference to the tough-minded authority but ultimately intimate involvement of the BOJ in market practice in contrast to the relatively distant and hands-off approach of MOF (Riles 2004b).

Indeed, in both of the examples of technocratic practice in this chapter, what ultimately defines technocratic intervention is not so much abstraction and domination as it is an impulse toward *collaboration*. What these technocrats understood as the innovative, modern, advanced, cutting-edge approach to the distance between themselves and the market was to find some way to incorporate market participants' perspectives into regulatory practice, and also to use encounters between regulators and market participants to shape those perspectives. The aim of the UCC project was to make regulation conform more to market participants' daily activities. Likewise, the aim of regulators working toward a Japanese netting law was to give legal effect to already established market practice. In both cases, regulators went about achieving this goal by talking with market participants, working closely with them on committees—by doing a kind of ethnography of the market (Holmes 2009). Of course, like all ethnography this collaboration always occurred within a controlled framework in which the technocrat remained in charge of the collaborative experiment and set the guidelines for the conversation. But what I want to emphasize is the place of legal tools in the collaboration: in both cases, the point of contact—the basis for collaboration—was the mutual respect the two sides—state actors and market representatives— had for one another's legal expertise, and the shared vocabulary, the shared set of technical practices. In the Japanese case, BOJ staff and the back-office staff of banks could enjoy debating legal arguments together in informal study groups that eventually produced the theory of the new law. In the UCC case, the drafters could appreciate market participants' own ways of structuring transactions as analogous to, and indeed in their view preferable to, existing legal categories, and they could work closely with these individuals in the drafting process (Twining 1973).

One could find many more examples of such an impulse toward collaboration. The currently fashionable "New Governance" literature, for example, gains its appeal from the way it gives a structure to this desire for collaboration. Its stated policy is to devolve power to local participants (Jorges and Neyer 1997).[19] And like the technocrats discussed in this chapter, the proponents of New Governance do not typically envision that collaboration extends so far as involving participants in the design of the experiment itself. To do so, from proponents' point of view, would break the technical frame, give up the game, turn an expert process into something amorphous and confusing. New Governance makes collaboration into a technical methodology of technocratic governance of its own. This has already led to concerns about the undemocratic, aloof, and arrogant nature of New Governance (Nickel 2006; Walters 2004, 34).

We noted in the last chapter that private and public governance are necessarily mutually implicated in many ways. So here is one concrete way this is the case, then. To be a technocrat, it seems, is to insist on one's own distance from the workings of the market, but also to harbor a desire for deep involvement with market "realities." Technocratic governance embodies an aspiration toward *collaboration*—an aspiration to be involved, without entirely abandoning one's distance. Indeed, in the two examples we explored, collaboration was the key project and modality of legal expertise. In the two cases discussed in this chapter this aspiration for collaboration found expression in the actual intellectual connections technocrats formed with the agents of private governance at the level of the technical legal details. Legal technique became the social, institutional, and intellectual hinge of public and private.

Notes

1. This observation fits into a line of work on regulatory environments that highlights how prevailing ideas shape the diagnosis of regulatory problems and provide participants with symbolic resources for contestation (Campbell 1998; Fligstein 2001; Stryker 2000).

2. Dewey, quoted in Eames 1977, 90–91:

> In the relationship of cause and effect there is the relation of the responses to each other in the sense of dependence, involving the adjustment of the steps to be taken with reference to the thing to be carried out. The arrangement, which may appear at one time in terms of means and end, appears at another time in terms of cause and effect. We have here a relationship of dependence of one response on another, a necessary relation that lies inside a larger system. It depends upon what we are going to do whether we select this means or another one, one causal series or another.

3. At the time of my fieldwork, for example, the top one-third of the class of the University of Tokyo law department, excluding the handful who become ac-

ademics and the 10% who became qualified lawyers, became bureaucrats. Miyazawa and Otsuka (2002, 183) report that in 1995 all of the top bureaucrats at the Ministry of Finance, likewise, were University of Tokyo law faculty graduates, and that in 1996, "the Finance Ministry proudly announced that the proportion of Tokyo law graduates to be employed by them in 1996 was smaller than before, and that even two women were included—nevertheless, of the seventeen new recruits, a total of eleven were from the University of Tokyo, with six of those being from the Law School."

4. Schwartz writes that "the flip side of a functional loyalty and sense of belonging *within* ministries is a dysfunctional us-versus-them attitude *among* ministries that creates tensions and hinders cooperation" (1998, 20). As Haley notes, in this situation of "fragmented authority, dispersed power and intense rivalry" that exists among them, "[t]hose who emerge from the fray on top are those who best seize and manipulate opportunities to act as go-betweens, alliance-makers, mediators, and architects of consensus" (1998, 475–76). See also Samuels 1986; Muramatsu and Krauss 1987.

5. The 1997 Bank of Japan law took steps toward bank autonomy but left considerable authority to the Ministry of Finance. It states that "due consideration shall be given to the autonomy of the Bank's business operations"; Bank of Japan Act Article 5(2) (1997). But it also allows the minister of finance and minister for economic and fiscal policy to send representatives to the meetings of the bank's board of governors (Article [2]) and requires MOF approval for numerous aspects of regulatory policy (e.g., Article 39).

6. Upham (1996, 402) argues that the private involvement in administrative authority is intimately tied to the "informal" character of Japanese law: "In many instances, formal law is irrelevant." By "formal law," he means authority governed by statute and subject to meaningful judicial review. Likewise, Haley (1986, 108–9) describes administrative guidance as "informal law enforcement" in contrast to "formal regulation." Nakagawa (2000) usefully specifies this term by parsing the differing meanings of formality and informality in the United States and Japan. In contrast, Miller's (1996, 20) usage of the term "preclearance" to describe discussions between parties prior to the announcement of policies does not necessarily carry the connotation of informality.

7. Until recently, Japanese bureaucrats usually retired to prearranged positions at the titular head of private corporations from which they continued to serve as conduits between government and industry.

8. This issue has not been tested in the Japanese courts. In fact, despite the global significance of netting agreements there is remarkably little case law anywhere addressing their validity. A U.S. court has considered whether the netting provision conflicts with Thai law. See *Finance One v Lehman Brothers*, 414 F.3d 325 (2005).

9. 11 U.S.C. § 561 (1994).

10. Bankruptcy Law 1922.

11. The "Zenginkyo" (its full name is Zenkoku Ginko Kyokai Rengokai) is the principal association of Japanese "city banks." Its activities include making proposals to the government and other parties concerned with issues relating to banks, rationalization and standardization of banks' operating procedures, operation of payment and settlement systems, and research, statistics, and education. At the time of my fieldwork, the leadership of the Zengingkyo rotated among the Sumitomo Bank, Daiichi Kangyo Bank, Fuji Bank, and the Tokyo Mitsubishi Bank. See, generally, the Zenginkyo Web site: http://www.zenginkyo.or.jp/en/gaiyo/gai01.htm. For a survey of the history of the Zenginkyo, see Calder 1993, 154–58.

12. The system was still "primitive," according to employees interviewed in 1998, and could only process 70–80% of the relevant data because it was not networked with the bank's branches. Moreover, the system could only calculate present value of positions for "plain vanilla" swaps; it could not calculate the present value of more "exotic" instruments.

13. See, generally, the Institute for Monetary and Economic Studies Web site: http://www.imes.boj.or.jp/english/index.html.

14. For debates surrounding the Japanese bureaucracy's system of "administrative guidance" (*gyosei shido*), see, e.g., Rosenbluth 1989, 21; Ramseyer and Nakazato 1998, 205–11; and Johnson 1982, 242–74.

15. "With regard to the regulation of financial markets in Japan, bureaucrats in administrative branches have long played a predominant role" (Kanda 1996, 305).

16. See, e.g., Schwartz 1998, 170–71, where he argues that in the context of turf wars between banks and their bureaucratic allies on the one hand, and securities firms and their bureaucratic allies on the other over the introduction of financial futures, "[i]t was precisely because the LDP was close to the contestants that it sat out the battle" and left it to MOF to carve out a compromise; Rosenbluth (1989, 26–38) finds that in matters of financial regulation, politicians often defer to the Ministry of Finance. This is clearly less true today, in wake of scandals associated with the Ministry and the conversations surrounding the Big Bang than when Rosenbluth conducted her research. Nevertheless, the netting case suggests that while politicians are deeply implicated in the "larger questions" of bank bailouts and corruption within the bureaucracy, they continue to leave the technical regulatory issues to the bureaucrats.

17. As the sociologist Miguel Centeno has suggested, "We must understand this perspective not as an ideology of answers or issues but as an ideology of method. . . . That is, what an elite shares is an epistemological rather than an economic ideology" (1994, 211).

18. As the governor of the Bank of Japan recently put it, "The central bank . . . maintains an engrained institutional culture emphasizing the importance of re-

search. The central bank also has access to information through its contacts with market participants. . . . All of these elements provide a strong foundation for effective system-wide analysis" (Shirakawa 2009b).

19. For Benkler, the goal of institutional design is to promote cooperation (2009). In experimentalist approaches to governance, "the central design issue is to make it possible for regulators, rating bodies, investor groups and other stakeholders to co-learn with investment banks, inventors of new financial instruments, and economists, and also to review, test, and rapidly update assumptions, measures and rules as circumstances change" (Schneiberg and Bartley 2010, 295). One advantage of privately implemented regulation is that the regulator is better able to cooperate with the regulated (Balleisen 2009, 16). One of the innovations of this approach to financial regulation is its focus on "behavior change" (Schneiberg and Bartley 2008, 42).

CHAPTER THREE

Unwinding Technocracy

S o far, we have taken a series of steps toward a new understanding of global private law as a set of knowledge practices with transformative consequences and effects. In chapter 1, I argued that the material and analytical practices that characterize global private governance are better imagined as routinized knowledge practices and as devices for making limits than as a system of norms. In chapter 2, I explored two examples of legal expertise at work in the alter ego of global private governance, the regulatory state. In both cases, what defines public and private forms of regulation—its similarities and differences, points of overlap and points of divergence—is a set of approaches to expert legal knowledge.

If expert knowledge is constitutive of the regulatory state, then it stands to reason that an attack on the legitimacy of the regulatory state will take the form of an attack on the particular kind of knowledge that defines it. And this is exactly what has happened over the last thirty years of neoliberal critiques. The legal instruments described in the last chapter have come under attack as of late, as calls for "transparency" from the state take the form of assaults on the character of technocratic knowledge.

Among the legal scholars and bureaucrats who are the subjects of this study, perhaps the best-known critic of the state as an instantiation of technocratic knowledge in financial market regulation and policy circles is the free market advocate Friedrich Hayek. In his classic text, *The Rule of Law*, Hayek famously decried the engineer mentality of the technocrat who believes he has "complete control of the particular little world with which he is concerned . . . a man whose supreme ambition is to turn the world round him into an enormous machine" (1975, 101–2).

This chapter considers this line of attack on the technocratic state framed as a problem of bureaucratic rationality through an ethnographic account of one instance of crisis surrounding the authority, legitimacy, and efficacy of governmental regulation of the market. The bureaucrats described in this chapter are officials at the Bank of Japan (BOJ), Japan's central bank, and are responsible for the payment system by which funds move from one bank account to another in the economy; as such, they would seem to be archetypal producers of technocratic knowledge. Weber (1966, 325) himself identified central bankers' manipulation of procedural policies such as the workings of the payment system as examples of bureaucratic "domination."

We will see that the Hayekian view of technocracy as a knowledge practice that inherently faces its own limits elucidates much about the character of the particular regulatory state I will describe. In fact, this thesis replicates and amplifies a way of thinking about bureaucracy often heard among these technocrats themselves. Faith in technocracy and careful attention to its calibration have long been hallmarks of Japanese politics in the twentieth century (Dimock 1968; Koschmann 2002; Morris-Suzuki 1994; Okimoto 1989; Tobioka 1993; Traweek 1999; Tsutsui 1998). But beginning in the 1990s, journalistic and policy studies accounts of Japanese bureaucracy popularized the Hayekian critique of technocratic knowledge. One typical volume, for example, asserts that "power in Japan is masked" (Mikuni and Murphy 2002, 38) and emphasizes that the failures of Japanese bureaucracy are the product of a culturally specific but ultimately misguided faith in bureaucracy (Lambsdorff, Taube, and Schramn 2005, 5). Others have repeatedly decried the ultimate tendency of the bureaucracy toward self-dealing and corruption (Carpenter 2003, 3; Mikuni and Murphy 2002; Scott 1972, 15).

In the 1990s and 2000s, one further line of critique of technocratic knowledge came from a powerful and widely circulating body of economic theory of regulation known as public choice theory (Buchanan and Tullock 1962; Gunning 2003).[1] According to this theory, regulatory policy is the product of interest group influence on regulators who, acting in their own self-interest rather than in the public interest, produce the regulation that powerful interest groups want in return for these groups' financial or political support. For the legal scholar Richard Epstein, for example, Hayek

> overstates the level of ignorance that we have, and thus underestimates the dangers of government intervention driven by knowledge of partisan advantage. . . . With partial knowledge I can put self-interest to work in the politi-

cal sphere just as I can put it to work in the economic sphere. Truth be known, that is where Hayek goes wrong. We (collectively) may not know enough to manage a complex economic system from the center, but we (individually) do know enough to seek to rig the rules of the game to cut in our favor. Imperfect information coupled with confined self-interest offers a better set of behavioral assumptions about individual actors and social processes. (1999, 299)

One might imagine that such an attack on the legitimacy of bureaucratic activity would have been greeted with scorn, or at least skepticism, among bureaucrats themselves. But in fact, in the 1990s and 2000s, among bureaucracies in numerous industrialized countries, a commitment to these theories emerged as a source of policy, a basis for personal motivation, and ground for political struggles within and between regulatory entities.[2] In Japan, the negative views of bureaucrats and their motivations at the heart of public choice theory have also seriously impacted the attractiveness of the bureaucracy as a career choice for elite university graduates (Milhaupt and West 2003; Riles and Uchida 2009).

If public choice economic theory and Hayekian social thought are primarily neoliberal projects, the attack on technocracy—the location of the critique of technocratic power in the categories of bureaucratic knowledge—is as much a project of the Left as of the Right. In Japan, one of the core platforms of the center-left political coalition that succeeded in unseating the venerable Liberal Democratic Party in 2009 was a promise to reduce the power of bureaucrats and, indeed, once in power the new government has sought to bring bureaucrats under the firm control of elected politicians (Dickie 2009; Fackler 2010). In the United States, likewise, the current progressive agenda for financial reform includes a critical appraisal of "regulators' incentives" (Carnell 2010).[3]

Just as public choice theory rephrased Hayekian social thought as technical economic analysis, leftist critiques of the technocratic state have been rephrased as problems of economic and political science analysis on the one hand, and problems for global grassroots social activism on the other—as problems of *transparency* (cf. Strathern 2000b; West and Sanders 2003). Indeed, one of the key intellectual imports of the Japanese Big Bang financial reforms of the 1990s (described below) was a new critique of bureaucratic corruption and associated progressive calls for "transparency, democracy and political accountability" in the bureaucratic process (Azfar, Lee, and Swamy 2001).

Susan Rose-Ackerman's entry on corruption in the *Palgrave Diction-ary of the Economics of the Law* provides an example of this progressive economic critique of the political process. Rose-Ackerman describes corruption as "negatively correlated with other measures of bureaucratic efficiency" and a "symptom of other underlying problems."[4] The solution she proposes is a formalist legal and bureaucratic one, "The response should be both to simplify the . . . laws to reduce bureaucratic discretion and to reorganize the bureaucracy to improve oversight and incentives for good performance" (1998, 517, 521).[5]

In the context of the regulation of financial markets, these lines of ar-gument translated into a quite seamless attack on the legitimacy of the regulatory state. For example, in a working paper series on bank super-vision and corruption and lending, the economists Thorsten Beck, Asli Demirgüç-Kunt, and Ross Levine argue that while the Bank for Interna-tional Settlements (BIS), IMF, and World Bank are pushing countries to strengthen direct oversight of banks, the evidence does not support this recommendation. "Rather, supervisory power is positively associated with corruption in bank lending. We find that supervisory power is linked to poor legal system development, low levels of government effectiveness, and high levels of national corruption" (Beck, Demirgüç-Kunt, and Levine 2006, 2134; Larmour and Wolanin 2001, xii; Rose-Ackerman 1999, 2).

In Japan in the late 1990s, these critiques were instantiated and pop-ularized by the media, the prosecutor's office, and supervisors in the fi-nancial bureaucracy, in the form of individual "corruption scandals," in which Japanese bureaucrats were discovered to have accepted en-tertainment from their clients (West 2006). In January 1998 two senior officials of the Ministry of Finance were arrested for accepting enter-tainment from the Sumitomo Bank and the Bank of Tokyo-Mitsubishi and hundreds of other bureaucrats were investigated and reprimanded.[6] A month later, the head of the BOJ's Capital Markets Division was arrested for accepting similar entertainment—dinner on eighty-nine occasions—from the Industrial Bank of Japan and Sanwa Bank. The ac-cused insisted at the time that he had "never received excess entertain-ment" and indeed, if he and others were motivated by a desire to sell government favors and secrets for personal gain, they should rather have been accused of gross incompetence in pricing the value of these secrets to industry at the cost of a series of nice, but certainly not top flight To-kyo meals (WuDunn 1998, 1). But this kind of self-defense only fueled the aura of arrogance surrounding the accusations. The scandals played out on the nightly news, as camera crews arrived on the scene to document investigators by the dozens raiding the Ministry and the Central Bank and emerging with cartons of files (Tett 1998, 4). Politicians issued daily statements of dismay at the disappointing moral character of the bureaucracy. The scandal atmosphere was enlivened by the suicides of a politician and former Finance Ministry official implicated accused of bribery.[7] Ultimately, the governor of the BOJ resigned and a number of bureaucrats and employees of private banks were indicted.

There is an argument that under the standard definition of corruption as an illegal payment to a public agent to obtain a benefit (Rose-Ackerman 1997, 33), what the vast majority of accused BOJ or Ministry of Finance bureaucrats did was not, in fact, corruption. Although the total amounts spent by individual banks on the entertainment of bureaucrats were in the tens of thousands of dollars, if one accepted bureaucrats' assertion that they had reason to meet with industry executives as often as they did, the amounts spent on dinner were not unusual by Tokyo standards. Whether these costs were reasonable or not is certainly a complex and context-dependent evaluation.

More important, up until the period of the prosecutions, there were no clear rules stipulating that accepting entertainment from members of the public was contrary to the bribery law, and no prior prosecutions had set a precedent for such an interpretation of the law.[8] Indeed, it would have been somewhat paranoid of a bureaucrat only a short period before to have raised concerns that what was not only an institutional norm but a set of activities directed by his superiors might expose him or her to criminal liability.

In recent years, a number of anthropologists, legal theorists, and social theorists have begun to observe how well-meaning efforts to achieve "transparency" have had far less democratic and emancipatory consequences for modern political and social life than transparency advocates might have hoped (Espeland and Vannebo 2007; Harrington and Turem 2006; Hoskin 1996; Westbrook 2004b).[9] They have pointed in particular to the way transparency is a slippery concept, full of internal contradictions.[10] My discussion here will build on this work but take the question in a slightly different direction—away from a critique of transparency per se and toward an appreciation of the unintended consequences of economic theory on technocratic life and practice.

I should emphasize that I do not seek in any way to defend corrupt officials or to suggest that some notion of cultural relativism stands in the way of a normative critique of unjust behavior by public agents.[11] As in the United States and elsewhere, there are public officials in Japan who sacrifice public trust and the dignity of their office for private gain. Nor do I mean to imply that Japanese bureaucrats, or Japanese people more generally, are so culturally "different" that Western ideas cannot make sense to them or that their activities cannot be analyzed in interest group terms.[12] Like Americans—indeed, perhaps even more so—Japanese political actors, in government and in the private sector, have a refined sense of the "game" of politics and are skilled at manipulating policies and institutional practices to achieve their own ends. My point is rather to ask a different question: what difference does it make when certain academic terms become the currency of politics?

What interests me in this chapter are the features of an ideological shift in which the technocratic state described in the previous chapter has been reframed, in Japan and in many other contexts, as posing a serious problem of transparency and corruption. To the extent that actors define themselves according to a set of prescribed roles that public choice specifies for public officials, it is reasonable to expect that these ideas in turn are affecting the character of bureaucratic practice.[13]

It is therefore not surprising that in the aftermath of the Asian financial crisis of the late 1990s and the consciousness of so-called systemic risk it amplified, the failures of technocratic knowledge were very much at the forefront of these technocrats' own minds. In the face of both the inability of sophisticated economic models to predict economic crisis or provide solutions to recent market problems (Eisenbeis 1997) and current efforts by global banks to privatize the payment system and, hence, to do away with bureaucratic regulation altogether (*American Banker* 1997), these central bankers were anxious about their own powerlessness vis-à-vis the market they were expected to manage. I describe how one set of regulators became interested in Hayekian political theory, public choice theory, and transparency theory, and the consequences of these interpretations for regulatory policy. Academic models of bureaucratic action can serve as powerful ideologies that shape bureaucrats' views of their work and their motivations for doing it. These particular technocrats addressed this crisis by creating a regulatory machine that, they hoped, would obviate as much as possible the need for human planning altogether.

An appreciation of how actors deploy economic tools for describing and predicting their own behavior in turn helps us to understand the social, economic, personal, and institutional consequences of these models.[14] The first theme of this chapter therefore concerns the consequences of academic theory for the regulation of the market. In contrast to often-heard claims that academic ideas are too distant from policy and regulatory practice to have much impact, I show how such ideas shaped the very parameters of regulatory politics, framing the contours of the possible.

But those theories came to be instantiated in bureaucratic thought and practice in ways far beyond the intentions or imaginations of their academic creators. In particular, the importation of legal and economic theory, as a so-called legal transplant to Japan, resulted in a quiet and unnoticed transformation of public choice from a *critique* to a *dream*—an aspiration to be achieved. This all should give academic readers some pause—some sense of responsibility for the consequences, intended and unintended of our theories, as they circulate globally.

The ultimate outcome of this influx of academic ideas was a particular bureaucratic sensibility and practice—something that I call the "unwinding" of technocratic knowledge. Rethinking deregulation as "unwinding"—a particular transformation of the regulatory apparatus— will provide us with a richer vocabulary of regulation and deregulation, and ultimately can help us perceive a new set of options for the governance of markets.

The Bureaucracy and the Big Bang

In the 1990s the Japanese financial system was in the midst of a major reform, a so-called Big Bang (Ministry of Finance Japan 1999a) named after the United Kingdom's "Big Bang" of the 1980s (Ministry of Finance Japan, 1999b). Its official aim was to

> contribute to the vitalization of the national economy by vitalizing the financial sector's intermediation and settlement functions. For this purpose, a) establishing a market that properly reflect[s] users' preference[s], and, b) supplying funds to growth industries for the next generation and overseas countries, and using personal financial assets efficiently, should be promoted. (Finance System Research Council 1997, 1)

The package of reforms included a tight schedule of legal reforms and policy and institutional changes to be implemented between 1997 and 2001 in three general categories: "liberalization and diversification of products, businesses and organizational structures"; "preparing infrastructure and rules for markets and transactions"; and "ensuring the soundness of the financial system."[15]

By any standard, the reforms were sweeping in scope. Foreign exchange controls were abolished as of April 1, 1998 (Ministry of Finance Japan 1997). Many of the regulatory barriers between banks, securities firms, and insurance companies were eliminated.[16] Banks were given permission to transact in equity derivatives,[17] and in a reversal of past policy (Calder 1991, 23), a wide range of entities was given permission to sell investment trust products (the Japanese equivalent of mutual funds) to public investors or engage in foreign exchange transactions (Patrikis 1998, 585). One of the stated objectives of this deregulation was "reducing risks in the settlement system" (Finance System Research Council 1997, 6), the subject of the particular regulatory reform described in more detail below.

The Big Bang also aimed to respond to foreigners' longstanding complaints about barriers to their access to the Japanese financial markets. As the buzz-words of the financial reforms, "free, fair and global" (Keizai shingikai [Economic Council] 1996), indicate, in the mind of government and private reformists alike, the reform of the Japanese markets was intimately tied to the globalization of those markets. As the Securities and Exchange Council (1997, 1) put it:

> Globally, there have been large reforms in securities markets around the world. By contrast, in Japan, in the boom-and-bust of the financial bubble during the past decade, innovation in the securities market had slowed. . . . There is an urgent need to make the Japanese market more attractive and competitive internationally, to reconstruct a dynamic capital market, and thereby to allow investors and issuers to enjoy the full benefits of an advanced capital market.

The 1990s saw a series of devastating financial market shocks and bankruptcies in Japan. In 1997 the collapse of Asian markets and currencies highlighted the powerlessness of national governments to protect their national economies in the face of global financial trends. As financial institutions found themselves in dire economic straits and under new pressure from foreign shareholders and creditors to do business with regulators in a more arms-length way, they became less willing to comply with regulators' informal "requests" (Milhaupt and West 2006, 413–14). Since 1995 the BOJ had for the first time allowed several Japanese banks to fail—as one Japanese commentator put it, "the reverse side of the coin of liberalization" (Yoshii 1998, 207). As a result, Moody's, the American bond rating company, dramatically downgraded the bonds of most Japanese banks and had even downgraded Japanese government bonds in what bureaucrats took as a profound national embarrassment (Dore 1999, 66).[18]

One of the principal aims of the Big Bang was to alter the way regulatory oversight occurred in the financial sector. Most notably, the BOJ was reorganized to render banking policy more "transparent," and to increase its independence from the Ministry of Finance (Bank of Japan Act 1997).[19] The Ministry of Finance's authority over financial regulation and economic planning was divided between that Ministry and a newly established Financial Services Agency located in the Office of the Prime Minister.[20]

The *shingikai* responsible for reviewing the regulation of the economy put it as a matter of global competitiveness:

> Efforts should be made to make the Tokyo market a competitive, international one able to stand shoulder to shoulder with those in New York and London as one of the three largest financial centers in the world. The Japanese financial industry must not be allowed to become an empty shell. (General Committee of the Securities and Exchange Council, 1996)

The list of criticisms of the committee charged with proposing reforms at the BOJ, for example, capture the flavor of the critique:

> The nationalistic tint of the bank's objective; autonomy (the governor's weak position, the government's general oversight authority, etc.), transparency (accountability, etc.), ambiguity in policies for supervising banks; and ambiguity in stipulations for providing credit to the government. (Takahashi 1997, 3)

In this, they echoed the litany of critiques that appeared in popular and academic commentaries during this period. The bureaucracy as an institution came under vocal attack from domestic and foreign media, politicians, and academics for failing to maintain the proper distance from events in the market. In the press and in the academic journals, calls for "freeing the invisible hand" (Porter and Hirotaka 1999) associated the intimacy of the architects of the market and the market participants under the administrative guidance system with a precapitalist past. The following newspaper article captures the general sentiment in typical tones:

> Banks and financial firms have made an effort to get information ahead of their rivals and outflank the competition in the process, but Japanese banks and financial institutions have been marked by their habit of garnering information through the back door. . . . Japanese bureaucrats, along with those at private financial firms, must learn to play by the rules of international finance if they hope to win the trust of the market and compete on an ever fiercer global field. (*Asia Pulse* 1998)

This was more than simply a matter of opening markets to foreigners. In popular conversation in Tokyo in the 1990s and early 2000s, one heard frequent references to a "second occupation" in allusion to the American postwar occupation of fifty years earlier. In making this connection, speakers had in mind not only the massive influx of American and European investment firms eager to enter into alliances with Japanese firms or to sell their products to Japanese investors, but also the influx of American ideas and ideals (Miyazaki 2006b). Indeed, the Big Bang was modeled at every level on American and UK regulatory systems.

The sentiment among central bankers was only a reflection of wider doubts about Japanese-style management and regulation in all sectors of the market and government. In this context of massive structural reform, ideas about the causes of regulatory failures became of great interest within both the political and bureaucratic branches of government. Just as the economic bubble of the 1980s had led commentators around the world to ponder the cultural causes of the "Asian Miracle," the crisis of the 1990s precipitated a sense that the "Asian way" was somehow to blame (cf. Anderson and Campbell 2000; Krugman 1998; Pomerleano 1998; Rose-Ackerman 1999). Accompanying the "free, fair, and global" slogan in popular and policy discourses were a litany of critiques of Japanese economic and regulatory practices and institutions and of Japanese society at large (Lipset and Lenz 2000).[21] Bureaucrats, journalists, and academics trained in American economic theories such as public choice began to critique the distinctive qualities of the Japanese market and regulatory practices, namely the relationship between banks, firms and the government (Lanyi and Lee 1999).

In these analyses, the reform of the bureaucracy is described again and again as the last step in the Big Bang—the ultimate act of reform that, unlike others, cannot be achieved by the introduction of new legislation alone. Consider a typical evaluation by a foreign Japan specialist:

> The obvious villains in this performance are the mandarins of Japan's Ministry of Finance, who have attempted to control both the stock market slide and the banking disasters with conspicuous lack of success. Accustomed to twirl the wheels and turn the levers of Japan's financial system from their Kasumigaseki headquarters, MOF's bureaucrats had failed to reckon with a new freewheeling international financial game whose players have little regard for national boundaries or protective ministries. All their efforts to re-window the hothouse economy failed. It had simply grown too big and too complex for their traditional guidance mechanisms to handle. (Gibney 1998, 7)

In the aftermath of the Asian financial crisis and the consciousness of so-called systemic risk it amplified, and in the wake of popular and academic critiques of bureaucratic planning, therefore, many central bankers experienced a kind of crisis of faith in their high-prestige identity and hence their authority to lead. One source was the growing appreciation by central bankers around the world of the limitations of the economic models that were the source of central bankers' expertise to offer useful predictions or fine-tuned policy solutions to recent market problems.[22] Another was the increasing integration of Japanese markets into foreign markets, which in turn forced the bureaucrats to confront actions by private parties in Europe and the United States who did not share Japanese bankers' deference toward their regulators. These included calls for new regulatory paradigms in which the payments functions of central banks would be privatized and the national boundaries of regulatory systems would be reimagined. In particular, leading international banks were planning their own private settlement bank outside the scope of central bank authority altogether that would severely constrain central banks' ability to use the interest rate they charge on intraday credit to members to set monetary policy (Taylor 1998).

From Economic Policy to Individual Corruption

This loss of confidence within the bureaucracy also had another source. The high-profile corruption investigations and dismissals culminated in a new Bank of Japan Law and ensuing regulations (Bank of Japan Act 1997).[23] The BOJ instituted a strict policy concerning contact between employees and outsiders: henceforth, every meeting between a BOJ official and an outsider would need to be cleared in advance with the manager of the division. Even when outside contact was approved, bureaucrats would be required to pay their share of any meals or drinks consumed in the course of the encounter.[24] In the years that followed, a handful of BOJ employees were dismissed each year for violating these rules.

In interviews, in conversations I observed, and also in their internal writings about the regulatory process, market participants painted a very different picture of these "corrupt" practices. Bankers emphasized the intimate involvement of the BOJ in the problems of Japanese banks and its willingness to share the burden of maturing Japanese financial institutions. Was it not supposed to be a good thing for regulators to understand the market and its practices? The market could not be learned in books, they insisted; effective planning was dependent on close personal relationships between *people* in industry and government at every level (cf. Blair and Stout 2001; Holmes 2009).

In the old system, I was told, bureaucrats also held formal encounters with their clients on office premises. Sometimes these meetings took place literally in front of the desk of the division manager, who sat at his desk pretending to read the newspaper, as his junior carefully executed the interview within his earshot. Usually on the night of the meeting, however, the clients would treat the junior bureaucrat to dinner (with his superior's tacit knowledge and approval), and after several rounds of drinks and conversations about a standard set of light topics, the conversation would turn back to the matter of that day. In that context, both sides would take pleasure in breaking through the boundaries of formality they had created for themselves earlier and "speaking in a straightforward way." Promises would be made that would serve as the basis of later action. The important point here is that something more than a benefit was at stake; both sides saw each encounter as an opportunity to cultivate a relationship that was valuable and even enjoyable for its own sake and also valuable in the future.[25]

The more senior staff in particular complained about the constraints the new transparency policy had placed upon their work. Their task depended on gathering information, on knowing what was happening in the economy, on having a sense of problems and working out solutions before they mushroomed out of control (Pempel and Muramatsu 1995, 68). If they waited to address the banks' inadequate capitalization or the absence of proper risk-management systems until everything had become public and stock prices had plummeted, they would surely be blamed by the press, the public, the politicians, the other ministries, for failing to act quickly enough. On the other hand, since the institution of the new policy, the flow of information from industry to the central bank had been reduced to a trickle. "We don't know anything about the market anymore," one senior banker lamented to me.

Senior executives at private banks I interviewed described the encounters in parallel ways. They pointed out that bank executives often serve as semi-public figures; they represent industry on government committees and participate in drafting regulations and making policies. In this role they are expected to speak for industry as a whole and work together with bureaucrats on the larger systemic issues surrounding the market. Although to an American corporate executive the notion of working for a benefit to the industry as a whole might raise "free rider problems," this policy work was one of the great perks, the interesting work that came at the height of a successful career. As part of this work, one was expected to meet with one's peers in industry over golf games and dinners. My informants in both government and industry insisted again and again that it would be impossible to have frank discussions at their offices; the only option was to meet in private and on neutral territory at a restaurant, bar, or private club. It was these encounters that now had emerged as "corruption."

Now there is room for legitimate debate about the relative merits and demerits of Japan's administrative guidance system. On one side of the debate, public choice theory raises concerns that regulation in such a system will be produced for the sole benefit of insiders (Bishop 1997) resulting in a government-supported cartel of sorts (Mueller 1989, 229). Market participants' own views of their closeness to some regulators corroborated these concerns: they emphasized for example the difference between the Ministry of Finance and the BOJ. "The BOJ is a supporter, not a regulator," one banker told me. "They want to push us to do something, not hold us back from doing things." The BOJ was viewed within the industry as something of an intercessor, interested in grasping the issues in depth, and was perceived as proactive, in contrast to MOF's reactive style. As one prominent industry figure put it,

> The Bank of Japan is more supportive. Its staff wants to understand the fundamentals, not just solve the immediate problem at hand. We use them to lobby the Ministry of Finance. MOF wants to know what is the fastest, cleanest way to make a problem go away, not what are the long-term consequences of the problem, or what is the issue about as a whole. You have to convince them that by solving one problem you are not touching regulation in other areas. I suppose [the staff of the BOJ] feel they have to understand everything about the industry because if they don't, MOF will accuse them. But no one can accuse MOF.

As a result, BOJ bureaucrats were proud of the fact that there are many instances in which regulation was supplied in the form and with the specific content that market players wanted.

But if the result of administrative guidance was regulation that served the interest of large financial players, the public choice explanation rooted in payoffs from interest groups to bureaucrats is far less satisfactory. My own efforts to test bureaucrats' level of awareness about the differing effects of particular financial regulations on constituencies other than the large domestic and international banks, or of the trade-offs in the benefits to one group at the expense of another at stake in particular pieces of legislation, suggests that the interests of other stakeholders (including smaller players in the financial markets, consumers, employees of financial institutions, and taxpayers) were too diffuse to garner the sustained attention of these regulators (Macey 1989). Indeed, my efforts to probe the effects of the pieces of financial legislation and regulatory policy I studied for small banks, consumers, and employees often seemed to strike my informants within the bureaucracy as downright odd. The fact that such questions were entirely outside the purview of rational policy debate for these bureaucrats tells us much about the ideological framework in which policy was being made and its implicit constituencies. It suggests that bureaucrats' orientation toward market insiders had less to do with particular pecuniary or political incentives to favor these insiders than with their more general and personally held ideological orientation, itself a product of their own high degree of intellectual inculcation in neoliberal economic and political theories.

In any case, more recently, the public choice critique of administrative guidance has itself come in for reevaluation. If in the last two decades academic observers have mostly portrayed administrative guidance as a flawed and outdated approach to governance, recently, the fashion in policy, journalistic, and academic circles has swung the other way, toward thinking about new forms of public-private regulatory cooperation. In this context, ironically, the very system of Japanese administrative guidance that had seemed so outdated might emerge as a possible model and example. The example of regulatory intervention in order to avoid financial crisis discussed in chapters 2 and 5 suggests that in certain cases and situations, at least, *ex ante*, informal and coordinated public private regulation can indeed be efficient and innovative.

How then did a serious and complex question of what might be the best model of regulation—formal rules backed by *ex post* sanctions or informal guidance characterized by proactive bargaining and collective government-industry problem solving—become framed as a question of individual and even criminal blame? The answer, I think, lies in a confluence of theories and political forces. First, politicians, who had been repeatedly accused of being swayed by contributions and entertainment themselves, had their own purposes in emphasizing the corruption scandal in the bureaucracy (Nakasone 1998, 42). One practical objective of politicians was to rein in BOJ executives' recent attempts to set monetary policy independently of political interference. There is an irony here: the independence of the Central Bank is a central tenet of the package of market reforms pushed on Japan and other countries by development consultants. Yet politicians and their supporters marshaled Western anticorruption rhetoric in order to undermine the BOJ's efforts to follow the Western capitalist model of central bank independence. At a more straightforward level, politicians also saw in the corruption scandal an opportunity to increase their own popularity by attacking the bureaucracy, an institution that inspired as much envy as it did respect (Nakamoto and Tett 1998, 6). A second cause of the anticorruption drive was the interministry and generational struggles within bureaucracy.

But in addition to political interests, the theories themselves also helped to define the political struggles. In particular, the public choice critique of bureaucracy, and the policy solutions it prescribed, gained powerful and committed converts among BOJ employees in their forties or younger, many of whom had received some education in economics, law, or government in the United States. These young bureaucrats

attacked the administrative guidance practices of their superiors that relied on regulation through private or unwritten directives from the bureaucracy and championed reforms that would institute American-style
disclosure mechanisms. They found allies also among the academics
they selected to advise the BOJ on reform.

Younger bank employees I knew severely criticized their seniors for
what they saw as unethical behavior. In their view, accepting entertainment from clients represented a deviation from true bureaucratic practice, defined by the procurement and dissemination of knowledge on a
"rational" basis. At the end of an evening at a local restaurant, after dividing the bill exactly down to the last yen, and then requesting a receipt
from the restaurant demonstrating she had done so, Shimizu, a bank employee in her early thirties, defended the policy with a zeal that went
beyond institutional allegiances. The policy was an inconvenience, she
argued, but it kept things "objective." It was also the only way of countering the tendency of bureaucrats toward arrogance and hegemonic behavior. This cult of rationality in the Weberian sense was one emblem of
the "Western" orientation that younger bureaucrats proudly proclaimed
(Dore 1999; Fife 1995). That is, the way political interests became defined and aligned was also shaped by the particular way foreign ideas
were imported and consumed in the context of the financial crisis.

The same could be said of the role of foreign players. Public choice
theories of deregulation would predict that reforms respond to either a
"demand for deregulation" (Keeler 1984) by domestic and foreign financial institutions or a demand for new regulation tailored to suit the interests of these institutions (Rosenbluth 1989, 5, 53; Upham 1996, 420–25;
see also Ito 1995). Yet what was the explanation for this demand? The
superficial explanation—the one assumed usually without evidence or
comment in discussions of Japanese regulatory reforms—is that foreign
financial institutions, nervous about the opaque quality of Japanese administrative guidance, pushed for formal legislation that restricts bureaucratic influence in jurisdictions like Japan. It is sometimes claimed
that a lack of information about "foreign markets" like Japan prompts
the executives and legal counsel of global investment banks in New York
or London to favor formal rules over bureaucratic standards. Yet if one
assumes, with this hypothesis, such a lack of information, it would be
impossible for decisionmakers in New York or London to know, a pri-
ori, whether they should favor rules or standards, judicially or admin-
istratively guided governance. More important, given the level of inter-

penetration of the global financial markets—and given that, in practice, these markets are clustered in a few cities around the globe such that each of these cities is easily staffed by the handful of institutional players in these markets—it is somewhat preposterous to assume this level of confusion about foreign regulatory structures. Records concerning bribery scandals involving Japanese bureaucrats released to the public during this period demonstrate, moreover, that foreign interests are by no means shut out of the more illicit aspects of "informal" conversations between regulators and industry. All of the employees of foreign banks I interviewed insisted that while it may have been possible to make the claim that foreigners did not have sufficient access to the government in the early 1980s, by the 2000s foreign players had acquired the personnel and knowledge necessary to play the game as well as their Japanese institutional counterparts.

Nevertheless, the Japanese and foreign representatives of foreign market participants I knew often expressed disdain for the "irrationality" of aspects of Japanese political and bureaucratic practice, and a strong "demand" for reform. One could understand this phenomenon in one of two ways. In the first, foreign firms that are substantively insiders even though they formally look like outsiders learn to deploy public choice arguments to gain advantage for themselves. A second possibility not entirely incompatible with the first, and one more plausible to me, is that the authors of such statements, as devotees of public choice ideology in its various academic and popularized versions, actually believed them. That is, such standard sketches of what was good and bad regulation, what was an ideal market, and what ailed Japan circulated ubiquitously in the financial culture and were repeated, casually over drinks, or formally in boardroom presentations, often without much reflection about their application to the actual concrete issues the individuals had before them.

In formal and informal conversations about regulation, it often felt as though a simplified, popularized version of the public choice critique was the right answer—the answer everyone could agree on, with a smile and a shrug, before moving on. And indeed, the argument was everywhere. Transparency International, for example, states in its sourcebook that

> While corruption is defined as "the misuse of public power for private profit," it can also be described as representing non-compliance with the "arm's

length" principle, under which no personal or family relationship should play any role in economic decision-making, be it by private economic agents or by government officials. (Pope 1997, 9)

Under this definition, the entire Japanese system of regulation through administrative guidance could arguably be defined as "corrupt." That such definitions are actively promoted by prestigious nongovernmental organizations, such as the World Bank (Florini 1999; Vishwanath and Kaufmann 1999), think tanks, and university public policy centers such as Harvard's Transparency Policy Project (Fung, Graham, Weil, and Fagotto 2004; Weil 2002), should go some of the way toward an explanation of why policy discussions about regulatory reform were reframed as matters of corruption.

While the Big Bang was clearly a response to a demand for deregulation, then, my own observation is that this demand was in turn the product of complex forces. It was not just that conditions had changed such that domestic and foreign players would now be better off in some purely material way with changed rules. Or rather, what regulatory regime would best suit their material interests was always somewhat opaque and open to interpretation. Advantages could be seen on both sides, as could hassles and uncertainties. The demand for deregulation was also constructed by debates in the press, the academy, filtered through conversations among practitioners that recycled back into the academic and popular literature and in turn were amplified in particular ways by politicians and bureaucrats in Japan and abroad.

Real Time

I now want to show how far-reaching and surprising were the consequences of this influx of theories by turning to an aspect of what central banks do that would seem to have nothing at all to do with corruption scandals or even with deregulation, the activities of the Payments Systems Division at the BOJ. Indeed, I suspect that I was given access to this aspect of bank activities precisely because they were regarded as the least controversial—the place where even the most ardent critics of the regulatory state would agree that there was legitimate room for government coordination. Moreover, this particular unit, headed by an energetic, extremely capable, scrupulously ethical, and broad-minded bureaucrat, was understandably a source of pride at the Bank. But as we will see, even this model unit felt the subtle pressures of neoliberal critiques of the regulatory state. The staff's actions over the period of my research cannot be understood outside the contexts of such theories.

The payments system is the all-important technology by which funds move from one party to another. Every day banks transfer through the BOJ's payment system 120 trillion yen (approximately US$ 1.26 trillion) in more than 30,000 transactions (Bank of Japan 2007–8) that represent the aggregate of millions of their clients' individual orders.[26] They do this by instructing the BOJ to debit or credit the accounts each bank holds with the central bank through its electronic clearing system for large-scale fund transfers known as BOJ-NET (Saito 1994, 224–25).[27] BOJ-NET transfers funds and Japanese government bonds from the accounts of member institutions (1595 as of 2005). It serves as a direct payment transfer system for large "wholesale" fund transfers and also as the final source of clearing for fund transfers between participants in the domestic retail payment system (Zengin System) administered by the Federation of Bankers Associations (Zenginkyo) as well as the Foreign Exchange Clearing System administered by the Tokyo Bankers Association.[28] BOJ-NET is administrated by the BOJ's Payments Systems Division, and its head, whom I will call Sato, a graduate of the University of Tokyo and Harvard's Kennedy School of Government.

At the time of my fieldwork, BOJ-NET was a so-called designated-time net settlement system (DTNS). Banks accumulated obligations to one another throughout the day and then calculated the balance of who owed what to whom at one designated time each day. This netting mechanism, engineered by the Payments Systems Division, was perceived by its architects as a small technocratic triumph, an example of the contributions of planning to the smooth functioning of the market (Kaufman 1996, 826). It was far cheaper and more convenient to "net out" what each owed the other at regular intervals (Matsuo 2003, 2004a, 2004b). The central bankers therefore had laboriously worked out the details of a system by which banks extended each other credit throughout the day and settled all their transactions at once, at a designated time.

But like all systems, it depended on coordination among its components (the member banks). By participating in the clearing system, each bank implicitly agreed to extend credit to the others from the time a notice of payment was received until the time of the actual settlement. As one economist put it, this informal credit system served as the "lubricant of the financial system" since it allowed for smooth transactions in the absence of physical payment (Folkerts-Landau, Garber, and Schoenmaker 1997, 25). The "advance" of designated time, as a system, then, had two dimensions. On the one hand, it represented conceptual sophistication—an understanding that net balances were functionally equivalent to the sum total of individual transactions. On the other hand, it represented a kind of regulatory sophistication—state-coordinated cooperation in the service of a common good.

At the time of my fieldwork the Payments Systems Division staff was planning a change to an entirely new kind of system known as "real-time gross settlement" (RTGS). As the name suggests, real-time gross settlement, which went into operation on January 4, 2001, demanded that market participants cease to extend time to one another to fulfill their commitments. In the new system, each transaction would be settled individually, and in full, at the moment the order to transfer funds was given (Bank of Japan 1998). By fixing each market transaction as an independent moment that created its own rights and obligations, each transaction would be separated and accounted for in real time.

This reform entailed a particular collusion of law and technology (cf. Callon 1998b). RTGS required a series of complex computer networks and programs and operators. But it was also a product of the notion that, as an American central banker put it, one could "substitute rules and other mechanisms to control customer risk-taking incentives" (Eisenbeis 1997, 48). The structure of the division reflected this understanding: one team was devoted to computer systems issues such as the improving speed of data-transfer RTGS clearing system, and another to legal issues such as working out the enforceability of collateralization agreements across borders.

Bureaucrats presented RTGS as a step forward, a technocratic advance. But on closer examination there was something puzzling about it. This was most apparent in the opposition RTGS generated among economists and market participants: employees of the banks that used the payment system, who by now had come to see how DTNS saved them money, complained loudly that it would be far more costly to clear their transactions individually, in real time, because they would have to raise funds to meet each individual payment throughout the day. Economists, likewise, insisted that DTNS was the wiser system because it saved money and avoided delays (Angelini 1998; Kahn and Roberds 1998; VanHoose 1991).[29] Real-time gross settlement was not so much an innovation, therefore, as the unwinding of planning expertise, a return to how things had been prior to technocratic interventions that had produced designated time net settlement in the first place. By settling each transaction in real time, RTGS replaced the bureaucratic coordination that was the very hallmark of technocratic intervention, and which market participants had grown to rely upon, with millions of discrete and individualized units of rights and obligations, now processed automatically by machine.[30]

It is worth pausing for a moment to appreciate just how radical a solution to systemic risk RTGS was. First, it would seem to contradict the public choice notion that regulators will seize any opportunity to expand their field of influence and power. It would have been possible for the payments division, upon becoming aware of the risks associated with DTNS, for example, to take these risks as an invitation to a higher order or greater degree of planning. If systemic risk derived from the ability of risk to cross borders, for example, one could imagine regulators calling for a greater degree of coordination, a linkage of national systems. Or attention to the limits of calculability in predicting risk might call for a finer set of bureaucratic plans, or a more developed set of economic models.[31]

Yet RTGS represented not an expansion, but a kind of self-cannibalization of bureaucratic coordination and policymaking. Where DTNS was the outcome of a common understanding of the market as a system coordinated by bureaucrats—all the market participants shared an understanding of the circulation of funds through the market and agreed to net out their transactions and clear them at the end of the day in the manner bureaucrats prescribed—RTGS represented an unwinding of systemic thought, a going back to an earlier moment of one-for-one exchange. The move to RTGS was a policy that negated policy itself. So why RTGS? Wherein lay the appeal, for its bureaucratic proponents?

An Antidote to the Limits of Human Capacities:
Responding to the Hayekian Critique

In November 1996 the Payments Systems Division circulated a document to member banks and government ministries. The document was a crucial building block in the creation of the policy, from the division members' point of view. The document focused on three problems. The first was "systemic risk":

> When there is an insufficient balance after netting it is unclear what particular transaction caused this problem because the payments are approached as a sum total. The assumption under this system is that all the banks that are expected to settle in a given day can meet their obligations. If even one bank cannot make its payments, it is possible that the entire system would be halted. (Bank of Japan 1996, 20–21)

If Sato saw RTGS as one step in the advancement of rational policymaking, in other words, the arguments he and other central bankers deployed for RTGS highlighted the powerlessness of bureaucratic knowledge in the face of its creation: systemic risk was ultimately incalculable. The problem was not simply one of computational complexity; some of the "risks" involved—the uncertainty over what law might apply to a particular bank failure or how that law would be interpreted, for example—were altogether unquantifiable.[32] For these bureaucrats, the concept of systemic risk flagged the same limits of economic reasoning that had so preoccupied Hayek in his critique of technocratic thought.

To Sato and his colleagues, RTGS was an antidote to the anxieties surrounding the financial crises of the 1990s I have described. RTGS responded to a desire for safe policy, policy that produced less risk even at higher costs. Henceforth, it would not be necessary to plan for systemic crises in the payments system since RTGS would act as a kind of fuse box to prevent the failure of one bank from causing the failure of another. The future failure of individual Japanese banks would be "contained" (Folkerts-Landau, Garber, and Schoenmaker 1997, 1). Like the bank's policy on contact with outsiders, in other words, real time represented a defensive strategy—it responded to bureaucrats' own Hayekian doubts about their ability to plan by minimizing the consequences of market failure and hence envisioning a system in which there would be less need for government planning altogether.[33]

But by giving up the system, the central bank was also giving up one of its important means of intervention in the economy (Sato 1998). Hence, there would be neither the need for nor the tools of technocratic intervention. In true Hayekian form, Sato had an almost utopian vision of the devolution of bank power that would accompany the reform.

He had a deep curiosity and even a certain degree of hope about what kinds of systems and practices private parties might spontaneously invent if left to their own devices. The initial chaos of RTGS would eventually give way to a deeper level of order guided by "market practice," he argued:

> Under RTGS, in which there is no settlement time, one may imagine that financial institutions' intraday liquidity may be destabilized because settlements are performed in no particular order during the period of time when the central bank's settlement service is available. . . . However, in practice, among market participants, a practice of aiming at a fixed period of time for particular kinds of transactions that are the objects of settlement can evolve and *a certain order can be created.* (For example, in the United States, settlements for federal funds transactions are concentrated during certain periods in the morning and the evening, while settlements for repo transactions involving Treasury bonds are concentrated during a certain period of time in the morning.) Even if settlements are concentrated during a certain period of time the merits of RTGS will not be lost at all because [under RTGS] net balances are not calculated or settled at a particular time as in fixed time net settlement. (Bank of Japan 1996, 125; emphasis added)

Sato actively encouraged market participants to develop private solutions to clearing such as opening accounts with one another's banks to decrease their reliance on the central bank altogether. "Sometimes they say these issues should not be fixed as a market practice but through guidelines from the BOJ. But we refuse. We say, we're going to prepare a very flat table. And what kinds of plates and saucers you put on it is your own work," he told me, proudly. The initial chaos of real time, Sato argued, would eventually give way to a deeper level of order guided by "market practice." The difference would be that this new order would emerge on its own, from the aggregation of the actions of individuals rather than as an artifact of his and others' planning. This was the Hayekian ambition for deregulation at its best.

Even in a policy as mundane and uncontroversial as the redesign of a payment system, therefore, we find the influences of certain academic critiques of the regulatory state, filtered through popular sources and private conversations into a form of generalized common sense about what "good policy" might look like and what a highly competent, sophis-

ticated bureaucratic team aiming to produce the very best results might
aim to do.

Eliminating Undue Influence:
Responding to Calls for Transparency

For regulators, the problem of "systemic risk" engendered by one party's
failure to meet its obligations in the context of a system of deeply inter-
connected market participants also implicated the wider political debate
about inappropriate intimacy between regulator and regulated in the
Japanese administrative state described above. In a more general sense,
RTGS promised to eliminate the very possibility of inappropriate regulatory behavior simply by reducing the opportunity for bureaucrats to
exert influence in the market at all. In neoclassical economic terms, the
proper response to systemic risk was for each bank to make careful judgments about how much credit it would extend to every other bank.

From the point of view of many bureaucrats and market participants,
bank failures were ultimately the proximate effects or outcomes of final
decisions taken by BOJ bureaucrats not to rescue a failing bank. They
were outcomes of their choice to adhere to a particular view of the regulator's role. Until 1995 the government had always stepped in to rescue failing banks, so that market participants did not take seriously the
threat of losses associated with intraday credit (Rochet and Tirole 1996,
735). This in turn made it difficult for the BOJ to impose what the economic literature called "market discipline"—to exercise authority by *refusing to intervene* in moments of crisis. This idea that the Bank should
not interfere to save failing institutions was the product of the influx of
economic analyses of markets and bureaucracies into decisionmaking.
DTNS, then, exposed a contradiction in central bankers' view of their
task. On the one hand, as architects of the system, they wanted it to become self-sustaining. Yet their own commitment to the system precluded
them from allowing the market to fail even as (according to their neoclassical economic theory) their benevolent intervention threatened the
system's very vitality.

As Sato suggested, RTGS would at last make it possible for the central bank to withdraw from the system and therefore to exercise the
power of "market discipline" precisely by tying its own hands. Sato was
particularly interested in the changes RTGS would bring for what he

called "the location of power in the market." The advent of RTGS would eliminate a special class of money brokers known as "tanshi," to whom the BOJ gave a monopoly in certain kinds of payments transactions in exchange for allowing the Bank to use them to manipulate short-term lending rates. The move to RTGS therefore meant the loss of an important source of leverage for the Bank (Sato 1998, 1). For Sato, RTGS meant that by replacing his own planning with an automated system for handling risk he could finally conform to his own model of rationality. By curbing his authority to direct policy he imagined that he could end the intimacy of the government as market creator and the governed as market participant. Anxious reflection about the regulator's own place in the market would become increasingly superfluous.

"The Global Standard": Responding to Calls to Internationalize

A second problem raised by the BOJ report concerned the international ramifications of Japan's continued reliance on what it depicted as an outmoded system:

> The world's national central banks, aiming at the reduction of systemic risk, are adopting RTGS as their own settlement systems. . . . Unless we change our current reliance on fixed time settlement, the Japanese Yen will be left behind. (Folkerts-Landau, Garber, and Schoenmaker 1997, 1)

As Sato continually reminded his colleagues, RTGS was a "global trend" (cf. Johnson 1998, 47; Drucker 1998, 77). It had been championed by central bankers at meetings of the Bank for International Settlements (Committee on Payment and Settlement Systems 1997) and enshrined as an objective in important statements of collective banking policy such as the Lamfalussy Report (Committee on Payment and Settlement Systems, 1990). Since the early 1990s, there had been numerous meetings of central bankers dedicated to the benefits of RTGS,[34] and Sato had first learned about RTGS at these meetings. He enjoyed the "club" of central bankers, as he called it, and was committed to spreading the values and ideas of what some have termed an emerging "epistemic community" of central bankers to Japan (Kapstein 1992, 265). RTGS for Sato was part of the path to an advanced economy regulated according to "global standards" (Shukuwa 2002).

Creating Rational Actors: From Models to Dreams

But there was one subtle piece to Sato's ambitions for RTGS that did not quite fit into the neat picture of good regulation promoted by public choice on the one hand and transparency theory on the other. Ultimately, it was the potential impact of real time on the personal character of market participants—whom he talked about in this context as citizens—that most intrigued Sato. He excitedly described how real time would encourage "self-responsibility" by requiring each entity to post collateral for the full value of its transactions in advance. Sato reflected in vivid detail to me about how, under designated time, bankers could just sit in their offices smoking away until the time of settlement each day. Under the new system, however, every second would count, and bankers would be forced to become far more alert, efficient, and nimble in their thinking. Indeed, one of the stated purposes of the shift to RTGS was to force market participants to internalize the costs of their actions, that is, to change the behavior of individuals by encouraging what the official BOJ document termed the "self-responsibility" of market participants (Bank of Japan 1996, 21).

In other words, the ultimate appeal of RTGS for its principal architect lay in its effects on the character of *people* in the market. Here again we see the influence of economic theory on bureaucratic vision. The language of this policy objective—a language of cost internalization— clearly bears the imprint of economic analysis. Yet there is a subtle but crucial difference between the way the economic literature might imagine that incentives change behavior and the ambitions of Sato and his colleagues. Where public choice theory and transparency theory assume that incentives work only because market participants and bureaucrats alike are rational actors, and hence responsive to incentives (cf. Hardin 1968), Sato sought to design policies that would actually *make people more rational*, in economic terms—more able to be incentivized in the first place.

Where did this ambition stem from? To begin with, we might note the role that an implicit model of the difference between East and West in general, and of the United States and East Asia in particular, plays in many economic theories of regulatory excess.[35] In *The International Handbook of the Economics of Corruption*, for example, the economists Daniel Kaufmann, Aart Kraay, and Massimo Mastruzzi (2006), make the claim that increased transparency, incentives for prevention and deterrence, and closer alliance with the private sphere are key mechanisms for "Africa and elsewhere [to] move *to the next stage of governance*" (95; emphasis added). Such an implicit suggestion that those in "Africa and elsewhere" are somehow behind the West—need to move to "the next stage"—would not be lost on the Japanese bureaucrats I knew, who were quite sensitive to negative comparisons with the West. For example, in conversations with law professors and bureaucrats, my interlocutors repeatedly turned to Max Weber's celebrated—but now discredited (Marsh 2000)—distinction between the rationality of modern German society and the collective, hierarchical forms of knowledge that he attributed to Asian societies (Weber 1978, 656). Usually, the reference was double-edged. On the one hand, my interlocutors recognized the arrogance and bias in such an interpretation of world history. On the other hand, however, they wished to emphasize that Japanese bureaucracy, and hence the Japanese person *could* be rational too (Hirai 1991). In other words, although they criticized paradigms in which bureaucratic rationality is a hallmark of Western identity, they also were profoundly absorbed by them.

This debate about rationality as an emblem of what defines the West, and what is "missing" in the East, has a long pedigree in Japan. As the historian Laura Hein (1994) has shown, the appeal to economic models is a progressive position in Japan with roots in anti-imperialism. Hein has described how for postwar left-leaning economists in Japan, rationality, and especially the assumptions about the character of the individual in economic theory, served as a kind of anti-authoritarian position, a way of standing against the cultural statehood of the then-discredited imperial system. In appropriating this theme, these economists drew on a repertoire of ideas that had dominated debates among intellectuals in the Meiji era of opening to the West as well (Fukuzawa 1931). Throughout the postwar era, rationality, especially as embedded in economic theory, is associated with all that is international, Western, and hence progressive (Craig 2009, 120; Fukuzawa 1931; Kanda, Kobayashi, and Uchida 1986; Kawahama 1993a–d). Rationality in this sense has been the progressive reformist *goal*, not the assumed state of affairs.

Public choice theory and other prominent American critiques of the regulatory state in other words enshrine some deeply held American views about human nature and motivation, government, and the source of motivation that may be experienced in other modalities or valences by people elsewhere.[36] In his essay "The Empty Space of the Modern," the sociolegal scholar Takao Tanase (2001) attributes the obsession with what is lacking in Japanese society to the politics of legal modernization and its cognitive and emotional impact on the citizenry in modernizing states. Japanese citizens—like all citizens of modernizing states, he argues—live with profound self-doubt about whether, after all their modernizing efforts, they truly are "modern." This phenomenon is not "cultural" (in the sense of something "outside" of law): rather, he traces Japanese self-doubt to the way "law talk" is "loaded with the power of rationality, universality and the future while indigenous culture is declared irrational, parochial and backward." Hence the debate about whether the Japanese are "rational" or not is symptomatic of the enduring effects of the Western legalist ideology. He draws attention to an aspect of the diffusion of legal ideas that goes unrecognized in most comparative legal analysis—its cognitive or emotional toll, and associated ideologies of legal modernization. In his view, the enduring effect of legal transplants is a culture of self-doubt, in which Japanese people are condemned to continually comparing themselves negatively to others and asking questions about their "rationality."

Such questions about agency, personhood and citizenship—about what is the proper way to be and act in one's institutional capacities, and how in turn one's work might foster a society of properly ordered persons—were particularly salient for the bureaucrats I knew. In the context of the power of institutions to define selfhood in Japan[37] these are vital concerns. Indeed, the reward many of the bureaucrats I knew confessed to desiring most of all was something subtle and elusive—a desire for a sense of satisfaction that they were contributing in a meaningful way to some notion of the social good (Rubin 2002). In conversations, people often referred to their "dreams" (*yume*)—dreams for themselves, but also for Japan. Many bureaucrats I knew talked with passion, in their off hours or casual moments, about their dreams of what Japanese markets, and Japanese people, might become. For Sato, creating rational actors was such a dream.

There is a certain dreaminess to being a technocrat, at least in Japan. Technocratic thought goes hand in hand with dreams: dreaming is an act of setting oneself apart from the world as it is lived day to day. It is small-scale, personal utopianism, predicated on a distance between the world as others see it and the world as it could be. As such it is very much like planning—it is in fact the precondition to technocratic planning. In the hands of technocrats, academic theories have a propensity to become political dreams.

As Sato's own dream suggests, these dreams are not necessarily progressive, transformative, or emancipatory; they can be deeply conservative and even destructive impulses. But they are nevertheless a reality of the bureaucratic style. And this dreaminess in turn fed into very practical concerns: where bureaucratic authority depends on the bureaucrat's ability to convince market participants to comply with policies, the Western discourse of rationality central bankers adhered to so passionately served as a powerful source of their own authority in their consultations with market participants.

In this context, in the 1990s and 2000s it was a standard move for so-called opinion leaders—an ethically empowered move, and one met with appreciation by the press and the public—to bash Japan and Japanese people for their lack of rationalism. A passage from an article by a prominent former bureaucrat captures the way the deregulation debate was cast as a matter of anti-authoritarianism, a problem with Japanese identity and culture, and even antifascism. In an article entitled "Deregulating Japan's Soul" (1998), Masao Miyamoto lays the blame on the "mind control" of Japanese society that begins with its school system. He associates all regulation with a Japanese social disease:

> "Mind control" and regulations have something in common: they both restrict human behavior. Japanese organizations seek people who can be manipulated to obey the rules of "the village" or organization. And the bureaucracy ideally wants its citizens to behave as if they had been castrated, like a gentle flock of sheep. School is the place where such ideal people are created. There students are placed under "mind control" so that they become masochistic and begin to believe that suffering equals pleasure. Personal sacrifice becomes a virtue. This basic thinking was prevalent during World War II. (74)

Quoting Plato's *Republic*, he continues with a lesson about deregulation:

> "The people are enslaved in chains, deprived of the right to move about. With the sun shining brightly from behind, they look at their shadows on the walls as if these shadows represented life itself. They are led to believe that the shadows are reality." . . . By substituting "regulation" for "shadow," it is pos-

sible to see the similarity between Plato's depiction of these men in the cave and the current state of Japanese society. The public, on the one hand, hopes that regulations are lifted. Yet on the other, they are afraid of freedom. While calling for deregulation, they are afraid of the freedom to become independent. (77)

This ambition to rationalize the Japanese self also became one of the central explicit goals of the entire regulatory reform project. For example, in its final report, the government's Justice System Reform Council, charged with overhauling the legal system, described Japan's dramatic legal reforms as a cultural engineering project aimed at remaking the very nature of Japanese selfhood (creating self-responsible individual persons) and of the relationship between the market, the citizens, and the state. As the report puts it, the success of the reforms depended upon the willingness of citizens to transform themselves from "governed objects to governing subjects":

> This is a transformation in which the people will break out of viewing the government as the ruler (the authority) and instead will take heavy responsibility for governance themselves, and in which the government will convert itself into one that responds to such people. (Council Report 2001, 1:1)

I do not want to imply that this cult of rationality was completely seamless. Eisuke Sakakibara, then Japan's Vice Minister of Finance, took a different view:

> I am not a "nationalist" in any sense of the word. However, I do take strong exception to the current fashion of advocating national policies that are merely extrapolations of the philosophy of Western corporate consultants or of our own consultants in the heady "bubble" days of the 1980s. It was pseudorationalism and shallow "innovations" of the business school style of management that distorted the liberal economic system of the 1980s. . . . It is therefore all the more bizarre to see the Japanese media fawn upon proposals to alter the Japanese sociopolitical structure in accordance with the very tenets of unbridled individualism and laissez-faire that have so distorted Japanese society over the past decade. (1998, 80)

Nevertheless, the sheer fact that Sakakibara must begin his comment with the statement, "I am not a nationalist," gives some sense of the political climate of accusation in which these debates took place. Critiques of the pro-individualist position were quickly and easily glossed as conservativism, or fear of change. The effect of all this is that once administrative guidance or corruption is framed as an Asian problem, as a deviation from Western-style rationality, it assumes a momentum of its own.[38]

My experience suggests that public choice is read in light of this tradition by Japanese bureaucrats and academics as encapsulating values to be achieved rather than an accurate model of the world as it is (what the anthropologist Clifford Geertz long ago termed a "model for" rather than a "model of"; 1973, 93). In other words, many Japanese consumers of economic theories of bureaucratic agency notice in them a different set of assumptions and read those *assumptions*, as much as the argument, as a kind of *aspiration*, rather than as a qualification of the applicability of the model to the Japanese situation (Feldman 2006). The model then serves to suggest that the problem with Japan is that it is *not yet* a society in which one could assume the things that American economists might off-handedly assume to hold true about their world (Miyazaki 2006b). This is one source of the moral empowerment bureaucrats find in their devotion to bureaucratic practice. It also explains the surprise of some of my academic colleagues in Japan when I mentioned that in the United States, public choice theory is often associated more with conservative than progressive political positions.

This brings us to the relationship between public choice theories and the individuation of blame for corruption as a mode of policy discourse. The BOJ's policy on contact with outsiders was intended to purify the act of planning from its social roots, now, in the wake of financial crises and criticisms of "Japanese capitalism," newly constructed as a problem of individual conduct. It was the intimacy between bureaucratic knowledge and social relations that had been rendered apparent through its association with "corruption" and its opposition to rationality. By blaming individuals, prosecutors were making a "performative" statement (Austin 1975)—they were performing their commitment to the values of rational individualism.

The result was the creation of a kind of roulette atmosphere in which who would take the individual blame for future policy shifts could not be predicted in advance. Hence bureaucrats became increasingly motivated by fear of blame rather than desire to expand their power, to solve problems, or enhance their own wealth or prestige.[39] The ironic result of taking the rational actor models too literally, then, was to distance the bureaucracy from the market rather than bringing it into line with the market, as economic theories of the regulatory process had envisioned.

Indeed, it is worth pausing to realize how far this state of affairs actually strays from the ambitions that motivate economic theories of regulatory action. Many advocates of transparency in the political process would explicitly disavow the notion that corruption is simply a problem of rooting out and scapegoating the offending individuals. They would insist instead that "combating corruption is not an end in itself," but a structural problem, connected to the broader goal "of creating a more effective government" (Rose-Ackerman 1997, 34). Likewise, in the ideal public choice world, the effect of public choice theory on bureaucrats would be to cause them to accept their proper role as agents subservient to the legislature. This is not what happened in the case of the reform of Japan's payment system, however. As a result of their adoption of economic tools of analysis, these bureaucrats adopted a different set of *objectives* for their plans. Their newfound objective was to create a world in which people (both bureaucrats and market participants) would behave more like rational profit-maximizing individuals and less like the negative stereotypes of Japanese corporate employees. Ironically, it is difficult to imagine a more extreme agency problem, in public choice terms, than the situation in which the agent aims to fundamentally alter the character, identity, or aspirations of the principal.

What Kind of Transplants?

In the Japan of the late 1990s and 2000s, then, a rich *policy question* about the proper style of financial regulation (formal rules or informal processes?) took the form of an endless litany of *individual accusations* of "corruption." The status quo of *ex ante* informal regulatory practice was cast as a set of rampant but individualized deviations from an imagined status quo of formal, arms-length regulation. This was possible because of the way the assumptions of public choice theory were read in Japan owing to the political history of concepts such as rationality or individual autonomy since the Meiji period, and in the postwar era in particular. In other words, the language of public choice and transparency, as it was received and used by its Japanese consumers, created the very kind of coalition of interests that public choice theorists analyze.

My larger aim has been to show how it is possible to adopt economic analysis and the assumptions about the world it enshrines as a set of *ideals or dreams*, a model to be emulated, rather than as a model of reality. Doing so deploys the substance of the very same theory to entirely different political effects. This has implications for the longstanding debate about "legal transplants" (Watson 1993) or the process of transmission or diffusion of legal knowledge, practices, and institutions from one society or jurisdiction to another. Gunther Teubner (1998) has pointed out that foreign transplants (which he prefers to term "irritants") do not simply enter a new legal system as whole entities but rather set in motion a long and turbulent set of reactions within the host legal system that both reshape the host legal system and the transplanted law. My contribution to this conversation is to urge attention not simply to the substance of any legal import, and how it might be transformed or transform what it encounters, but to the modality, affect, or register in which it is imported. As anthropologists have long understood, a "model of" is very different indeed than a "model for." It has different consequences and different uses, inspires in different ways, and conceals different implicit or unarticulated ambitions, agendas, and hopes. In substance the two are identical but, put into motion, they produce entirely different results.

Before we dismiss this as a rash and peculiar Japanese solution, it is worth remembering that the move to RTGS was a global trend (Johnson 1998; Kodres 1996), first implemented by the U.S. Federal Reserve in the aftermath of the bank failures of the 1980s—a defensive bureaucratic response to another earlier period of crisis. Likewise, the Japanese experience with rationality—an experience of rationality as something to be attained rather than as an innate starting assumption of policymaking—is not uniquely Japanese (cf. Chakrabarty 2000, 29). Nor in fact is Sato's ultimate dream of transforming the selves of private actors: in recent years, the fashion in regulatory theory has swung very much toward solutions from behavioral economics that seek to "nudge" private actors to internalize the "proper" values by shaping their preferences (Sunstein and Thaler 2009). All this suggests that the Japanese case serves not as an example of a strange and distant alternative to the West but rather as a useful comparative example that highlights dimensions of bureaucratic behavior around the world that nevertheless may escape attention in the domestic context (Drucker 1998, Milhaupt 1997, 867; West 1994, 1439).

Unwinding Technocracy

What I have described is, in one sense, a quotidian episode of financial deregulation: one state-coordinated system is displaced by another state system whose objective is to be much less interventionist and much more predictable, and hence to place the responsibility for decisionmaking on private market participants rather than public regulators. But if the moves that define deregulation are quotidian, they are also poorly observed and grossly underestimated. Hidden in plain view, these practices offer a treasure trove for understanding the regulatory state and its transformative possibilities.

Consider the concept of systemic risk at the heart of the real-time reform project. Although systemic risk indexed bureaucratic failure, its very discovery was in itself a kind of technocratic achievement. When regulators think about the payment system, they think about the payment system as a whole, as if seen from a distance or from above, with all its component parts, participants, glitches, and capabilities (Mitchell 1998). They think about the market as something to plan. In Sato's own account, for example, he and his colleagues looked at the payment system in a different way than market participants looked at it. As planners, they could see what market participants themselves could not see—aggregate trends, macro, or systemic issues. Hence they would not have expected market participants, who, in their view, did not think about the market in systemic terms, to have an adequate appreciation of systemic risk. It could only be detected through careful contemplation of their system as an integrated and objectified whole (Douglas and Wildavsky 1983; Riles 2000; Stinchcombe 2001).

Regulators deploy their tools upon the market from a distance—this is their comparative advantage; they are able to see problems and solutions by virtue of the fact that they are a step removed from the market. Now in the neoliberal conversation about the proper place of government regulation in the markets, it is precisely this distance between regulators and the markets that has become the problem, the liability of regulators.

As we saw, regulators were caught in the cross-fire of two different criticisms. On the one hand, they were criticized for being too far removed from day-to-day activities in the market. In the Hayekian view, regulators were always a step behind actual innovations in the market, always just a little out of touch. In this view, distance from the market—

technocratic perspective—makes it impossible to regulate effectively. On the other hand, regulators were also criticized for failing to keep the proper distance from the market—for being too intimately involved, personally and professionally, with particular individuals and institutions in the market. Once distance became the defining feature of planning, the metric by which planning was defined and evaluated, there was no perfect distance from which to plan.

From this perspective, let's now turn to deregulation. In this episode, we saw, deregulation was framed as putting an end to state interference in the market. But in practice it entailed not so much an end to state intervention as a transformation of the role of the state, from a visible quotidian force to a less visible but arguably far more consequential role of shaping the very nature, preferences, and objectives of the private actors who populated the market. This is deregulation as transformation rather than disappearance. Taking my cue from the way RTGS was imagined to unwind the prior settlement system, I call this transformative move "unwinding."

I want to focus on unwinding as a response to the problem of a legitimacy deficit for regulatory intervention in the financial markets—as a response to the collapse of distance between the planner and the market. As with the unwinding of two tightly intertwined strings, the episode of unwinding I have described actually recreated a kind of distance—let's call it a synthetic distance—between the planner and the market. After the creation of RTGS, Sato was able to contemplate again how best to foster a successful economy even if he was surely aware that RTGS did not do away with the underlying problems and questions surrounding regulatory legitimacy in the first place. As we saw, the difference that unwinding made for him lay ultimately in the ability to make new kinds of subjects, new kinds of individuals in the market (Cohen 2008, 506). With the creation of "self-responsibility" in the market the very need for bureaucratic intervention would dissipate. The remarkable outcome of unwinding technocratic knowledge from the market, then, was to be the creation of an entirely different kind of market populated by new kinds of economic actors who would already be imbued with the planner's rational instincts—the ultimate rapprochement of state and market. Unwinding then is an escape from a current analytical, political and ethical trap without imagining that it is possible to truly escape the problem altogether. Unwinding is by definition movement in place rather than movement forward. It is a response to a situation in which one is too close, too tightly bound up with the thing one is trying to engage with, to make sense of it.

How does this metaphor help us to think differently about the possibilities for state regulation of markets or imagine new possible solutions to regulatory problems? In two principal ways. First, unwinding gives us a more vibrant, mobile, transformative picture of what is usually termed deregulation. The latter is used either with enthusiasm or melodrama (Westbrook 2010) to suggest a total destruction of the regulatory state. But unwinding sets us thinking about how the state and the nature and meaning of market intervention is not so much constructed and destroyed as it is continually morphing from one genre to another. This, in turn, recalibrates the politics of policy debates away from simple right/ left, pro-state/anti-state battles and toward a more imaginative conversation about the kinds of transformations and outcomes that can be hoped for, and associated policy options. It also gives us a vocabulary for thinking about some recent policy proposals for regulating the markets premised, even more explicitly than RTGS, on unwinding the power of the regulatory state and refocusing state power rather on the creation of new kinds of economic subjects and new kinds of economic relations.

Unwinding also helps us to think in richer ways about the place of academic ideas in regulatory practice. The dominant view in the United States, if not in Japan, is that in order for academic ideas to have an effect in the "real world" they must be "translated" into "policy proposals"— beyond this, academic thought is more or less irrelevant. But the Japanese experience with deregulation demonstrates on the contrary the profound impact of academic theories on the political climate. Academic ideas achieved something arguably far more potent than "policy proposals": they became the stuff of planners' dreams, defined planners' conception of themselves as ethical subjects, provided the meaning, purpose, and motivation for their work. Once inspired in this way by public choice, bureaucrats needed no assistance from academics to transform dreams into policy proposals. They were already experts in doing this. In other words, if we accept my description of the state as an accumulation of knowledge tools, then theory, models, and academic ideas must be seen as part of the toolbox. But at the same time, this should be a cautionary tale. For what bureaucrats "took" from public choice was ultimately subtly but consequentially different from what public choice theorists thought they were offering. Recast as dreams—ambitions for transforming society—the assumptions underlying public choice models of societies populated by rational actors neatly pursuing their self-interest left no room for the very dreams that motivated the creators of public choice models—dreams of small states and free markets.

All of this suggests that it is too easy and comfortable for academics to assert that their ideas have no impact and hence that they can be absolved of responsibility for the accidents of the past, or the limitations of future solutions. Here is a neat example of how economic actors engage in theory building alongside, and even in conversation with, economists. But it also suggests that in others' hands, academic ideas necessarily take on implications, shapes, and modalities quite different from those their original proponents could have imagined, let alone intended. For these central bankers, the seemingly distant question of corruption became inseparable from the crisis of rationality surrounding their own loss of faith in the predictive capacities of their models. What is most interesting is that the multiple possible uses and interpretations of economic analyses of financial regulatory policy apparently went unnoticed by *both* sides—academics and policymakers—as they talked in what they perceived as a shared language.

Economists are now accustomed to thinking about the effects "learning" can have on human behavior (Langley and Simon 1981; Simon 1975). But to include in the "stuff" of learning the economic model itself is to build a second "loop" into the learning model that takes into account actors' ability to learn not simply from repeat plays of "the game" but from outside "theories" *about* their game. Conversely, this requires acknowledging that all academic arguments for or against a particular vision of how regulation comes to exist are not "just" arguments but the artifacts of particular interests, alliances and disputes (cf. Dezalay and Garth 1996). A model that incorporates this assumption necessarily treats the academy and the bureaucracy/judiciary as a singular collaborative and hence requires the theorist to treat him- or herself as part of what is being modeled. This introduces what anthropologists and sociologists call "reflexivity" into the analysis. It breaks the frame of the economic model, so to speak, and asks us all to think more about the model and the model-makers as factors that have real-world effects.

Notes

1. For debates about public choice theory in Japan and its applications to the bureaucracy, see Hayashida 1995; Kurokawa 1998; Yoshida 1998.

2. Leight credits a similar underlying commitment to public choice ideals among financial regulators in the United States for many of the deregulation policies of the 1990s and 2000s. As she comments, "It is perhaps the supreme irony of the success of the capture theory of regulation that it has succeeded in making capture itself somewhat superfluous" (2010, 6).

3. There is a long tradition of progressive scholarly critiques of bureaucrats as well. In his classic mid-century critique of U.S. politics, Theodore Roszak assails the "technocracy" as "that society in which those who govern justify themselves by appeal to technical experts who, in turn, justify themselves by appeal to scientific forms of knowledge. And beyond the authority of science there is no appeal" (1969, 8). Like other theorists of his time (e.g., Meynaud 1969), Roszak follows Hannah Arendt (1979), Herbert Marcuse (1964), and Max Weber (1968) to focus on the way technocratic power is "the product of knowledge and extraordinary performance" (Winner 1977, 139). Recent work revives this tradition to show, for example, how the assumptions and inner workings of bureaucratic knowledge impede citizen participation (Espeland 1994; Fischer 1990).

4. Yet at the same time, corruption for her is primarily an economic issue. As Barry Hindess puts it, "Rose-Ackerman's treatment of corruption as if it were first and foremost an issue of financial gain and economic effect might not deny the existence of these other forms of corruption, but it does suggest that they should be seen as something of a sideline" (Hindess 2001, 3; Rose-Ackerman 1999).

5. In contrast, recent work in economics suggests that efficiency and corruption are not necessarily correlated in such a direct way (Banerjee, Hanna, and Mullainathan 2009).

6. It was clear that these two banks were not acting in an aberrant manner. Many of the other "city banks" in Tokyo were also implicated. See Sugawara 1998, 11.

7. The scandal "provide[d] [Prime Minister] Hashimoto with a powerful weapon in his campaign to achieve administrative reform in Japan and to shift the power from the bureaucracy to the political establishment" (*Financial Times* 1998).

8. No one was accused of accepting cash payments; what was at issue in these cases was entertainment expenses. Articles 197 and 198 of the Japanese Penal Code simply ban bribery without defining the term further (Penal Code 1907, articles 197, 198).

9. Marilyn Strathern (2000a) speaks of a new "culture" of accountability, with a capacity to hold the moral and the financial aspects of modern social and institutional life together. Some critics have described this culture of accountability as a new form of coercion ("coercive accountability") in which noncompliance no longer is an option (Shore and Wright 2000, 81).

10. Michael Power (1997, 52) notes how the breadth of the transparency ideal

allows it to be demonstrated and performed in diverse ways: "Accountability for effectiveness is therefore a vague ideal and can be operationalized in a number of different ways with very different emphases and related bodies of knowledge. Making effectiveness auditable is closely bound up with defining performance and installing a management system to measure that performance." Anthropologists likewise have described transparency as an "organizational vision," a "gaze" (Garsten and Lindh de Montoya 2008, 4) rather than a principle. As such, transparency becomes "polysemic" (Grossman, Luque, and Muniesa 2008, 99)—it may assume disparate meanings to different audiences. As for the internal contradictions of the concept, Hetherington, for instance, reflects on how much transparency rhetoric actually shares with its nemesis, corruption:

> The new democratic premise that transparency is an antidote to populist corruption relies on a simple opposition between two ways of organizing the relationship between the state, the citizenry and documents. Both transparency and populism are forms of inclusion. Populism produces citizens through semi-private networks of gift-giving, including the gifts of documents that solidify the linkage between state and citizen. By contrast, transparency produces citizens by extending the public sphere of deliberation about government through the circulation of *information about* government. (2008, 47; emphasis in the original)

11. In other words, I do not engage with the literature on the "morality" of corruption. See, e.g., Rose-Ackerman 1999; Donagan 1979; French 1979; Walzer 1973.

12. The critique of stereotypes of Japanese law as culturally different from Euro-American law has been the subject of considerable recent writing in Japanese legal studies. See, e.g., Ramseyer 1991; West 1994, 1997.

13. This focus draws on anthropologists' findings about bureaucrats' adoption of the language and models of rationalism. Anthropological studies of bureaucracy have analyzed the systems of categorization bureaucrats deploy and the political and social effects of these systems (Fife 1995; Hertzog 1999; Herzfeld 1992), such as the demarcation of the sphere of science and scientific reasoning from other arena of knowledge production (Nader 1996, 2).

14. "The form of a legal pronouncement might affect citizens' preferences, and thus the effect of the law on behavior. Specifically, legal form might affect the extent that citizens feel 'endowed' with a legal entitlement" (cf. Korobkin 2000, 51).

15. The laws are the Law Concerning the Reorganization of Laws Relevant to Financial System Reforms (Financial System Reform Law); the Law Concerning the Liquidation of Specified Assets Through Special Purpose Companies; the Law Concerning the Reorganization of Laws Relevant to the Enactment of

the Law Concerning the Liquidation of Specified Assets Through Special Purpose Companies (the SPC Laws); and the Law Concerning Close-out Netting in Specified Financial Transactions Engaged in by Financial and Other Institutions (the netting law). See generally Ono, Kanda, Tanaka, Yamada, and Wani 1998, 26–27. As Ronald Dore (1999, 40) has put it:

> What . . . all these slogans add up to is a general belief that (1) the principles according to which the typical neoclassical economics textbook says the economy are to work are a priori correct principles, (2) those principles are best exemplified in the American economy, (3) the rightness of those principles is further confirmed by American success, and (4) Japan's present plight is not just a cyclical phenomenon and a debt-deflation hangover from the bubble; it is the natural and wholly just retribution visited on Japan for not following these principles.

Scott and Wellons (1998, 472) have argued that "the Big Bang apparently rejected the unique Japanese financial system that had worked so well until the late 1980s."

16. Many of these regulatory barriers have their origins in the laws and policies instituted by General MacArthur after World War II. See Rosenbluth 1989, 40–41.

17. See Amendments to the Banking Law, Article 10(2)(2), *Kanpo Gogai* no. 120, June 15, 1998, p. 199; Law concerning Reorganization of Laws Relevant to the Financial System Reforms, Law no. 107 of 1998.

18. For a critique of the power of bond rating agencies and the criteria of evaluation they deploy, see Partnoy 1999.

19. See the Bank of Japan Act 1997. The new law came into effect in April 1998.

20. See Financial Supervisory Agency Establishment Law 1997. The initial staff of the FSA came almost entirely from the Ministry of Finance. However, the agency hired a number of regulators from the private sector as well and also brought in a small number of bureaucrats from other ministries.

21. Economists clearly claimed that a lack of transparency and disclosure contributed to the Asian economic crisis. Rahman (1998), for example, argues that most of the corporations and banks in the five East Asian countries did not follow international accounting standards in reporting those financial transactions that appear to have been responsible for triggering the financial crisis. Mehrez and Kaufmann (1999) also illustrate how poor transparency combined with new and deregulated financial markets may lead to unsustainable investment and large exposures and vulnerability of financial institutions.

22. As Robert Eisenbeis, director of research at the Federal Reserve in Atlanta, put it: "[S]ystems, instruments, and markets are evolving faster than the

political entities can bring their various rules and regulations into harmony despite the many initiatives that have been undertaken" (1997, 50).

23. Article 29 of the Bank of Japan Act reads: "The Bank of Japan's executives and staff shall not leak secrets which they have learned in performing their duties, or use such secrets for their own interest. These requirements are equally applicable after they leave the Bank." See also Article 32: "In light of the public nature of its business, and in order to ensure appropriate discharge of duties by the Bank of Japan's executives and staff, the Bank shall establish rules regarding ethical discipline of its executives and staff, such as the obligations to devote themselves to their duties and to separate themselves from private enterprises."

24. One indication of the degree to which all this was taken appears in the rules' explicit acknowledgment that it is acceptable for bureaucrats to keep small mementos given them by foreign governments on international trips such as coffee mugs or ballpoint pens. This is according to Article 6 of the National Public Official Moral Code, which reads, "Certain high-level national government officials are obliged to report any gifts or benefits from business entities if the value of such gifts or benefits exceeds ¥5,000" (approximately US$56). The UCPA does not explicitly permit "facilitation payments." However, the guidelines provide that, since small facilitation payments "are not made for the purpose of procuring administrative service which the payer would otherwise have no right to receive; are solely for the purpose of facilitating procedures the benefit of which the payer is rightfully entitled; and are considered acceptable under the OECD Convention they should also be considered acceptable under the UCPA Fusei kyoso boshiho" (The Unfair Competition Prevention Act [UCPA]) 1993, Act no. 47, as amended September 28, 1998).

25. The anthropologist Mayfair Mei-hui Yang (1988, 411) has made a similar point with respect to the uses of "guanxi" in China and its distinctions from corruption.

26. Every forty-eight hours, BOJ-NET turned over an amount equal to Japan's GNP (Borio and Van den Bergh 1993, 5).

27. BOJ-NET is used for fund settlement among financial institutions, settlement of credit and debit positions from other settlement systems such as the retail funds transfer system or foreign exchange clearing system (privately run systems), and the purchase and sale of government bonds. See Bank for International Settlements 1993, 255. In 1992 BOJ-NET handled 3,710,000 transactions for a value of 35,892 trillion yen (283–84).

28. The Federation of Bankers Associations of Japan (*Zenkoku Ginko Kyokai Rengokai* or *Zenginkyo*) is the principal representative body of banks in relations between the government and the industry. Its 148 member banks are represented on a series of committees. The chairmanship rotates among the most prominent "City Banks" for a one-year term. See http://www.zenginkyo .or.jp/en/gaiyo/gai01.htm. During its term, that bank's staff will chair each of the

many subcommittees established to consider particular problems facing the industry. Thus, the bank's staff at various levels will be occupied during the year with committee work. The Federation operates the Zengin System of interbank payment and settlement, which is an electronic fund-transfer network incorporating all depository institutions in Japan. It operates the Foreign Exchange Yen Settlement System. The Federation has no foreign members. It sends representatives to BIS negotiations on capital adequacy requirements.

29. To economists, the question of who was initially to blame for systemic risk was the wrong question because risk was something that could not help but be shared among all participants in the system. Formal economic modeling suggested that there were many benefits to net settlement: Net settlement reduces "gridlock"—the possibility that each bank could not meet its demands until it received a payment from the other. Net settlement also creates credit constraints, and avoids trading delays (Angelini 1998; Kahn, Andrews, and Roberds 1999). For this reason, economists were deeply divided about the wisdom of RTGS. See, e.g., VanHoose 1991.

30. The division's understanding of the natures and uses of law harked back to a classical mode of legal reasoning increasingly prevalent in the international financial sector. In this understanding, "rights" were ontologically coherent units independent of the institutions that enforced them. They were imagined to "vest" at the precise place and time in which the events that brought them into being occurred. In this case, the transfer of funds from one account to another in "real time" created a right to those funds held by the transferee at the split second of the book entry.

31. In the same way, James Ferguson has shown how the neoliberal state is often something "more" than the state described by Jim Scott in *Seeing like a State* (cf. Ferguson 2005; Scott 1998).

32. As one central banker put it:

> At present, concern about such clearing and settlement systems stems from the sheer size of the potential losses rather than from a true understanding of well-articulated scenarios on how the risks would be played out. . . . Measuring and monitoring these interrelated exposures across the world, across different markets and time zones, is a truly daunting modeling and monitoring problem. It is made even more so by the dynamic and continual evolution of new instruments and markets. (Eisenbeis 1997, 46–48)

In this sense, RTGS responded to the general distrust of bureaucrats' competence to tame the market through planning and regulation. Indeed, RTGS and the policy concerning contact with outsiders represented similar strategies of "risk minimization," ways of isolating future dangers to themselves and the market rather than strategies of innovation (Pempel and Muramatsu 1995, 71).

33. Centeno argues that neoliberalism and technocracy go hand in hand. He attributes this to the fact that many technocrats ultimately share Hayek's distrust of democracy (1998, 36, 37).

34. That is to say that central bankers were actively promoting RTGS as a global trend. The most important forum for such meetings has been the Bank for International Settlements.

35. This heuristic has a long tradition in legal scholarship that touches on the rule of law in Asian or "Oriental" societies. See Maine 1931; Wigmore 1897; Unger 1977; and David 1983. For a critical analysis of this tradition, see generally Chiba 1989.

36. Some public choice theorists have recognized that the theory's assumptions about bureaucratic motivation are relatively unsophisticated, untested, and most likely quite culturally specific. In concluding that the functional equivalent of the residual as a source of motivation in public choice is the possibility of bureaucratic slack, for example, Terry Moe acknowledges that this is only a hunch that is difficult to prove. Moreover, he acknowledges that (even American) bureaucrats are probably less motivated by pecuniary gain than other "types" such as entrepreneurs and in fact that there are different "types" of bureaucrats (e.g., political appointees, career officials) who are no doubt motivated differently (1984, 763–74). William West, drawing on James Freeman, goes further to emphasize that the "factors which undermine the legitimacy of administrative policymaking" are profoundly shaped by "aspects of our national character, such as a concern with bureaucratization, ambivalence toward government intervention, and a lack of faith in bureaucratic expertise" attributable to multiple sources, "including American anti-intellectualism, the perception that administrators do not have a monopoly on useful information, and the realization that administrative choices often rest on value judgments" (1984, 341).

37. As the anthropologist Nakane Chie (1972) has argued, where in certain societies persons are defined by demographic traits such as class or cultural affinity, Japanese in the postwar era have defined themselves by the institutions to which they devote their labor.

38. Amy Borovoy (2001, 95) has discussed the powerful effects of the introduction to Japan of popular psychology, with its American emphases on bounded individualism, on its largely female consumers. Notions such as "codependence" emerge as "a language for social criticism," she argues.

39. Wendy Espeland (2000) has explored the uses of public choice models within one bureau at the U.S. Department of the Interior. Her ethnography points to the appeal of these ideas: a bureau already under attack seeks to insulate itself from public criticism, and within that bureau, the marginal figures ("consultants") who are assigned politically sensitive tasks of determining pub-

lic opinion about a particular policy seek to insulate themselves from the game of roulette in which a particular bureaucrat is made to take the blame for a policy. In the example Espeland describes, as in this case, the appeal of the theory is rolled up with the appeal of technology—of sanitizing and insulating the political marketplace by constructing a machine to manage them (in her case, creating quantitative indexes of preferences and then building a Web-based interactive computer program to enable the public to register its views as "inputs"). Espeland points out how this model of participation excludes those who cannot define their political interest as a matter of preference. Espeland does not claim that the consultants who adopted public choice models purposely sought to emaciate the political process. Rather, she points to the unintended consequences of the adoption of these models as the particular media for dialogue between government and its citizen-stakeholders (cf. MacLennan 1997, 195).

CHAPTER FOUR

Placeholders

Engaging the Hayekian Critique of Financial Regulation

Since Friedrich Hayek, debates about the proper relationship between the state and the market, and about the optimal design of regulatory institutions, often turn on assumptions about the workings of legal expertise—and in particular about the difference between public expertise (bureaucratic knowledge) and private expertise (private law). Hayek's central attack on state regulation and argument for market regulation through private law has been adopted uncritically by a wide array of policy-makers and academics across the political spectrum. These arguments are worth engaging because, as I show in chapter 3, they are not just academic arguments: they have had concrete effects in the financial markets, as they have been taken on by market participants and regulators themselves as justifications or criticisms of what they do.

At its core, Hayek's argument is a temporal one: bureaucrats are by definition analyzing events that have already transpired, and economic planning, therefore, is always one step behind the real-time movements of the market (Hayek 1952). Hence effective market planning is impossible. Moreover, the abstraction of economic planning distorts the true complexity of the market, and therefore cannot possibly make accurate predictions about the future (Bockman and Eyal 2002; Reddy and Heuty 2008). In a world in which "preferences and opportunities are constantly changing in response to new information" efforts to centralize information always lag behind the ever-changing information itself (Anderson 2008, 247). Hayek's conservative belief that the knowledge of bureaucratic planning is no match for the temporality of capitalism has a progressive parallel in the anxious claims of present-day theorists of capitalism that the Keynesian state is under attack because of the hyper-mobility of capital (Wolf 1999, 230).

Hayek argues that private ordering is superior, in contrast, because it is of the moment, happening in real time. In a world in which it is impossible to know the future, *price*, as a private and real-time system of co-ordinating information, creates order out of the "unintended actions of millions of economic actors" (Beaulier, Boettke, and Coyne 2004, 211) in a way that is more accurate and efficient than state-sponsored efforts to centralize information. Where state planning undermines and distorts the market price system of information coordination, moreover, private property rules facilitate it. Regulation, in other words, is only legitimate if it is *ex post*—through the adjudication of private property and contractual rights after the fact—not *ex ante*—through regulatory or fiscal policy that dictates particular courses of private action in advance.

As mentioned in the previous chapter, Hayek's description of the limitations of bureaucratic planning resonates with the sense of powerlessness and frustration experienced by many of the government officials I knew. It is important to recognize also that Hayek's ideological argument about the limits of traditional technocratic rationality has been demonstrated empirically again and again by social theorists and anthropologists and sociologists of bureaucracy who do not share Hayek's political motivations (cf. Beck 1992; Clarke 1999; Giddens 1991).

But Hayek's rich and suggestive account of the limits of public legal expertise in regulating the market *ex ante* is far less complete when it comes to the strengths of private legal reasoning.[1] I submit that the ideological dimension of Hayek's argument lies not in his attention to the limitations of technocratic reasoning per se but rather in the way he slips from observations that public legal reasoning has certain temporal weaknesses to a simple assumption that private reasoning must have equivalent temporal strengths. The slippage from a critique of public regulation to an undefended endorsement of private regulation has also been remarkably common among legal theorists over the last two decades.

This chapter takes on Hayekian arguments against government regulation through a detailed examination of real-world examples of how public and private legal technologies manage the temporal dimensions of risk in the over-the-counter (OTC) derivatives markets. The specific examples are: the usage of collateral on the private law side (chapter 1), and the usage of real-time gross settlement (RTGS) payment settlement

systems on the public side (chapter 3). I choose these two examples because they are paradigms of private and public regulation: if collateralization is a core element of private market self-regulation, the administration of the payment system is one of the few functions that even many
ardent defenders of free markets would allocate to the state. Global swap
markets function outside state control in many ways. But they still rely
on state institutions to clear their transactions. The standard view is that
at a very minimum, the state must do this. And yet even this last bastion
of state action has become increasingly controversial: Hayek himself late
in his career launched an attack on it as nothing more than a monopoly over currency for the benefit of governments (Hayek 1976a), and at
the time of my fieldwork, market participants had plans to create a private clearing system for their transactions entirely outside the purview
of state institutions.

This chapter is about time, therefore—how legal reason deals with
the future, and about the temporal dimensions of legal knowledge of the
market. Here, Hayek's insight is prescient: time—the relationship of present to past and future—is indeed the key challenge for markets and their
regulation. Ultimately, information about past market transactions can
never fully predict future market problems or opportunities. Assets have
value (positive or negative) that is by definition only discoverable over
time and can never be fully predicted in advance. Or, to put it another
way, relationships between market participants with respect to those assets unfold in time in ways that can never be fully anticipated or ensured.
In Roscoe Pound's words, "In a commercial age wealth is largely made
up of promises" (1945, 2).

At the same time, theorists of finance have shown that the notion of
"real time"—the focus on the moment, and the imperative to be up to
the moment, is in fact a quite recent sociotechnical creation, a product
of market technologies and institutional relationships themselves rather
than a mere external constraint on these. The philosopher of markets
de Goede argues for example that the very notion of the future as something that must be hedged against is a historically and culturally specific
understanding of time particular to late capitalism and made possible by
the development of such things as the Dow Jones Index, which enabled
investors to visualize their investments in time (de Goede 2005; see also
Greenhouse 1996, 49; Hope 2006). Likewise, the historian of markets
Alex Preda (2002) shows how the development of the ticker tape machine, which produced and disseminated price information in real time,

fundamentally changed the way time was conceptualized in the market. This literature suggests that rather than view time as a neutral arbiter and constraint on markets and their regulation, as Hayek does, we might think about the definition of time as another ideological battleground, a kind of market politics. Towards the end of this chapter I will suggest that from this point of view we can begin to see the production and manipulation of time through private law technique as a kind of analog to regulation, and hence also as a resource for market governance.

I begin by reviewing the circumstances surrounding the Bank of Japan's transition to a RTGS payments system described in the previous chapter, as a quotidian example of the problem that time creates for the public regulation of the financial markets.

Public Governance and the Problem of Time

As explained in the previous chapter, payment systems are the digital, legal, and institutional apparatuses by which money is actually transferred from one bank to another. Until the late 1990s, Japan's payment system cleared payments on a "net" basis at several designated times during the day (DTNS—designated-time net settlement). However, this very act of coordination created a new danger of its own: If one bank was unable to meet its obligations to pay others at the designated time, this could leave others without the cash to meet their own obligations and, hence, create a "domino effect" (Folkerts-Landau, Garber, and Schoenmaker 1996, 1) that would lead to systemic failure (Bank of Japan 2006). The previous chapter therefore chronicles central bankers' creation of a new "real time" payment system that would clear transactions one by one, in real time.

As we saw, behind this reform was an anxiety on regulators' part about their ability to plan—that is, to predict the future of the market and address problems *ex ante*, before they occurred. Like Hayek, they struggled with the temporal incongruity between the retrospective methods of positivist science and the prospective demands of the market (Hayek 1952; cf. Miyazaki 2003). Regulators lacked confidence about the knowability of even the very immediate, near future of the market—the danger of DTNS was that, on a particular morning, an unknown market crisis might be lurking before the next designated time of net settlement that afternoon.

Here we have a practical example of how time creates a problem of legitimacy for state regulation of markets. Critics and proponents of public governance have long commented on the "inevitable tension between democratic control of public policy, including regulatory policy, and regulation of experts" (Shapiro 2004, 343). As described in the previous chapter, this tension has often been recast as a problem of bureaucratic experts pursuing their own self-interest rather than the wider public interest. But in fact, the problem of bureaucratic legitimacy is deeply intertwined with the problem of the knowability of the market. As we saw, what counted as corruption was in many cases a pragmatic effort to know the market in advance—to gather and act upon market information before it became public and hence already incorporated into prices.

As a technology of governance, then, RTGS is one kind of response to financial crisis—a public regulatory response, but a defensive one, grounded in regulators' anxieties about their inability to plan for the future. We might think of RTGS as an institutional embrace of Hayek's critique of the possibility of government planning. Hayek's claims concerning the temporal difficulties associated with government planning seem borne out by the experience of these central bankers. Here we can see how the temporal challenges of regulation identified by Hayek create a deficit of legitimacy for the state and its regulatory apparatus.

One final point before we contrast technocratic knowledge with private governance technology: did the Real Time governance machine live up to its promises? Could it really obviate the need for planning for the future, get the government out of the day-to-day management of the market, and hence take the politics out of regulation through automation? In fact, almost as soon as RTGS was on the drawing board, it became clear that the state would remain deeply involved. A diagram, drawn for me by the head of the Payments and Settlement Division, dramatically illustrates how time continues to pose a problem: where would market participants get the necessary liquidity to clear their transactions in real time? The system would have to depend on massive loans from the government—so-called daylight overdrafts from the central bank (see fig. 3).

The Real Time machine did not eliminate the need for state interference in markets nor did it automate the politics of regulation. In this respect, it is no different from many other efforts to automate regulation studied by sociologists of markets, such as automated trading mechanisms on stock exchanges (cf. Muniesa 2000). But this does not

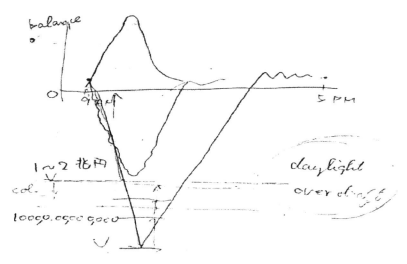

FIGURE 3. Schematic depiction of the liquidity problem created by RTGS, drawn by Sato

mean the project was a failure. On the contrary, the feedback loop between regulatory theory and regulatory practice described in the previous chapter rendered this project absolutely crucial to the legitimacy of
the central bank. If little changed as a matter of economic substance,
as a matter of political form, the central bank moved from opacity to
transparency.

Private Governance and the Problem of Time

This material suggests that Hayek was indeed on to something in his diagnosis of technocratic planning as a modality of thinking about market
governance. If this is so, then it may be time to think about alternative
modalities of state intervention in markets than technocratic planning. I
will return to this point at the close of this chapter.

For all his sophisticated critiques of public regulation, however, Hayek
has surprisingly little to say about how exactly private law governs the
market. In *The Mystery of Capital*, likewise, Hernando De Soto (2000)
writes only of the security of private transactions, bolstered by collateral, without giving any picture of how collateral magically makes everything so secure. I now want to extend the Hayekian discussion of the
public to the private by turning to the example of the nature and uses of

collateral in the global private swap markets. Here we will see that similar problems of time pervade private legal regulation. How then does private law govern? What are the techniques and sources of its authority and legitimacy?

As it turns out, there is also a temporal problem at the heart of the swap transaction. In order to see how this is so, lets reconsider from a slightly different perspective the mechanics of swap transactions laid out in more detail in chapter 1. We might think of the swap as a temporally stretched form of the classic market exchange—a market exchange with an attenuated but definite temporal horizon. That is, the swap has a definite future point of exit, specified in the initial swap agreement as the future date of the close-out. But unlike in the classical model of market transactions, that point of exit does not happen immediately; it happens at some mutually agreed future time. In this respect, the swap may at first seem unusual from the point of view of standard theories of capitalism in which exchange is immediate (I give you money and you give me widgets) and involves no personal or economic commitment on either side beyond this. But, in fact, many forms of market exchange work precisely by means of a time lag between the two sides of an exchange. Examples include the ordinary loan, to be repaid at some future time, merchant relations surrounding the sale of goods on account, and in a more general sense all arrangements in which payment is made at the conclusion of an agreed period of mutual involvement, from the purchase of food in a restaurant to a employee's monthly paycheck. This instability is simply more volatile in the case of the swap, as the size of the obligation and even who is the creditor and who is the debtor shifts back and forth over the course of the maturation of the swap, with market movements (Johnson 2000, 45).

In practice, this raises all kinds of problems—risks—surrounding the future reliability of one's exchange partner and the future interpretation of the relationship. If a trader at Paribas Bank agrees with a trader at Sanwa Bank to swap a certain amount of currency at a certain price at a year's time, what assurance does the risk management staff at Paribas have that Sanwa will be willing or able, in a year, to fulfill its side of the bargain? In the "meantime" (Wiegman 2000, 822), before the close-out of the swap the parties to a swap are *involved*. Their fates are intermingled. Their fortunes influence one another, and their actions have consequences for one another. In the meantime, we might say, the parties govern one another and submit to being governed.

Now, in the view of Friedrich Hayek, and in more recent times of Hernando De Soto and the many other proponents of property rights as an antidote to government regulation, this is precisely where collateral comes in, as a "method for dealing in property for the purpose of securing the payment of a debt" (Garrard 1938, 356). As detailed in chapter 1, in the textbook explanations, collateral is a tool for foreclosing those uncertainties, those risks. Collateral is a tool for *placing limits* on those mutual entanglements: If Sanwa Bank posts collateral today, risk management staff were fond of pointing out, Paribas does not have to think further about Sanwa's whereabouts tomorrow, to inquire about whether it has its financial house in order, to know the messy details of what executives are on the outs with government regulators, or whether its traders are competent and above board. Paribas's risk-management staff only needs to know that their positions are fully collateralized. Specifically, ISDA's collateral regime commits the parties to a rigid system of collateral calls to be made and responded to in specific ways when certain "thresholds" are reached (ISDA 2005, 54). This could serve as a textbook example of the Hayekian model of the evolution of private regulation. As Richard Epstein puts it, "According to Hayek, it is the capacity for error in particular cases that impels individuals within the spontaneous order to gear their conduct by certain standard rules and practices, the precise reason for which they cannot fully understand" (2000, 276). This view that private law doctrines and techniques can stand as a bulwark against the complexity and indeterminacy of the market is known as legal formalism.[2]

But, in fact, property lawyers know that property produces more entanglement, not less. Contrary to De Soto's simplistic claim (2009) that the very existence of registered property rights produces clarity and certainty about the delineation of powers and obligations (and hence that the only necessary reform of the financial markets is the creation of an adequate registration system for property in derivatives), most of property law is in fact about the enormous ambiguities that surround what powers and obligations flow from titled property ownership. If I own a piece of land, does that mean I have a right to build a factory on it that billows smoke onto neighboring property? If I own a shopping mall, does that mean I have the right to exclude protestors from demonstrating there? If I can be understood to own my body, does that mean I have the right to sell my organs (cf. Alexander 1997; Alexander and Penalver 2008; Penalver 2005; Penalver and Katyal 2007)? As Duncan Kennedy and Frank Michelman pointed out in their landmark 1980 article, formal property law increases certainty for some but reduces it for others; it increases certainty about some expectations but decreases certainty about others. The real issue is whose certainty do you want to maximize, and about what (722–25).

What is true of property in general is all the more true of collateral: collateral has long been recognized as a special kind of property right.[3] Collateral is a species of *ius in re aliena* in Roman law, rights in others' property, which "impose restrictions on the exercise of the rights of ownership by the owner" (Berger 1953, 27; Pound 1959, 185). In property law, we sometimes speak of certain kinds of property arrangements as a "commons" (Dagan and Heller 2001, 552) in which multiple parties' rights of access encourage each to exploit resources as much as possible in the short run and to shirk their obligations to maintain the property onto other owners. We also speak of situations in which multiple parties have legitimate rights to exclude others as an "anti-commons"— resulting in the underuse of an asset as no one can make use of it without being certain that others might claim that they are in fact entitled to exclusive use of it. In this vocabulary, collateral is a kind of temporally delineated commons, or anticommons, depending on the specific rules governing the particular transaction. In the near future—that is, for a set period of time in the future delineated by the time when the debt is to be repaid—there are two hands on the baton, so to speak, each with legitimate claims that can either chill the other from using the collateral or encourage each to exploit it as much as possible in the short-term to the detriment of long-term use. In fact, in the financial markets the pledgor and the pledgee both have rights and obligations vis-à-vis the collateral and these rights and obligations are entangled, not delineated.

There is another aspect to the collateral relationship beyond the relational matter of intertwined rights I have just described, and one that distinguishes it somewhat from the traditional commons examples—parks, condominiums, and so on. Collateral is fundamentally a hierarchical relationship: the debtor-pledgor is in a position of structural weakness vis-à-vis the creditor-pledgee. That is, the pledgor cannot exit the relationship until it satisfies the underlying debt or obligation, and until it does its assets are hostage, so to speak, to the pledgee. Conversely, parties often post collateral in order to enter into debts or obligations that are crucial to them financially or otherwise. To borrow a term from political theory, posting collateral is an act of sacrifice (Bataille 1991). Although it is possible for both parties to post collateral in relation to a given swap, the amount and quality of collateral will rarely be identical, and in any case each posting is legally and hence economically independent. Unlike the underlying swap it is not offset by reciprocal postings of equal value.

In the derivatives world this reality of hierarchy is reflected in the fact that the rules regarding the management of collateral are written by and for the benefit of dealers—parties who are more often than not collateral-takers rather than collateral givers. This is what makes ISDA's official claim that collateral is an egalitarian institution so remarkably ideological: "Collateralization equalizes the disparity in creditworthiness between parties" (ISDA 2005, 21). An intuitive appreciation of the hierarchies inherent in collateral relations is what perhaps led one early commentator to describe the pledgor-pledgee relationship with respect to collateral as raising problems analogous to the relationship of the trustee to the trust property in trust law—a relationship designed to address possible problems of abuse created by inequalities of power or information.[4] Collateral, then, is a compact for a short-term political arrangement (cf. de Goede 2005), a kind of private constitution with a time horizon—something perhaps best analyzed alongside other short-term private and hierarchical political institutions like indentured servitude (Kelly 1991).

And like all constitutions, collateral stages further problems of governance. Take, for example, the issue at stake in the AIG case, of how to value the collateral during the period of the swap. As the market fluctuates day by day, minute by minute, how should the collateral's value be calculated? Who should have the authority to make these calculations? How often should they be made? And what consequences should flow from them—under what circumstances should the collateral-holder have the right to demand more collateral from its counterparty as a result of a decrease in the original collateral's value? This latter issue raises the very same risks as the swap itself since it is only because the parties have differing valuation methods resulting in differing views of market value that they are willing to take opposing sides in a swap transaction.

Far from separating the interests of Sanwa and Paribas, then, collateralization involves them in a particular way—in the management, the care for, this *thing*, as this political relationship is reified now, the collateral. Any understanding of private governance methods then must begin with an understanding of the relational quality of obligations—of entangled, not delineated, rights. As a substantive political or epistemological matter, property poses problems of governance as much as it resolves them.

In summary, there is no reason to believe that either private or public forms of regulation are actually more effective than the other as a stopgap against the future uncertainties in the market—there is no magic fuse box for separating one person's risk off from another. Politically speaking, private and public genres of regulation are not nearly as distinct as Hayek and his followers would like to suggest.[5] Neither can inherently make the vast political problems at stake in the management of the near future disappear. As George Soros has put it, "Market fundamentalists blame market failures on the fallibility of the regulators, and they are half right: Both markets and regulators are fallible" (2009, 78).

But this generates another puzzle: as we saw, there is nevertheless a kind of "Hayekian" perception, by market participants and government officials alike, that private devices for limiting future risk such as collateral are more legitimate. How then does private law govern? What are the techniques and sources of its authority and legitimacy? Here I turn to some aspects of private law as a genre of knowledge.

An Example: The Legality of Rehypothecation of Collateral in the Derivatives Market

In order to understand how collateral, as a private legal technology, handles the temporal uncertainties surrounding market risk—uncertainties that, as we saw in the previous section, are simply transposed in property law into legal uncertainties surrounding overlapping property rights and obligations—we need to immerse ourselves first in what those uncertainties look like in the derivatives market. One example concerns the problems surrounding so-called rights of rehypothecation (Johnson 1997, 966) alluded to in chapter 1. Suppose once again that the Sanwa Bank and the Paribas Bank enter into a swap transaction through their traders, and Paribas insists that Sanwa post collateral to cover the transaction. If, within the coming year, Sanwa Bank should prove unable to meet its obligations, Paribas will lay full claim to the collateral. But what about right now, in the present? What can Paribas do with the collateral? Can it use it as collateral of its own in other swaps?[6] How must the collateral be maintained and accounted for?[7]

In practice, rehypothecation is a tool of large dealers rather than derivatives end-users (such as airlines or manufacturers hedging against
future fluctuations in the cost of a key input such as the price of oil). "Although the right is mutual, it is unlikely that the end user would have the
financial acumen to fully take advantage of the right" (Johnson 2000,
51). The value of a right to rehypothecate, from the collateral-taker's
point of view, is that it can put the collateral to some financial use during the time it holds it. In theory (that is, assuming the counterfactual—
transparent pricing), this should drive down the price of swap transactions by ensuring that all assets are being used to their fullest potential
at all times, rather than having large amounts of wealth parked and un-
usable as collateral at any given time (Mann 1997). There is now a complex market and set of transactional models and procedures for trading
in collateral available to derivatives dealers who wish to use it (Gangahar 2002). As one commentator has noted, "Granting a right of rehypothecation has become a requirement to do business with certain counterparties in the derivatives area" (Johnson 1997, 1000).

But of course the collateral-holder's use of the collateral brings with
it risks of its own. In the example above, suppose that Paribas rehypoth-
ecates the collateral to Bank of America, and then encounters financial difficulties that preclude it from recuperating the collateral by the
time of the completion of the original swap in order to return it to Sanwa
Bank? In allowing Paribas to rehypothecate in this way, Sanwa runs the
risk of so-called rehypothecation failure—the risk that the collateral will
not be returned, or that what is returned will not be of identical value.

Hence the legal (as well as political and economic) question about
what to do with the collateral in the "meantime" of the swap transaction—what power to accord the collateral-holder and what powers to
reserve to the pledgor. These are precisely questions raised by the intertwined and political nature of property rights, as described in the previous section. Traditionally, a party holding another's collateral had certain "duties of care" that prevented it from transferring the collateral to
a third party, for example, without permission. By the late 1980s, however the dealers in the derivatives industry had obtained an amendment to the U.S. Uniform Commercial Code and Bankruptcy Code (11
U.S.C.) to explicitly permit rehypothecation. But there was no analogous
provision in the Japanese Civil Code.

The standard ISDA collateral documentation has an exceedingly direct and simple solution to this question. It simply grants the collateral-

holder "the right to: (i) sell, pledge, re-hypothecate, assign, invest, use, commingle or otherwise dispose of, or otherwise use in its business any Posted Pledging Collateral it holds, free from any claim or right of any nature whatsoever of the Pledgor" (1994, para. 6[c]) and imposes on the collateral-taker only the obligation to return equivalent securities at the close of the swap. This simple clause and its uses—an example of techni- cal legal practice of an exceedingly mundane kind—is more sophisticated and consequential than first meets the eye. I will take it as an example of a technical private law solution to the problem of the "meantime"— the problem of the entanglement of interests, risks, powers, and obliga- tions in time.

This solution to the problem of entangled rights in the near future, borrowed from the common law of property and memorialized in the ISDA section quoted above, can be understood as a *placeholder*: in the meantime, that is, for the near future, the parties simply agree to act as if the holder of the collateral (the pledgee) already has clear and com- plete rights over the collateral (as if the parties are no longer trapped in the messy "meantime"). As one commentator long ago put it, one can think of such a transaction as a "conditional sale of it as security for the payment of a debt or the performance of some obligation. The condi- tion is that the sale shall be void upon the performance of the condition named" (Jones 1881, 1).[8] A *conditional sale*: for now, it is a sale, but in the future, who knows? The sale could be rendered void by the repay- ment of the debt, for example—but this does not stop us from thinking of it as a sale, *for now*. For the near future, the parties agree to treat the col- lateral as if it were the pledgee's—with the caveat that this treatment will be subject to later re-evaluation if it turns out to be an inappropriate de- scription of the state of affairs.

Now is this an entirely accurate description of the present state of the rights and obligations of the parties? Not in any abstract or logical sense. For all the reasons discussed in the previous section, the pow- ers and obligations of the pledgor and pledgee are actually intertwined. But one of the interesting features of the placeholder is where it puts our attention—on the provisionally settled present, and on the near future. The assumption here is that all that we can really know at the moment is this near future. We will leave final outcomes to unfold as they may. How else to understand the illogical and ungrammatical temporality of the following concluding statement to one canonical twentieth-century account of the law of collateral securities: "a debtor who has put up collateral should *never* expect to have it again, or its value, *until* he pays the debt; and the most he can ask is that the value be credited upon the debt" (Garrard 1938, 379; emphasis added).

This placeholder—this provisional conclusion for the meantime—of course raises all kinds of secondary problems and questions. One important set of questions concerns the interface between state law and private contracts—will this agreement actually be enforceable? What law applies? To what extent must the parties' private assumptions about the state of affairs conform to a larger legal framework? Under New York law, the repledge of collateral—the granting of a security interest in the collateral to a third party—could be done with few formalities and the pledgee had broad latitude with the collateral in its possession. The derivatives industry had succeeded in including express rights of rehypothecation in the 1998 revision to the Uniform Commercial Code, which was then adopted into law by New York (Kettering 1999, 1113–16).[9]

But courts in other jurisdictions perhaps less beholden to the financial services industry, recognizing the problems of intertwined property powers and obligations, had long required more formalities to validly pledge or repledge collateral, and also gave greater weight to the legal rights of the pledgor—and hence placed more limitations on the right of the pledgee to repledge the collateral. In the United Kingdom, for example, the pledgor retains the right to transfer the asset while it is pledged and the pledgee has very specific duties of care with respect to collateral in its possession, including an obligation to secure the pledgor's consent before transferring the collateral to a third party (Bridge 2002, 176–77). In Japan, likewise, the Civil Code imposed on the pledgee a duty to exercise good care with respect to the collateral (Civil Code Section 298)[10] and liability to the pledgor for any damages caused by repledging the collateral without the pledgor's consent (Civil Code Sections 350, 348, 398; Office of the Prime Minister and Ministry of Finance 1998, Article 1; Netting Law 1998).[11]

Lawyers for dealers in the UK derivatives industry had circumvented these requirements by structuring collateral transactions as "title transfers."[12] These differences in the national treatment of collateral rights and duties then raised all kinds of further questions about what law might apply to a collateral transaction, where many transactions involve parties from different jurisdictions, and where collateral may be posted through intermediaries in yet other jurisdictions or take the form of particular government bonds or be denominated in particular currencies (Kettering 1999, 1114–16). One traditional rule of private international law suggests that the law of the place of the collateral should control—but where "is" collateral of this kind located (Hval 1997)? Another traditional rule would defer to the parties' choice of applicable law, at least with respect to some issues (Borchers 1998, 186–87). But when would a court find such deference appropriate and when would it be deemed inappropriate? ISDA's own lawyers favored applying the law of the "place of the relevant intermediary"—the law of the custodian bank holding the collateral (ISDA 2005, 45) and they had succeeded in having this view incorporated into the European Union's Collateral Directive (see chapter 1). But even this left considerable ambiguity—where "is" a certain custodian bank when it has offices globally, its accounts are maintained electronically, and it is incorporated in one location and has its principal place of business in another?

During the period of my fieldwork these problems became the subject of a flurry of legal argumentation about how to fit this private law placeholder within the existing framework of Japanese law. One option would be to frame a collateral transaction as a title transfer, as in the United Kingdom. But there were several problems with this approach. First, structuring the collateral transaction as an outright transfer had potentially negative tax consequences for the parties. Second, a controversy had arisen about the formal legal consequences of such a structure for the availability of netting (discussed further in the next chapter) between the collateral value and the value of the exposure since under Japanese law a collateral transaction is a separate "transaction" not explicitly protected by Japan's netting law (Office of the Prime Minister and Ministry of Finance 1998). Finally, "repledge is what Americans are familiar with," one Japanese lawyer told me.

An informal group of Japanese lawyers from government, the banks, ISDA, and the large law firms ultimately crafted a makeshift solution to this problem. They advocated framing the collateral transaction as a special kind of loan, a loan for consumption with return of the same kind (*shohi taishaku*) (Civil Code Section 587; Office of the Prime Minister and Ministry of Finance 1998).[13] But this also did not put to rest arguments that collateral transactions might not be protected by the netting law. In this controversy, legal experts within the banks, most of whom were not qualified lawyers, found themselves outranked by the authority of *bengoshi* (lawyers who have passed the bar and are qualified to appear in court) who, to their frustration, made arguments that were in their view ultimately unhelpful to the practical interests of market participants. As one informant described it,

> A law firm advised [two large foreign banks] . . . that collateral should be stipulated as a transaction [meaning the benefits of netting would not be available]. . . . Even though their interpretation is right . . . lawyers—they know the market. But still they insist on their own argument. Their conclusion is that the netting law and set-off are totally different. There is no way to make collateral transactions fit. They are arguing for a literal translation of the Civil Code.

While all this contestation surely felt discouraging to those involved, it is actually a quite standard aspect of private technique. First comes a placeholder, agreed upon as such as between the parties. Then the existence of this placeholder raises secondary questions about its integration into state law—framed as problems "down the road" for the placeholder. What will happen if and when it is challenged in court, for example? This, in turn, gives rise to a plethora of legal moves—from lobbying for law reform to legal argumentation about what existing legal box to put the placeholder in (what is "deemed" to have occurred—a borrowing or a transfer?). I discuss all of these moves, and the complex sociology of the profession they activate, in the following chapter in greater detail. For now, I simply want to point out that in the midst of all this controversy the placeholder has become a kind of market reality of its own— something that needs to be dealt with, something that raises real-world consequential problems that demand lawyers', and perhaps judges', academics', and bureaucrats' attention. Moreover, in this massive effort to evaluate these "problems," the agreed understanding was that whatever clever legal characterizations of rehypothecation lawyers in the market produced, these only served as further placeholders of their own for future government lawmaking, whether in the form of legislation, court decisions, or administrative regulations.

Legal Fictions as Placeholders

So, what is collateral? It is simply a legal fiction—a fiction that the rights of the parties are well defined—nothing more and nothing less. In legal terms, a legal fiction is a statement that is consciously understood to be false, and hence is irrefutable (Fuller 1930a). Examples include the notion that a corporation is a person, or the fiction that an adopted parent is the biological parent of the adopted child (Yngvesson 2007).

As we saw, these provisional solutions in turn open up further problems. And at each stage of analysis, the trick is the same: when we reach the question of whether collateral is a fiction of Japanese or New York law, the parties simply assert, and expect (for the meantime, at least), that the law of New York applies and that this law will uphold their obligations. To be more precise, then, collateral is a chain of such legal fictions, each taking over from the next in time, as one fiction (such as the fiction that the pledgee already has full rights to the collateral) gives rise to questions and problems (does this fiction contradict national private and public law?) which then demands the creation of further fictions (it will be "deemed" that the posting of collateral is a transfer, or alternatively, it will be "deemed" that it is a special kind of loan).

Why would market participants believe in something so fictional? The answer is that they don't, at least in the traditional sense of "belief." For them, these fictions are just techniques, tools, means to an end. From the point of view of those who deploy them, legal fictions are more like machines than stories—they are practical interventions with concrete consequences. The legal fiction to which lawyers appeal in rehypothecation—the fiction that the future moment of the swap's completion has already arrived—does not pretend to resolve, in actuality, the indeterminacy of future risks associated with one's investment—it is rather a command, or a mutual agreement, simply to act "As If." When I say that legal fictions are technicalities or techniques of private law, therefore, I mean that they are *nonrepresentational*: in contrast to many other kinds of language, the fiction that the collateral-taker has an unfettered right to repledge does not "mean" anything at all (which is not to say that it is not a highly consequential utterance—it surely is) (Riles 2003; Ross 1957, 821).

Thus the legal fiction is not really so much an epistemological claim as it is a special kind of pause, for the moment. In mathematics, a placeholder is a "symbol, frequently an empty box, used in teaching to denote a missing quantity or operator in an expression." One creates a placeholder in order provisionally to overlook it. In other words, it is a technique for working with and in the meantime. As such it has no particular content or meaning, except that it defines and manages the near future— the time for which this particular commitment holds true. But it is also a political device, a kind of collective commitment: The original meaning of the term was overtly political—"a person who acts as deputy for another; a lieutenant, a proxy. A person who holds office, esp. in the government or in government service."[14]

This is important: one of the most consequential differences between technocratic planning (of the kind critiqued by Hayek) and legal technique lies precisely in the nature of representation. Technocratic legal knowledge *communicates* something: bureaucratic plans can be read and critiqued as messages about who and what is politically important or not; about what is sanctioned or favored or not; about what will happen next, and where the problems lie. And these messages in turn often become subjects of heated political contestation that lead to crises of legitimacy for the regulatory state.[15] In contrast, private law is mostly "indifferent" to what it represents in this epistemological sense (although it certainly represents in the political sense of the term).[16]

Over the course of the deployment of these As Ifs, they come to take on a cultural reality of their own. In day-to-day thought, the means comes to take over the end (Riles 2004a; Vaihinger 2001). The fictions become practical, technical scripts for the management of the parties' relationship. These fictions—which are just as problematically related to market "realities" as government planning technologies—nevertheless come to be much more readily accepted predictors, and indeed creators of market realities.

In traditional social scientific parlance and associated forms of technocratic management, anything that is fictional is by definition illegitimate,[17] and there is in fact a longstanding debate in legal theory about whether legal fictions are the engines of legal progress or lawyerly tools of obfuscation (Riles 2009). For critics (going back most notably to Jeremy Bentham) legal fictions are cynical tricks on the part of insiders to pull the wool over the eyes of unsuspecting outsiders who lack the expertise to understand, for example, that the mere assertion that collateral rights are well defined does not really make them so. I will only point out here that this critique confuses two separate questions. First there is the question of whether such legal fictions favor insiders (such as swap dealers) at the expense of outsiders (end-users of swaps, or the market as a whole). This is, of course, a legitimate question and a complex one. But it is a different question from whether legal fictions are cynical farces, something asserted by insiders with a wink and a nod, knowing that only an outsider would truly believe in such a thing. This latter question assumes, once again, that what is really at issue in the legal fiction is the truth or falsity of the thing—that the challenging dimension of the legal fiction is the epistemological one. In fact, precisely because the fiction is more tool than text, the truth or falsity of its content is really beside the point from its users' point of view. What matters rather is what possibilities for action it opens up or forecloses.

But my point is more empirical than normative: observation in the swap markets reveals that legal fictions—rule forms that create what they express—do have practical legitimacy from the point of view of actors in the market, and this legitimacy is enduring, even at times of crisis. In response to the temporal problem of finance—the inability on the part of either market participants or regulators to plan—the technique here is to act as if the parties could just know in the present what the future holds. I now want to think about these fictions from a different point of view than the traditional focus on truth and falsity, therefore—I want to focus on their temporal quality.

The Temporality of Legal Technique

In the last section, I suggested that rather than call collateral a legal fiction, we call it a placeholder. The claim that it is as if the pledgee already has full rights to the collateral is simply a provisional claim, one that holds for the meantime, that is, for the near future. As such, it is quite anti-utopian: legal technique has little to say about, little interest in, the utopian time of the distant future. In contrast, it directs endless attention and produces great fascination about all the possible intricacies surrounding the near future, the moment just beyond the present one.

Now, this placeholder is a material, sociotechnical phenomenon, not simply a concept. As we saw in chapter 1, documents, and the sociotechnical relations they engender, are a particularly consequential node of this activity. As suggested, the forms used to define collateral relations are not just instantiations of legal doctrine or government policy, as legal theory would have it, nor are they simply textual descriptions of legal arguments. Rather, they are elements of a singular sociotechnical network that includes legal doctrine, legal policy, and legal argumentation.

We can give this point a bit more precision by focusing on the role of documents, as material artifacts, in the temporality of the placeholder. Forms such as the ISDA collateral agreement are made to be filled in:

they are mundane scripts for future action (form-filling) (Miyazaki 2006a, 210). As Mario Biagioli (2006, 127) has suggested, a documents serves as a "hinge between two distinct moments."[18] Documents then are tools that work in, and with time.

The placeholder's central feature is that it forecloses a question (like "what are the rights of these parties relative to this collateral?") for the moment—not by resolving it, but by papering over it—by creating a provisional solution subject to future reevaluation. In this sense, the placeholder is the opposite of ways of thinking about the future such as philosophical pragmatism that focus attention on the ambiguity or open-endedness of the present (Rorty 1989). That is, unlike pragmatists who see the present as an open zone of endless possibility and unpredictability, the placeholder treats the present and the near future as actually already determined, its ambiguity as already resolved.

Likewise, the placeholder is a very different approach from prominent technocratic ways of thinking about "preparedness" for possible future risk. It has become common for market regulatory agencies to create simulations of financial crises as a way of preparing for what cannot be known in advance. The central bankers I knew were deeply interested in such simulations. The Bank for International Settlements likewise has calculated capital adequacy requirements on the basis of such simulations (often as performed by private banks themselves). Now such simulation also relies heavily on practices of both fictionality and documentation: Clarke terms the scenarios that result from such simulations "rationality badges" (1999, 16)—signals to the public and to regulators themselves that things are under control. Although they are ostensibly about the future, they are really more for political consumption in the present.

In contrast, the placeholder makes no assurances about the security of the future—in fact, it says nothing at all about what might happen in the future. Its "rationality badge" is only for the present. Crucially, the placeholder is always deployed in an As If modality—the assumption is only a working assumption. It is not even a hypothesis since hypotheses exist to be tested against reality; the As If points instead inward, away from reality, simply to itself (Fuller 1930b, 902).[19]

I propose that we think of these technical legal fictions that proliferate in every corner of financial law as technologies of collaboration in time—between those in the present and those in the future. A statement written into a standard derivatives contract such as "the pledgee has full rights to the collateral" is made with the clear appreciation that it will be subject to later reevaluation, renegotiation, or downright abandonment in the future, that is, by those to whom one is handing it off. When one completes and files the document it is for others to do with as appropriate for their time. This is the irony, the farce we might even say, of collateral—as a guarantee of something that by definition cannot be guaranteed, that is, the politics of the future. But it is a consequential farce, because just as regulators' fictional simulations of future financial crises really do shape the limits and possibilities of state power over the market in the present, collateral as a placeholder calls forth a particular "we"— the we whom, *for the moment*, the As If assumption holds (Teubner 2004b). In this sense, placeholders are private constitutional moments.

Perhaps this all sounds a bit too grand and theoretical—too distant from the technical and financial realities of collateral. But the ultimate insight of this book is that there is far more at work in the mundane techniques of private law—far more epistemological complexity, far more political imaginativeness—than the existing ways of thinking about financial regulation are even willing to entertain, let alone address.

Indeed, what we have done is to give substance to Hayek's impressionistic arguments on behalf of the temporality of the private. In essence, Hayek's own argument for private law technologies was a negative argument—private law was what technocratic market regulation was not. Hayek and his followers do little more than assert with wonder that private actions result cumulatively in collective good without much explanation of how this might be the case. Like the solution deployed by the technocrats described in the previous chapter, Hayek's private law is more a fuse box than an engine. It is an argument for a limited form of regulation premised on the assumption that all that the law can do is to cause as little harm as possible, to literally work in a collateral role, on the sidelines of market action, as guarantor but nothing more.

I have tried to provide a richer account of the political and epistemological possibilities that inhere in the temporality of private law technique, an account that is positive, not simply negative. Collateral in this account is both a technology and a kind of politics, both a means to an end and a special kind of relationality. Most of all, collateral is a compact for a politics of the near future, of the meantime of the exchange, itself defined by the way it is also a handoff to the time beyond the near future, that is, to what and who cannot and should not, be predicted and controlled from the point of view of the present (Teubner 2004b).

Private Legal Techniques for Public Regulatory Purposes

So does this mean that, as Hayek and his followers assert, private regulation is inherently superior to public regulation? The fallacy of the
Hayekian argument is the assumption that these "private" technologies
can only be deployed by private actors. In fact, there is nothing inherently private or public about the techniques associated with private law.
Indeed, Hayek himself implicitly admitted as much when he described
the control states assert over markets in the form of national currencies
as resting precisely on a *legal fiction*: "the legal fiction that there is one
clearly defined thing called 'money' that can be sharply distinguished
from other things" (1976a, 48).

I want to show how this might be so with an example of how financial

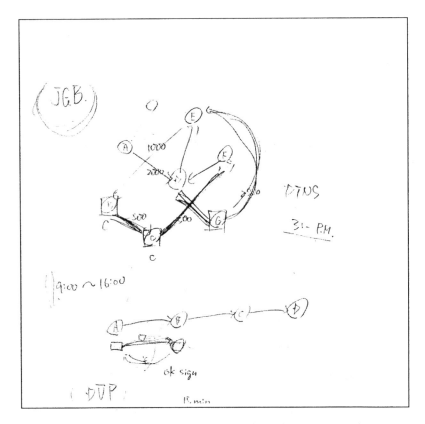

FIGURE 4. Schematic depiction of the solution to the liquidity problem, drawn by Sato

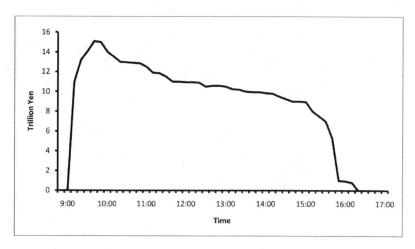

FIGURE 5. Outstanding balance of intraday overdrafts in the course of the day, May 14, 2001 (Bank of Japan 2001b, 16)

regulators in Japan redeployed the trick of the legal fiction and hence regained legitimacy in their own eyes and in the eyes of market participants. The example concerns an ingenious solution the Payments and Settlements Division devised to the problem of liquidity created by RTGS. As described earlier in this chapter, the problem was that Party A needed cash to pay Party C before it had received the payment it was owed on the same day by Party B. The old system, DTNS, had taken care of this liquidity problem by clearing all transactions simultaneously at 3:00 pm.

The solution they devised was this: As sketched out in the following diagram produced by the Division head, it was simply "deemed" before the fact that after the fact the transactions had occurred in proper order—A had first paid B, who then paid C, and so on. In other words, the solution was a legal fiction, a placeholder.[20]

Now functionally speaking, it will be obvious that this is not really different from DTNS nor is it different from a bank overdraft (see fig. 5). But if these other two solutions raised concerns about illegitimate interference in the market by regulators, the legal fiction was apprehended by market participants and regulators as a legitimate technical solution to a practical problem, nothing more (Bank of Japan 2001a; Omine 2001). Does this mean that it was a sham? Just a clever way of pulling the wool over the public's eyes? I think such an explanation would be too simple. The power of legal techniques lies in their ability to serve as placeholders—ways of leap-frogging over problems that by definition cannot be resolved in the short run. Legal fictions differ from lies, as Lon Fuller tells us, because everyone knows them to be fictions (1930a, 367). But along the way—and here lies the governance element—they begin to serve as pathways, scripts, private constitutions for particular kind of action.

Conclusion

To return to the central question of this chapter, then, if private law mechanisms of market governance and public law mechanisms of market governance are equally indeterminate, as a matter of the control they exercise on the ambiguity and risk associated with the future, how is it that private law governance does not suffer from the legitimacy deficit of technocratic regulatory practice?[21] Legitimacy is generated on a grand scale by transparency and political accountability. But on a day-to-day, mundane scale, legitimacy may also be generated by the availability of techniques that render the near future "workable." Here, we can think about legitimacy as the effect of techniques of standardization, simplification, entextualization, and reification that allow certain working truths to hold in certain conditions, for a certain amount of time (Callon 1998b). Counterintuitively, the force of these techniques may inhere in the way they serve as placeholders for, rather than reflections of, market realities. In this respect, legal technique creates its own forms of legitimacy and its own scripts for governance. As we saw, collateral is just such a technique—a tool for producing working truths, for the moment.

Let me be clear about what I am not advocating. First, I do not mean to suggest that transparency and accountability are not crucial elements of a stable financial system. Second, I am not advocating the actual privatization of regulation, including now fashionable experiments with delegating regulatory authority to private parties. As discussed further in the concluding chapter, these proposals assume, with Hayek, that there is something mysterious about governance that only private entities can do well. My point is exactly the opposite: there is nothing inherently private or public about the placeholder, as a device for governing the near future. The example of RTGS demonstrates that government regulators can effectively appropriate and redeploy traditionally private legal governance techniques on their own regulatory terrain. Here is an example, then, of how state regulation of markets might be revitalized with the methods of private law.

Notes

1. Unlike some of his latter-day followers, such as Hernando De Soto, however, Hayek displays a quite sophisticated understanding of the subtleties and internal tensions within the doctrines of private property law, its origins and purposes.

2. For some latter-day formalist arguments of this kind, see Alexander 1999, Scalia 1989, Schuck 1992, Wilson 1985.

3. Some commentators characterize collateral as more of a contractual right than a right in property. Interestingly, progressive and conservative commentators alike tend to assume that characterizing collateral as property will produce more conservative doctrinal outcomes while characterizing collateral as contract will produce more progressive outcomes (e.g., Harris and Mooney 1994)—an assumption the "progressive property school" would vigorously contest (Alexander 2009). Whether collateral is "actually" property or contract need not concern us here. Like many kinds of rights or doctrines it contains elements of both.

4. Colebrooke 1883, 117:

> The relation of the immediate parties to the contract, where negotiable instruments have been placed in the hands of a creditor by a debtor as collateral security, for the payment of a valid debt or obligation, resembles that of a trustee and cestui que trust. The responsibilities of the pledge to the pledgor are similar to those of a trustee: First, to collect and apply the securities at their maturity to the payment of the debt, . . . and secondly, to pay over the surplus, if any, to the plegor. The pledge is also likened to a trustee, as he may not deal with the trust property so as to destroy or impair its value.

5. I leave to one side another important Realist critique of the Hayek–De Soto line of argument, which is that there is no such thing as a truly private property regime in any case since all private property rights are ultimately defined and enforced by public authority. I leave this to one side because my focus is not upon the nature of private law in some existential sense but on the kind of thinking that traditionally characterizes private law—the moves, metaphors, and methods of analysis.

6. In practice, it is common to structure the repledge as a repurchase contract in which the collateral-taker sells the collateral to a third party and simultaneously agrees to buy it back at a future date (Johnson 1997, 968–69).

7. There are parallels as well as historical ties to the law and policy debates surrounding the rights of lenders in mortgages. For an historical survey, see Wigmore 1897 (also discussed in the introduction.)

8. Jones is careful to add the following caveat recognizing the interaction of private law and state law: "If the condition be not performed according to its terms, the thing mortgaged is irredeemable at law, though there may be a redemption in equity, or by force of statute" (Jones 1881, 1).

9. UCC 9–207(c)(3) and 9–314(c).

10. This includes a duty to collect and account for the fruits of the collateral during the pledge period (§ 297).

11. There are two kinds of sub-pledge under Japanese law: *sekinin tenshichi* (literally "responsibility sub-pledge") and *shodaku tenshichi* (literally "approval sub-pledge"). They are respectively covered by sections 348 and 350 of the *Minpo* (Civil Code). The main difference between the two types of sub-pledge is that in *sekinin tenshichi*, the pledgee sub-pledges without the pledgor's approval and in so doing assumes responsibility for any losses arising from the sub-pledge, even if the loss is caused by *force majeure*. *Minpo* (Civil Code), Law no. 89 of 1896, Article 348, "Pledgees may sub-pledge the Thing pledged within the duration of their rights, upon their own responsibility. In such cases, the pledgees shall be responsible for any loss arising from the pledge even if the same is caused by force majeure." In *shodaku tenshichi*, the pledgee gains the pledgor's approval first, and the pledgee is not responsible for losses arising from the sub-pledge caused by force majeure. The extent of the pledgee's liability in a *shodaku tenshichi* is determined between the pledgor and the pledgee.

12. The contrast between a pledge and a title transfer is described in ISDA documentation as follows:

> under a pledge, the collateral provider creates a security interest in favor of the collateral receiver in securities and/or cash. The securities and/or cash are typically delivered either directly to the receiver or to its custodian. The collateral provider generally continues to own the securities and/or cash, subject to the right of the receiver to sell the securities and/or take the cash if the collateral receiver defaults; whereas under title transfer, the collateral provider transfers full title in securities and/or cash to the collateral receiver and grants the collateral receiver the right to set off or net, on default of the collateral provider, the collateral receiver's net exposure to the collateral provider under the master agreement against the value of the securities and/or cash. Under this approach, the collateral receiver owns the collateral, without restriction, and the collateral provider, if it performs in

full, is only entitled to the return of fungible securities and/or re-
payment of cash in the same currency.

A pledge may require greater formality in its creation and
perfection than title transfer, possibly including (depending on
the various factors mentioned above) registration, filing or some
other form of notification of the pledge and other specific requirements as to the form and content of the document creating
the pledge. The formalities are necessary to 'perfect' the pledge,
that is, to ensure its formal validity and priority over any third
party with a purported claim to the collateral assets. (ISDA
2005, 38)

13. According to Civil Code Article 587, "A loan for consumption shall become effective when one of the parties receives money or other things from the
other party by promising that he/she will return by means of things that are the
same in kind, quality and quantity."

14. Oxford English Dictionary Online, http://www.oed.com.

15. In this definition not everything that bureaucrats or other state agents
do is technocratic, however. I have described the difference between state lawmaking that is representational and state law-making that is not representational
in more detail in another context (Riles 2003).

16. "The indifference of the text with regard to its referential meaning is what
allows the legal text to proliferate, exactly as the coded, preordained repetition
of a specific gesture or set of gestures allows Helen to weave the story of the war
into the epic" (de Man 1979, 286).

17. There are, of course, exceptions. One is the neo-institutional school of political science that focuses on the role of form, myth, symbol and ritual in generating political legitimacy.

18. His example is scientific records of authorship, but one could also think
of the archival quality of documents, which sometimes purposely and sometimes
unintentionally hinge the present to the past.

19. As Lon Fuller has also argued (1930a, 367), a legal fiction differs from a
hypothesis for Fuller because there is no question of proving its truth.

20. In 2006 the BOJ formalized this legal fiction in the form of a revised
RTGS system. The new system, presented as simply a technological upgrade,
complete with a name that invokes computer systems upgrades, RTGS-XG
(RTGS—neXt Generation), addresses the liquidity problem through an "algorithm" that searches for transactions that would be better reordered, and reor-
ders them (Bank of Japan 2005, 2006; Nakajima 2007, 2008; Ogura 2008). This
does not raise issues of transparency and legitimacy for its architects because
the system is automatic (the algorithm resides in a computer) and because mar-

ket participants can see their transactions in a queue and move to reorder them themselves. We might say that in this case the placeholder was a handoff to a machine. Science and technology studies (STS), of course, gives us reason to doubt whether computerizing such transactions actually depoliticizes them as it is suggested here.

21. I refer here to legitimacy as an empirical matter—as a matter of whether or not a governance regime is perceived as legitimate by its diverse stakeholders. Whether or not it is legitimate as a normative matter is a separate question.

CHAPTER FIVE

Virtual Transparency

The creation of a private sphere of transnational law beyond the reach of state authority demands the authority and institutions of the state itself (see chapters 1 and 2). Often, the very method of shielding private parties from national authority is another public act, a statute. "Deregulation" often takes the form of a corresponding "reregulation" (Mabuchi 1993, 130). In such cases, what looks like the devolution of state power to the global market actually brings into play a much more subtle and ambiguous coexistence of private and public authority and legitimacy. The vehicle for such law reform projects often is the legal transplant— the borrowing of legal concepts, doctrines, case law and statutes from one jurisdiction to another.

This chapter concerns one standard episode in legal transplantation, ISDA's Japanese campaign for the promulgation of a netting law that would validate derivatives dealers' contractual agreement to net out their obligations in the case of default. The project of creating this netting law was a stunningly explicit effort to tailor state authority to the desires of the market. The objective of the law was to ensure that in the event of bankruptcy, judges applying national law would not have the leeway to reach a legal interpretation contrary to the interests of the transnational derivatives industry. The proponents of this law, global banks, were pursuing similar campaigns through their global lobbying organization, the International Swaps and Derivatives Association (ISDA), in a number of countries around the world. The netting law then is an example of a class of law reform projects enacted around the world in the last twenty years that champion a neoliberal conception of the rule of law—primarily, uniform principles of freedom of contract.

To date, critical analyses of this type of episode in the global proliferation of neoliberalism take one of two forms. First, social theorists and legal scholars decry these legal reforms for the radical change they bring. Some comparative lawyers and critical legal scholars have commented with dismay on the pitfalls of "law and development" projects, in which legal models developed on one continent are simply repackaged and offered elsewhere, as they encounter local conditions which do not fit the standard form (Trubek and Galanter 1974; Twining 2000). Social theorists likewise have described these projects as imperial in ambition and scope (Ong 2006).

A second line of critical analysis argues rather that such reforms have limited impact because of their distance from local conditions. Some comparative lawyers have argued that the process of translating foreign law into local conditions so alters the law that it becomes something different altogether (Legrand 1997). Legal pluralists likewise emphasize that these imports represent only one kind of law, and often the least important kind (Chiba 1989; Merry 1988).

What is left out of these discussions of the substance of law reform projects and their relative merits is the nature of the "law" that circulates in these global projects of law reform—the kind of knowledge at stake in its production and implementation. Remarkably, legal pluralists, anthropologists, and comparative lawyers, all of whom share a commitment to local diversity, treat the form of law as a kind of universal when they discuss the global diffusion of neoliberal legal models. The variation of interest to them exists only in the content of the rules and the responses they generate locally.

But laws, and law, may have a very different character than the commonsense definition affords. Indeed, global law reform projects may play on, or make use of the fact that their audiences do not question that common sense definition of law. This may be the very source of their efficacy. A focus on legal knowledge, and in particular on its form, therefore becomes imperative to understanding the precise nature of the global power of rule of law reforms and of the political and cultural status of legal harmonization projects.

I want to focus on two different modalities of globalized legal knowledge at work in this example that are integral to global private governance—analogy-based legal interpretation and statutory construction. These modalities, or genres, are both paradigmatic ways of "doing" law reform, and they are usually imagined as alternatives. Their conflict and complementarity have consequences for the self-consciously "global" quality of the global financial regulation.

So what interests me in this chapter is the way the transnational and private market orientation of such neoliberal projects makes a mark on the law's *form*. We will see in particular how matters of legal epistemology are inseparable from matters of legal aesthetics. In this respect, this chapter develops and deepens our appreciation of the subtle epistemology of legal knowledge, and its consequences for governance explored in the previous chapter, by allowing us to see how such epistemology is sustained through form.

One of the features of this law is its professed achievement of bringing *transparency* to market regulation. In this respect, it sounds a theme that pervades many market-reform initiatives on both the right and the left. The idea behind the call for a statute to enforce netting agreements was that a statute would bind the judge in a way that mere legal arguments could not do, since in theory, as long as the language of the statute is straightforward and there is no question as to whether the statute applies to the case at hand, the judge must simply "apply the law." At first glance, transparency presents as standard, old-fashioned legal formalism and legal textualism—the view that the law's meaning is coherent and readily apprehensible from the language of the text.

But things are far more interesting than they first appear. We will see that the netting law is a kind of virtual transplant—an entity that does no more or less than evidence, reveal, or signal global legal harmonization and convergence (Carrier and Miller 1998; Massumi 2002). This does not mean that it is ineffective; on the contrary, it achieves an enormous amount, albeit not what is often described or implied as the core achievements of law reform. This virtual transplant also challenges the view that neoliberal reforms represent a break with the past, a radical "exception" to prior juridical practice (Larner, Le Heron, and Lewis 2007). This law's own triumphant claims to transparency then should give us some pause (Maurer 2005a; Westbrook 2004b). Transparency itself can be a technique for creating opacity.

This is important for debates in legal theory and law and society, and also for current policy debates. Simply put, the thrust of all of these debates is that law is out of touch with (economic, political, social) reality, and that legal form is something of a problem, if not an outright sham. The aim of law reform, it is said again and again, is to bring law closer to social, economic, and political realities. My hope is that a close encounter with an example of legal virtualism might give us greater appreciation for precisely what is not so real about the law.

Building a Solution to the Netting Problem

In chapter 2 I described how the netting problem came to be, and I explored how public and private legal actors worked together to address it. But to stop here, with an account of the actors, the interests, and the institutions involved would not capture what is most interesting about the netting problem and its resolution, from the actors' own point of view. Indeed, what is most unsatisfying about the netting problem from a sociolegal point of view—what would likely lead many a sociologist or political scientist to declare this case uninteresting, just technical stuff, precisely not the raw material of a new theory of private governance and new associated forms of political legitimacy—is that there was so little disagreement about the nature of the problem or the need for a solution. Although one could certainly imagine how the netting problem could have generated political controversy, given its potential distributive effects, in fact, it did not; it was a technical conversation among experts in government, the academy, and the private sector, all of whom agreed on the ultimate outcome they wished to reach. The issue was simply one of constructing the appropriate technical artifact to put the problem to rest.

This effort to address the "netting problem" involved extensive personal collaboration between lawyers for the banks, academics, bureaucrats, and a group of young graduates of Tokyo University's law faculty now in private practice at elite law firms (Dore 1999, 86; cf. Vogel 1994, 220). The Japanese and foreign banks coordinated most of their activities through Akihiro Wani, partner in the law firm of Mitsui, Yasuda, Wani and Maeda, and local counsel to ISDA. A graduate of the University of Tokyo Law Department, Mr. Wani also holds a master's degree in law from Columbia University Law School. Mr. Wani's entrée into the business was an internship at the Tokyo Mitsubishi bank in London in the 1980s. During his time in London, ISDA was in the process of creating its master agreements and he had the opportunity to learn about ISDA's activities first hand. He returned from London in November 1989 and through his connections with the Tokyo Mitsubishi Bank, a prominent member of ISDA Tokyo, Mr. Wani received the work of addressing the legality of close-out netting.

The firm was not one of Tokyo's blue-chip law firms. Yet it was at the center of almost all derivatives-related regulatory work on behalf of banks involved in the over-the-counter (OTC) markets in Tokyo. Virtually nothing happened between the government and the industry on the subject of derivatives without Mr. Wani being aware of and most likely involved in it. Derivatives specialists explained to me that to refer legal work elsewhere would be to forgo the benefits of Mr. Wani's extensive knowledge of what was actually going on based on his work for everyone *else* in the industry, not to mention his personal contacts in the government.

Mr. Wani's strategy for tackling the netting problem was dictated largely by ISDA's central offices in London and New York. Initially, Mr. Wani sought to acquire legal opinions from a respected Japanese jurist on the legality of netting. For this task, he selected Professor Koji Shindo, a senior specialist in civil procedure recently retired from one of Japan's most prestigious law departments, the law faculty of the University of Tokyo, to draft the legal opinions because of his skill at legal argument. Given his stature and age, and the dominance of University of Tokyo graduates on the bench, there was also the probability that a judge facing a question about the enforcement of netting agreements might even have been his student. Professor Shindo did not draft the ISDA opinions on his own. He was aided by several young associates of one of the most prominent law firms in Tokyo known for its international clientele.

Analogy

ISDA's representatives in Japan called upon Professor Shindo's expertise as a specialist in the technique of legal argumentation. I want to take seriously the value placed on Professor Shindo's expertise. What makes this kind of technical legal expertise—explicitly framed as "nonpolitical" but "expert"—so powerful and efficacious? In order to answer these questions, I turn to a close reading of the Shindo opinions.

The first solution to the netting problem was a legal argument: At the outset, participants in the swap market based their hope that close-out netting clauses were enforceable, as applied to swap transactions that had not yet reached maturity at the time of bankruptcy, on two legal opinions obtained by ISDA Japan.[1] Drafted by Professor Koji Shindo, the two legal opinions present sophisticated legal arguments for the proposition that netting contracts were already enforceable under existing Japanese law (Shindo 1996a, 1996b).

The intended audience for these documents was not the bureaucracy, the academy, or the industry, but the bench. As Professor Shindo himself insisted to me, the opinions deployed arguments strategically on the understanding that only particular kinds of arguments would succeed with the courts. As one banker put it, "you have to put it in terms non-finance people will understand." Professor Kanda agreed on this point: "In Japan, it is necessary to place much emphasis on pre-existing legal logic and to construct a logical argument step by step in order to convince the courts." These opinions are best understood therefore as exemplifications of a particular discourse appropriate to the hierarchical encounter between the supplicant and the judge. As Professor Shindo described the kind of reasoning appropriate to the task, "When one works as a lawyer, one needs to understand the immediate obstacle and resort to the best measure to overcome that obstacle. One needs to construct a legal argument that is invincible" (Shindo et al. 1994, 28, 33–34).

The first Shindo opinion (1996a, 135) concerns the enforceability of the 1987 ISDA Master Agreement (concerning currency and interest rate swaps) and was issued in 1993. The specific problem concerns the so-called right of election of bankruptcy trustees, under the bankruptcy and company reorganization laws of Japan, that is, the right to elect to either uphold or void contracts outstanding at the time of bankruptcy.[2] The main issue it addresses is whether close-out netting is nevertheless permissible under Article 104 of the bankruptcy law.[3] The argument is that if one *analogizes* netting to other permissible practices in bankruptcy law known as off-setting, netting is enforceable (Shindo 1996a). More precisely, through an analogy of close-out netting to off-setting under the bankruptcy law, Shindo argues, it is possible, first, to net out all transactions involving the same currencies and the same delivery dates, and then to net out all of the obligations resulting from the first stage of netting, so that in the end, the same functional effect as stipulated in the Master Agreement's close-out netting clause can be legally achieved. In other words, Shindo seeks a workable *analogy* for the contractual stipulations of the ISDA Master Agreement in existing Japanese law.

In building an analogy between netting in the ISDA contract and off-setting in the Japanese Civil Code, Shindo appeals to a core legal form: It has long been recognized that analogical thinking is a central element of all legal knowledge (cf. Kennedy 1997, Atiyah and Summers 1987).[4] In civil law regimes such as Japan, for example, analogies are commonly and explicitly used to fill in "gaps" between the sections of the code—to interpret the intent of the code as to questions, such as the enforceability of netting agreements, on which the code is silent (e.g., Langenbucher 1998, 481; Merryman 1985).[5] And in the common law case law-based system, analogy is understood to be even more important—the very foundation of the common law as celebrated by some and reviled by others.

The Shindo opinion presents multiple layers and levels of analogies. At the outset, Shindo suggests two alternative analogies to netting—two possible ways of conceptualizing netting under Japanese law. Each of these analogies quickly encounters problems, however, as the opinion acknowledges that netting is not in all respects just like either of the legal categories to which it is analogized. Each analogy yields a "remainder" (Strathern 1991, xxii). In each case, Shindo overcomes these remainders with dozens of further analogies between the character of swap transactions or the contractual terms of the Master Agreement, and particular sections of the bankruptcy law. At each stage, the repeated discovery that netting is both like and unlike sections of the bankruptcy law seems to demand yet further acts of analogizing, since no single analogy will in itself solve the "netting problem."[6]

What makes the opinion such a brilliant example of this style of legal knowledge is the astounding number of different legal categorizations that Shindo proposes and, in turn, analyzes. These alternative categorizations are arranged into a massive analytical structure that, taken as a whole, gives the effect of anticipating every possible argument, no matter how mundane or implausible it may be. The objective is to demonstrate that whatever analytical path one takes, one arrives at the same conclusion: netting is enforceable. The opinion opens with the assertion that netting may be explained from "two different roots." It then proceeds methodically through the "first problem," raised by the first analogy to "the second problem," and so on, raising and dismissing, at each stage, counterarguments and possible complications, and then moves on to the "second root" of the argument and repeats the same steps. I have diagramed a portion of the steps in the argument to give a sense of the analytical form.

The overall effect is both exhaustive and exhausting. Like an exercise in formal logic, the opinion asserts the obvious—what is uncontested—at every stage and the form of the argument gives its far more contentious claims an aura of uncontestability (Shindo 1996a, 147–49). Entering into

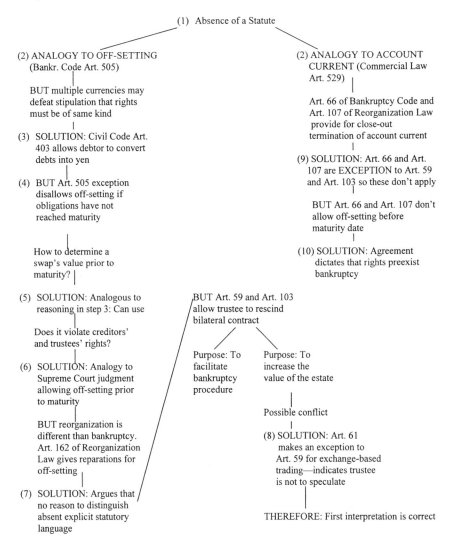

(1) Absence of a Statute

(2) ANALOGY TO OFF-SETTING
(Bankr. Code Art. 505)

BUT multiple currencies may
defeat stipulation that rights
must be of same kind

(3) SOLUTION: Civil Code Art.
403 allows debtor to convert
debts into yen

(4) BUT Art. 505 exception
disallows off-setting if
obligations have not
reached maturity

How to determine a
swap's value prior to
maturity?

(5) SOLUTION: Analogous to
reasoning in step 3: Can use

Does it violate creditors'
and trustees' rights?

(6) SOLUTION: Analogy to
Supreme Court judgment
allowing off-setting prior
to maturity

BUT reorganization is
different than bankruptcy.
Art. 162 of Reorganization
Law gives reparations for
off-setting

(7) SOLUTION: Argues that
no reason to distinguish
absent explicit statutory
language

(2) ANALOGY TO ACCOUNT
CURRENT (Commercial Law
Art. 529)

Art. 66 of Bankruptcy Code and
Art. 107 of Reorganization Law
provide for close-out
termination of account current

(9) SOLUTION: Art. 66 and Art.
107 are EXCEPTION to Art. 59
and Art. 103 so these don't apply

BUT Art. 66 and Art. 107 don't
allow off-setting before
maturity date

(10) SOLUTION: Agreement
dictates that rights preexist
bankruptcy

BUT Art. 59 and Art. 103
allow trustee to rescind
bilateral contract

Purpose: To   Purpose: To
facilitate   increase the
bankruptcy   value of the estate
procedure

Possible conflict

(8) SOLUTION: Art. 61
makes an exception to
Art. 59 for exchange-based
trading—indicates trustee
is not to speculate

THEREFORE: First interpretation is correct

FIGURE 6. The first Shindo opinion

a kind of dialogue with himself, Shindo raises every possible question
and concern: "Is it legal to determine the value of the contract before
the maturity date?" he asks, for example. Yes, he responds to his question, according to the same reasoning as the conversion of foreign currencies to Japanese yen in bankruptcy valuations as stipulated by the
code (Shindo 1996a, 144–47). The tone throughout is balanced and rea-

sonable: There are legitimate objections to the analysis, he concedes at numerous stages.

The second Shindo opinion performs an even more astounding feat of analogical thought. A year after the publication of the first Shindo opinion, ISDA again hired Professor Shindo and the Mori Sogo law firm to draft a second opinion (Shindo 1996b) on the legality of close-out netting under Section 6 of ISDA's 1992 Master Agreement. The 1992 Master Agreement's aim was to move beyond netting by novation (netting across like contracts with identical delivery dates) to allow for netting as between different kinds of financial products.[7] The first opinion's analogy of close-out netting to off-setting would not suffice in this case since under the Civil Code off-setting is traditionally limited to like products in bankruptcy. Shindo would need to make an even greater stretch to argue that netting by novation was also permissible under existing Japanese law.

Here Shindo couples the analogy with another device of legal logic, the rule/exception paradigm. The principal argument of the second opinion is that Article 61 of the bankruptcy law, which directs the trustee in bankruptcy to close out positions in exchange-traded products, creates an exception to the trustee's right of election in bankruptcy which should be extended (analogized) to swaps.[8] And because even this logic is not enough when it comes to corporate reorganizations rather than bankruptcies, because the company reorganization law has no equivalent to Article 61 of the bankruptcy law, Shindo adds that *by analogy* the argument should be extended to reorganization as well.

The bulk of the second Shindo opinion extends the legal form of argumentation to an analysis not of law per se, but of the practical economic nature of the products at issue. The opinion is divided into sections addressing different kinds of products and legal "scenarios." One small portion will provide a glimpse of the nature of the argument and of its effect (see fig. 7).

In the first scenario, close-out netting occurs prior to the execution of an options contract. Shindo approaches this scenario by dividing it again into four possible "situations."[9] Each is addressed in identically formulaic terms. Sentences are repeated from one paragraph to the next; the discussion of each situation even takes up the same amount of space on the page. All in all, the effect is of a perfectly symmetrical system of logic that the reader can picture as a massive decision tree. A summary of a small portion of the steps of the argument (outlined in fig. 7) will give a sense of its effect:

Close-Out Netting Before the Execution of an Options Contract

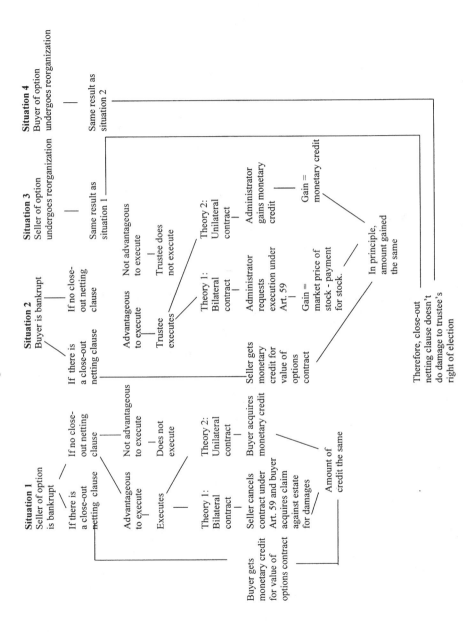

FIGURE 7. The second Shindo opinion

In Situation 1, the Seller of the option goes bankrupt before its execution. If it is disadvantageous for the buyer to execute the option, he will not do so. However, if it is advantageous to exercise the option, the buyer will execute. At that point, there are two ways to understand the result of the execution of the option. First, one might argue that a bilateral contract is created because one side has an obligation to deliver the securities, while the other side has an obligation to make a payment. If that is the case, the administrator of the bankrupt seller would choose to cancel the contract according to Article 59 of the bankruptcy law, and the buyer would acquire a claim for damages because of the cancellation. The amount of the damages would be decided according to market value.

If, however, one understands that as a result of exercising the option a unilateral contract is created, the buyer will acquire a monetary credit. Let's assume there is no close-out netting clause in the parties' agreement, in Theory 1 or 2, and call the economic gain the buyer obtains from the option "A." If there's a close-out netting agreement, the buyer will acquire a monetary credit whose value is the same as the market price of the options contract. Let's call this monetary value "B." B is a value that takes into account the chance that this options contract is not going to be exercised. Therefore, A and B should be identical values, and the enforcement of a close-out netting clause should not cause any substantial damage to the trustee's right of election. (Shindo 1996b, 185–86)

The argument traces its way through each of the alternative scenarios: Situation 2, in which the buyer of the option is the bankrupt party, is addressed in terms that track the previous paragraph's discussion almost word for word.[10] In situation 3, in which the seller of the option undergoes reorganization before the date of execution, the reasoning and outcome would be the same as that in situation 1. In situation 4, in which the buyer of the option undergoes reorganization before the date of execution, the reasoning and outcome would be as the same as in situation 2. The argument then moves on to each subsequent scenario and repeats the same structure. The rule-exception structure then produces a description of the practical functions of options and netting as much as an analysis of law. Geoffrey Samuel (2004, 46) terms such descriptions "virtual facts" because "they are factual modes which transcend actual factual reality."[11]

One of the intriguing aspects of the argument is the way this rule/ exception structure operates as a way of eliminating problematic rules. For example, two of the principal problems for Shindo's theory are

Bankruptcy Law Article 59 and Company Reorganization Law Article 103, which give the trustee the right to choose whether to cancel or execute contracts.[12] If the trustee has such an absolute right, a counterparty cannot enforce an obligation to net against a bankrupt party, since netting is in essence the enforcement of obligations. Shindo overcomes these problems with reference to Bankruptcy Law Article 66 and Company Reorganization Law Article 107, which stipulate that upon declaration of bankruptcy or inception of the reorganization process, running accounts are to be terminated and accounts are to be settled, creating one singular transaction. Citing various commentators, Shindo asserts that it is generally understood that articles 66 and 107 represent exceptions to articles 59 and 103. With a minor sleight of hand, he enlarges the point to claim that if articles 66 and 107 are applicable, there is therefore no room for trustees' rights. He proceeds to demonstrate that articles 66 and 107 are indeed applicable and therefore by the logic of "If A then Not B," articles 59 and 103 do not pose a problem for netting contracts.

The Shindo opinions present not one grand theory or argument, but rather a careful scaffolding of a seemingly infinite number of analogies, arranged in a rigid form of successive analysis of rules and their exceptions. The rigidity of this form of analogies embedded in rules and exceptions then belies—indeed enables—its expansive applications. This scaffolding generated a cumulative effect of an airtight, utterly complete argument, a legal fait accompli.

Through an awe-inspiring edifice of legal reasoning, then, the Shindo opinions argue that Japanese law *already* provided adequately for netting. In this way, the opinions make solid local sense of global phenomena. In this analogical approach, a baseline of difference—netting is new; it has not been part of the practice of bankruptcy up to now—provides the ground for the work of finding similarities: the categories that encompass netting as a theory are analogous, that is, formally "like" the theoretical categories of the bankruptcy law. Shindo's arguments are both similar to and different from existing legal arguments, variations from within an established genre of legal argumentation, invention within the parameters of convention (Wagner 1981).

Epistemology and Aesthetics of the Legal Analogy

Even Professor Shindo seemed bemused by my theoretical interest in his opinions. This discomfort with treating the work as theory is telling:

what is on display in the Shindo opinions is not theory but technique. One could say that such an appreciation of the qualities of a good legal analogy, of its clever and yet appropriate deployment, is the craft of legal knowledge (Riles 2004a). It is a craft performed and appreciated as if it were something far less than a craft—simply a device for balancing opposing political interests, or rendering the market more efficient, or improving human rights standards or conditions for scientific research. Heidegger (1977) called such things—the art at the heart of technical instrumentalism—*techne*.

Crucially, the opinions are not by any stretch of the imagination a blind application of legal rules, a slavish adherence to the letter of the law, as some critics of "legal formalism" assert. The opinions' inventive use of case law, for example, artfully disposes of countervailing arguments in judicial opinions.[13] The second opinion frequently inquires into the purposes behind particular sections of the code in order to extend its claims as far as necessary. Indeed, the arguments in the second opinion in essence are policy arguments. For example, having argued that the economic effects of enforcing or refusing to enforce a close-out netting clause would be identical, Shindo asserts that the risk of speculation on the part of the administrator, who is unlikely to have expertise in swap trading, gravitates toward upholding the validity of the close-out netting clause (Shindo 1996b, 187–88).

If Shindo's opinions make policy arguments, however, they do so in a particular *form*. That is, these functional policy arguments take the form of analogies or of formalistic discussions of rules and their exceptions. Consider, once again, Shindo's treatment of the problematic Article 59 of the Bankruptcy Law and Article 103 of the Company Reorganization Law that allow the trustee to rescind a bilateral contract, discussed above. One hypothesis about the purpose of Article 59, he asserts, is that it exists to protect both sides to the bilateral contract while also facilitating the process of bankruptcy. A second hypothesis would be that this article aims to give the trustee more rights and more choices. If one follows the first theory, he argues, these two articles do not conflict with the notion of off-setting. If one subscribes to the second understanding, however, there is a conflict. Shindo handles this problem by finding an exception to Article 59 in Article 61, which concerns exchange-based trading. The rationale is that it is not proper to allow the trustees to make speculative judgment. The existence of such an exception demonstrates that the first interpretation of the purpose behind Article 59 is the correct one (Shindo 1996a, 159). Acknowledging the existence of these alternative formulations of the purpose of the rule, Shindo uses doctrine to make sense of the purposes, that is, to determine which is ultimately correct. In other words, purposes are evidenced from the overall structure or form of the code, even if they are prior to and ultimately superior to the formal law itself.

In a conversation about this chapter, Shindo emphatically insisted to me that I not misrepresent his project as naïve conceptualism. And indeed, each of Shindo's analogies between aspects of netting practice and the categories of bankruptcy law, each invocation of a rule and its possible exceptions, as well as the larger argument that netting is enforceable in Japan, require a tentative and subtle suspension of belief. Analogical reasoning builds one As If upon the next such that, aesthetically, these As Ifs take on an aura of solidity in the aggregate. Each analogy nests inside another such that, as a totality, they provide a kind of context, or totality (Strathern 1990; Wagner 1977). This cascading structure of As If logic, in turn, recedes into further analogies: At the horizon of the legal arguments about netting, the practical economic theory of netting, likewise, consisted in theorizing separate transactions as if all had been one from the outset in much the same way. The As Ifs of law and the As Ifs of the market become a kind of virtual context each for the other that substantiate and sustain one another. In this mundane and technical artifact of legal knowledge, this small episode in the construction of private global governance, then, we have a far more epistemologically adventurous position than meets the eye.

Neoliberal Form

I now want to focus on a shift that occurred over the course of the collaboration between netting law reformers, from efforts to construct a legal *argument* that netting was enforceable under existing Japanese law to efforts to enact an entirely new *statute* affirming enforceability that would supersede all existing legal arguments. As we saw in the previous section, ISDA first addressed the problem of the enforceability of netting by turning to an eminent legal scholar for a legal opinion—a legal argument. But even as Professor Shindo was putting the finishing touches on his netting opinions—indeed, before the opinions had a chance to be tested in the market in any concrete way—a movement was afoot to devise a different kind of solution to the netting problem altogether: a statute, rather than a legal argument. Following ISDA's global strategy, Mr. Wani and others began to lobby for the enactment of a netting law. This new netting law ultimately was promulgated in June 1998 and took effect on December 1, 1998 (Netting Law 1998).

One way to think about the industry's shift in strategy is to see it as a move toward reification: The netting law takes an *objectified* form (a statute that is imagined to be something real, on the books, a thing in the world, not just a law professor's theory) (Strathern 1988, 171–90). And this object-like form of the law is taken to obviate the need for analogical thinking. Gone is the delicate metaphorical orientation of legal analogies. Netting is now secured by an actual law.

The new netting law was drafted by the staff of the Ministry of Finance's Financial Planning Bureau. However, at key junctures, Mr. Wani and other ISDA members provided information concerning industry practices and drafting assistance with the text of the new law. They even served as informal advisors to bureaucrats on the politics of getting the law passed. Although Mr. Wani described himself to me as a "lobbyist," using the English-language term, other core members of ISDA contest the characterization:

> We try not to be a lobbyist in the Western image. We are pressured by ISDA New York and London to be more outspoken but we always say to the government, "it would be ideal if we had this" (not, we must have this), and we hope that they will come to us for advice.

For the task of informally advising the Ministry of Finance, ISDA called especially on the advice of Professor Hideki Kanda. Like Professor Shindo, Professor Kanda was professor of law at the University of Tokyo, but he was a generation younger, and one of Japan's premier specialists in the more contemporary subject of financial law. Kanda was a ubiquitous member of ministerial committees on financial and commercial regulatory issues. He had made a name for himself importing to Japan the "Chicago School" of law and economics scholarship. One of the aims of this tradition, at least as practiced at that time, was to subordinate legal theory to neoclassical economic theory (Posner 1995). It asserted that law should be explicitly reorganized to serve the interests of efficiency in a free market economy, and it generally preferred that these reforms take place through statutes that directly speak the language of the market rather than through legal interpretations of existing law that seek to accommodate traditional legal thinking to market demands. As discussed in chapter 3, law and economics in Japan was also strongly aligned with an attack on the legitimacy of the administrative state. Statutes are preferred, in this view, because it is assumed that they constrain bureaucratic authority. Professor Kanda's support for a statutory solution to the netting problem, then, was in harmony with his more general positions on the character of law and legal reform. The two figures—Shindo and Kanda—then epitomize two generations of legal theory in Japan: The older, more traditional, generalist era of doctrinal legal analysis, and the younger, internationally minded, market-oriented approach grounded in the scholar's own extensive network of contacts overseas.

One could explain the events surrounding this incremental incident in private global governance sociologically—as a generational contest within the academy and the bureaucracy (e.g., Dezalay and Garth 2002). The sociolegal literature has repeatedly shown with respect to rule of law projects, the arguments for or against a particular solution to the netting problem I will now describe are not "just" arguments but the artifacts of particular interests, alliances, and disputes.[14] Indeed, the legal interpretation of existing statutes described in the first part of this chapter was the outcome of an alliance between BOJ bureaucrats and an older generation of Tokyo University Law Department academics, while the later turn to drafting an entirely new statute as the outcome of an alliance between the Ministry of Finance and a younger generation of academics from the same law faculty. Yet to focus solely on such "palace wars" would not do justice to how the dispute looked from these actors' point of view. To them, it was also a dispute about form.

Virtual Transparency

An earlier draft of the netting law produced by the Ministry of Finance had followed the line of argument outlined in Professor Shindo's legal opinion to explain the legality of netting by analogy to current bankruptcy law provisions. Yet the final draft abandoned Shindo's analogies. Instead, the netting law borrowed many of its concepts directly from a model netting act drafted by ISDA and posted at their Web site (ISDA 2002b).[15] ISDA intended its model netting act for possible adoption in every jurisdiction around the world in which swap trading occurs or might occur, irrespective of differences of law, politics, economics, or culture. The format of the law is simple and straightforward—there is no admission of issues of reception, translation, or accommodation to local conditions. It simply affirms that certain netting contracts are enforceable. And following the language of the model netting act, this is exactly what the Japanese netting law asserts as well. In the model law, and its enactment in Japan, we have the apotheosis of the private global law reform project—a global law, posted at a private Web site, and downloadable directly to national bureaucracies (ISDA 2002b).

On closer examination, however, there is something curious about this statute, something rather less than meets the eye. The text of the law itself is extremely brief, although somewhat baroque in drafting style. Article 1 makes the transnational market orientation of the law explicit by affirming that the ultimate purpose of the law is to "improve domestic and international trust in the functioning of our country's financial system and to contribute to the healthy development of the national economy" (Netting Law 1998, Article 1). Article 2 then simply adds that the "specified transactions" covered by the law are OTC derivatives transactions to be specified in a ministerial ordinance to be jointly issued by the Ministry of Finance and Prime Minister's Office.[16] Article 2(2) defines the financial institutions for whom netting will be enforceable. It lists certain specific kinds of institutions,[17] but also adds that "other legal entities" can also take advantage of netting. The law states that such "other entities" are once again to be specified in an ordinance to be jointly issued by the Ministry of Finance and Office of the Prime Minister.[18] Article 2-6 of the law explains the mechanics of close-out netting.[19]

Finally, Article 3 clarifies the relationship between close-out netting and bankruptcy and reorganization procedures:

> If a party which has been declared bankrupt or is undergoing reorganization is either a financial institution or the counterparty of a financial institution engaged in a specified financial transaction according to a master agreement that stipulates close-out netting, for all specified financial transactions engaged in according to the master agreement concerned, all the property or entitlements specified in the clauses below ... become one single entitlement that the party declared bankrupt or undergoing reorganization will possess according to the agreement, or one single entitlement that its counterparty will possess according to the agreement because of the occurrence of the reason for close-out netting concerning the declaration of bankruptcy or reorganization.

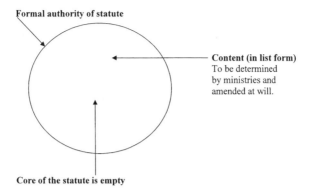

FIGURE 8. The virtual transparency of the netting law

What is most interesting, then, is the form that "transparency" takes here. The netting law consists of a very short text that asserts only that netting in certain "specified transactions" between certain "specified parties" will be enforceable. The work of specifying the key terms of the statute is left for a future date to the Ministry of Finance and the Financial Services Agency. The character of this law, then, can be captured in figure 8.

I call this virtual transparency because what we have here is a statute with a hollow core. We have the *form* of a statute, the *form* of something straightforward and in line with market conditions, but nothing more. The content of the statute remains largely unspecified.

Making White Things White

The lawyers involved in the swap markets I knew insisted with pride that the advantage of the law's form was that it was far more flexible (Martin 1994). First, unlike the Shindo opinions, they argued, it was not limited to those transactions that could be shoe-horned into a legal analogy to existing law. The form of this statute—its hollow core—allowed for a greater degree of flexibility than even other statutes. Where in the United States it is periodically necessary to return to Congress to request an amendment to the bankruptcy laws to ensure that new products are covered under those laws, in the Japanese case, I was repeatedly told, the bureaucracy could simply issue an amended list of "specified transactions" at any time, without going through the extensive procedures of amending legislation.

But what is also significant about this law is not what it achieves but what it refuses to achieve. As Professor Kanda put it, "From the point of view of financial institutions, in a sense, the law just makes white things white, but I think it is a new type of legislation and it is interesting." Professor Kanda refers here to the official position of bureaucrats and industry representatives that the netting law simply confirms the current enforceability of close-out netting agreements under the bankruptcy law. That is, by its own admission, and indeed insistence, the law does not alter social or economic practices, nor does it disturb existing rights and obligations as they are understood by the parties. The form of the statute—a statute with a hollow core—simply enshrines pre-existing authority and practice (together with its hallmark flexibility) (Strathern 2000b). The same bureaucracies as before retain responsibility under this statute; they are no more constrained than before. Their authority is formalized in the statute, however, and thus protected from interference by domestic courts and foreign lobby groups alike. In other words, the statute rephrases existing practices not by translating them but by simply replacing them with the empty form of "global standards."

Indeed, at one point or another, most of the people I knew who were involved in this reform—despite their tremendous investment of effort in the campaign for a netting law—insisted that the new legislation would not change much. For some, this was because at that time the failure of a major financial institution still seemed somewhat difficult to imagine, despite the government's repeated warnings that it would no longer protect banks from default. But for many others, this reflected an insight about how a new law might or might not alter how problems were addressed, when they became serious, in the market.

During the period of my fieldwork, a situation arose that tested how a default situation actually would be handled in Japan. In October 1998, only several weeks before the netting law was to come into effect, the government nationalized the failing Long-Term Credit Bank (LTCB) in order to prevent its financial collapse.[21] The nationalization of a counterparty is one of the events listed in the ISDA Master Agreement as allowing a party to terminate the agreement (ISDA 1992, 6). The nationalization of the bank therefore gave counterparties to swap transactions with LTCB cause to demand that all swaps be netted out and settled immediately. Since LTCB was heavily involved in the swap markets and most likely did not have the funds to cover its obligations, this had the potential to engender a chain of defaults on obligations.

Eager to forestall this sort of catastrophe, officials of the Ministry of Finance and the BOJ jointly summoned representatives from each of the banks that held outstanding swap contracts with LTCB. They assured these counterparties—first privately, and later, at the urging of the foreign banks, in public statements—that the government would assume all of the bank's outstanding obligations with termination dates within three years. On this basis, MOF and BOJ officials jointly and emphatically asked the counterparties not to declare a situation of default requiring close-out netting, as was their legal prerogative to do under the terms of the Master Agreement.

It was the ultimate example of informal administrative handling of a market crisis, precisely the opposite of rule-based legalism of the kind announced by the netting law. No counterparty did declare default, and most market insiders I knew described themselves as satisfied with the arrangement. The government's assumption of the obligations for a period of several years proved to be a far less expensive and more predictable way of resolving the problem than litigating claims under the terms of the netting law would have been even if, in rare cases, certain contracts with terms beyond three years would not necessarily be honored.[22] Many told me they felt the case established a precedent for how problems would be handled in the future, although one person commented that because this was not a case of the so-called sudden death of a financial institution, the government had time to rally the industry to its proposal in a way that might not be true the next time around. Nevertheless, there is an irony in this success. At the very moment at which formal legal solutions were reaching fruition, all of the parties concerned seemed most satisfied with the ultimate example of a government engineered solution from the days prior to "free, fair, and global."

Signaling and Comparing

The implications of this irony were not lost on market participants. Lawyers involved in netting issues usually doubted whether the law would bring about dramatic change in the actual process of settlement in the event of bankruptcy. One person involved in the negotiations over LTCB summed the situation up with a shrug: "Practically speaking, the informal system worked all right, but was still unclear. The market requires—or rather, Western people require—something more. It was not secured, not ruled by law."

When they reflected on incidents like the LTCB episode, people insisted that if the law was important, it was, as stated in Article 1 itself, for the sake of rendering Japanese regulation "transparent" to foreigners, not Japanese parties.[23] Making Japanese law accessible to foreigners was important because the markets depended on active foreign participation. The netting law was most of all important as a statement to the outside world. Formal law solidifies bureaucratic authority in an environment of shrinking bureaucratic resources at the same time as it satisfies foreigners' demands for transparency (Mabuchi 1993, 135).

The foreigners seen as demanding transparency of course were well aware of all of this. As mentioned in the previous chapter, foreign financial institutions are well enough staffed and resourced to acquire good local knowledge about the state of law reform projects in Japan. But a managing director of a transnational bank has his or her own transnational audiences. It is far easier to explain in a short briefing paper to executives back home or to a reporter for a financial publication or in an article aimed at global shareholders that there has been "progress" when one can point to the enactment of a statute. Informal ways of handling problems are messy, contextual, and by their nature not always open to public revelation. Informality cannot be revealed the way a law reveals itself. Conversely, the law's specificities would be of less interest to most of these audiences, as they tick through the list of reforms that have taken place in various jurisdictions around the world in which global financial players have interests. And yet, there must be some *evidence*, some *outwardly visible signal* of progress; the managing director cannot expect shareholders just to take his or her word for it that a certain jurisdiction is favorable to foreign interests. And so laws like the netting law provide something to put in the annual report. One of the achievements of virtual transparency, we might say then, is its ability to signal transparency itself. That is, the netting law evidenced the fact that there was a law, and that this law conformed to global standards. Although this may seem like a quite exotic and strange species of law, I venture that there are many elements of transnational law that have just this feature.[24]

But although the transnational projection of this law clearly is important, I want to quibble with the suggestion of my informants that this law was a performance solely for the benefit of foreign parties. For this claim ignores the uses and even pleasures of the form of this statute for its Japanese enthusiasts. In an article on the subject, Professor Kanda concludes that "the ideal is that we should have a legislative solution to this problem on the basis of an understanding that close-out netting is the termination of a contract or a settlement, just like the United States" (1998, 13). The phrase "just like the United States" is significant here: the defense of the statute was invariably cast in *comparative* terms. Kanda refers to the existence of this kind of legislation in the United States, Belgium, France, Germany, and Italy, and asserts that "our country finally joins the advanced nations" (1998, 18). I was often told by bureaucrats that the best way to win over other sections of the bureaucracy in support of a particular reform was to present a list of other countries that already had the legislation and to make the claim that Japan was "behind the curve."

The Ministry of Finance official responsible for drafting the netting law made the comparative argument for its significance in a graphical form that mirrored the simple formality of the statute itself. This form was not his own invention; a similar chart appears in many government documents produced in advance of law reform projects in Japan today. The empty space in the box corresponding to Japan poignantly makes the argument that Japan is lacking, lacking in a matter of "global standards" (see table 1).

One consequential aspect of this statute's form, in other words, is the kind of comparison it makes possible. Most comparative lawyers would surely decry this form of comparison as amateuristic and shallow—it is nothing more than a simple listing of whether countries "have" or "do not have" a particular element of law reform. But that is precisely the point from the view of the law's proponents: to compare a simple and straightforward entity, "Japan," to other "developed nations" without making analogies, without translating, without complexity and context. This kind of comparison itself takes on a kind of virtual quality (what does one really know about the law of Jurisdiction A if one knows it has a certain law on the books, a comparative lawyer will insist). But perhaps "knowledge" is really beside the point in this kind of technocratic comparison—what Graziadei terms the prestige factor in legal transplants (2006, 458) and David Nelkin (2006) calls "signaling conformity." Rather, the point is that one is able to think of one's daily work, the work of producing domestic legislation, as part of a larger transnational (and progressive historical) imperative: Netting laws are appearing everywhere in the civilized world; by helping to produce this law we are join-

TABLE I. **The legislation concerning the enforceability of close-out netting in derivatives trading in G7 countries (Yamana 1998, 23)**

Japan	(See table note)
United States	▶ 1989 Enactment of the Financial Institution Reform Recovery and Enforcement Act of 1989 Pub. L. No. 103-73, 103 Stat. 183 (1989) (FIRREA) ▶ 1990 Amendment to the Federal Bankruptcy Code ▶ 1991 Enactment of the Federal Deposit Insurance Corporation Improvement Act Pub. L. No. 105 Stat. 2336 (1991) (FDICIA)
Great Britain	▶ 1993 Opinion of the Financial Law Panel
Germany	▶ 1994 Enactment of the Second Financial Market Promotion Act ▶ 1999 Planned amendment to the Bankruptcy Code
France	▶ 1993 Enactment of the Law Concerning Securities Exchanges and Futures Markets
Italy	▶ 1998 Enactment of the Order Concerning Financial Intermediation
Canada	▶ 1992 Amendment to the Bankruptcy and Insolvency Act (BIA) and the Canada Deposit Insurance Corporation Act (CDIC)

Note: The enforceability remains based on interpretations in the Shindo Opinions.

ing the family of civilized neoliberal nations and speeding the project of global law reform in the service of markets. The "transparent" form of the netting law, therefore, is not just "what Western people require": it is also a device that enables the Japanese architects of the As If economic order to see their work, in direct, if empty transnational terms.

Tearing Down Law

Beyond its instrumental service to the interests of the global derivatives industry, the netting law was also imagined by many of its champions as the outcome of a critique of traditional legal reasoning. By the time I began to research the netting problem, some months before the new netting law was to take effect, it had become fairly commonplace, especially among young American-educated Japanese lawyers, to criticize the Shindo opinions. According to one young associate at a prominent law firm, the opinions were somewhat "technical, formalistic, or artificial. . . . If we were counsel, we would rely on various facts. The opinion doesn't work absolutely, but may be somewhat effective." The act of finding analogies, and the edifice it created, in other words, had come to seem somewhat excessive, contrived.

In a published dialogue, professors Shindo and Kanda elaborated on the differences in their approaches to the netting problem. Professor

Kanda argued that market participants think of netting as a process of marking transactions to market, not as a set of separate obligations to be offset at the time of bankruptcy, and Professor Shindo's analogies would create new problems later on.[25] He concluded that "I have always understood the offsetting argument as a kind of necessary evil. I'm not saying it's really bad, but it will face its own limits" (Shindo et al. 1994).

In response to Kanda's critique, Professor Shindo raises the problem of how to "translate" market participants' interests, concerns, and practices into legal categories.

> What you just said is understandable from the point of view of practitioners. From the point of view of the logic of the Bankruptcy Law, however, another kind of logic is necessary. . . . The transaction at issue is so distant from everyday experience for people like me. I feel that I was forced to engage in an argument without a full understanding of whether what I say reflects reality. But I have struggled to find an approach understandable to judges while being informed by Mr. Wani, [and other leading lawyers for global banks] of the reality of trading. I feel that I really have experienced the role of a cross-cultural interpreter. (Shindo et al. 1994, 26, 41)

The Shindo opinions represent a self-conscious exercise in translation, then (Langer 2004).[26] Shindo makes sense of foreign contractual terms and of the exotic transactions of the global derivatives markets in the existing categories of Japanese law; he approximates the terms of the transnational derivatives markets to the form and content of knowledge familiar to a local judge. As he put it, "In order to convince bankruptcy law scholars, although this may be pushing it in terms of logic, it is necessary to translate words or tools we are accustomed to using, one by one, and proceed" (Shindo et. al. 1994, 27).

It was precisely this act of translation that the netting law rejected. The netting law was self-consciously *new* in the way that it put aside legal analogies in favor of straightforward language. The term for this sense of newness was "transparency."[27] As Mr. Wani announced in a round-table discussion on the topic,

> We would like to show that Japan also explicitly has a law concerning close-out netting and has a transparent system that is visible from outside. . . . The reasoning up to now has been based on interpretation, but from now on it's going to be based on a law.

The appeal of the netting law, beyond its instrumental purposes, then, lay in its assault on another kind of legal knowledge—its tearing down of the delicate scaffolding of analogies in favor of something more straight-forward, something imagined as closer to reality. In a 1994 article advo-cating the need for a netting law, Professor Kanda argues that close-out netting should be understood in terms of "economic fundamentals":

> If you pay attention to the economic substance of close-out netting, close-out netting is a settlement of transactions and it is closer to the termination of a contract than to off-setting. To be more precise, it is termination plus settle-ment and as long as it is categorized as a form of settlement it is a realization of the contract at the time of termination. In short, it is an effort to mark the contract to market. (Kanda 1994, 12)

Kanda's point is that Shindo's analogies of netting to off-setting under the bankruptcy law are too far from the economic nature of the transac-tion. In contrast, a law that simply directs the judge to uphold netting contracts, without inquiring into how these contracts may or may not be analogizable to legitimate transactions under existing Japanese law, seemed more transparent, more straightforward.

Now this attack on "traditional" legal knowledge, this shift from le-gal reasoning to statutes and from translation to transparency, may seem momentous: it is tempting to describe the netting law as part of a kind of epochal shift from one modality of lawmaking, and one vision of politics, one vision of state legitimacy, one way of practicing the legal craft, to another—an exemplar of how neoliberalism has shifted the parameters of law and politics, as law was brought into line with market realities. As we saw, that is how the participants in this project themselves sought, at certain moments, to describe their activities.

But it is important to remember that the proponents of the netting law were all established jurists, elite lawyers, and legal experts within the bureaucracy, hardly legal outsiders. If the netting law signaled novelty, a fresh move away from lawyerly obfuscation, then this assault on legal knowledge was carried out by some of Japan's most important legal ex-perts themselves. The tearing down of legal knowledge, the assault on the "unreal" nature of legal analogies, on their distance from "economic fundamentals" in the netting law was simply the instantiation of one as-pect of legal knowledge, one standard move, alongside the production and refining of the legal analogies.

So I have presented what legal reformers treated as two contrasting kinds of legal knowledge. These two forms of law and knowledge appealed to different sources of authority and legitimacy. The "power" of the Shindo approach lay first in the biography of its author—the fact that it is backed by a grand figure of the Japanese legal academy—and second, the awesome quality of the logical apparatus Professor Shindo constructs in his opinions. In contrast, the effectiveness of the netting law lay in the way its multiple and more anonymous advocates (lobbyists, academics, bankers, bureaucrats) were normatively empowered by a sense of being on the side of progress and of globalization, and against the obfuscations of legal fictions. In the case of the Shindo opinions, the consumer of the legal fiction gains a detached appreciation for the scientific brilliance of the argument. In the case of the statute, however, the consumer is drawn into the project and becomes the advocate, the zealot, even, of global economic relations.

Where in the Shindo opinions the mode in which legal knowledge intersects with the transnational implications of Japanese law was locally oriented *interpretation*, in the netting law translation was displaced by global *comparison*. In the first case, knowledge was contextual; the point was to make sense of global forms in their local context. In the second case, knowledge was experienced as more immediate; it was imagined to be free of "cultural" specificity. The statute aims to be readable by foreigners and Japanese, lawyers and traders alike. It signals a vision of Japan as a transnational entity and of Japanese law as fundamentally implicated in and open to transnational capitalism.

At first glance, the netting law certainly presents a stark example of law in the service of global markets. Yet the neoliberal orientation is not what distinguishes the netting law from the Shindo opinions: Shindo shared this orientation with the proponents of the netting law and understood his work to serve the same financial interests as the law itself. The netting law and the Shindo opinions were undoubtedly *both* instruments of global market practices, artifacts of a confluence between the interests of international banks and those of lawyers and bureaucrats. Second, it would be inappropriate to describe the one as a more locally oriented form of knowledge than the other. Both artifacts—the Shindo opinions and the netting law—are transnational artifacts—efforts to respond to the problems and possibilities posed by Japan's entanglement in the global financial markets and the associated demands of foreign interests.

I want to suggest rather that we think of these two legal forms as posing two alternative genres of legal knowledge. We saw that Shindo's analogical reasoning worked with a delicate epistemology of As If. Now this
particular form, the "tree" of nested analogies, is by no means unique
to this case or to Japanese law or even to financial law. Shindo's argument—its style, its substance, its epistemological position—is not unique
to financial law, or global legal problems, or Japan. Indeed, Shindo had
been selected by ISDA because of his expertise in civil procedure, not financial law. His task was rather to produce an exemplary artifact of legal
knowledge, to do what a true legal expert does best. The Shindo opinions then can be read as specimens of standard legal thought.

What is at stake here, then, is not an epochal break between two opposing approaches, but rather an oscillation between two alternative possibilities of form. In a most practical sense, lawyers relied on both these
approaches—they appealed to the netting law to ensure their clients that
netting involving transactions covered by that law was enforceable, but
made arguments based on the Shindo opinions for transactions not covered by the law. In a more aesthetic sense, the netting law was dependent
on legal fictions for its aura of novelty, freshness, and transnationalism:
If there had been no technical legal arguments, no grand doctrinal structures to make local sense of global legal norms, the cry for bringing law
more into line with market realities would have had nothing to devas-
tate, and the straight, clean lines of this statute would have cut a far less
dramatic figure indeed.

Indeed, despite the contrast that outside observers might draw between these two genres of neoliberal legal knowledge, there was in fact
continual collaboration between the two. The most vociferous advocates
of the netting law had moments at which they professed that a statute
would change nothing relative to earlier legal arguments, and the same
figures at moments artfully deployed the technicalities of legal logic as
well. Likewise, Professor Shindo himself noted that the most satisfying
outcome of his work would be the enactment of a netting law.

This oscillation between seemingly incompatible approaches to law
reform is important because it helps us to understand how those involved
in the campaign for a netting law both believed in these reforms and
viewed them as simply a veneer for foreign consumption, a way of rendering Japanese regulation "transparent" to foreigners (cf. Dore 1999). The
trick of the statute was precisely the way in which at moments it inspired

passion and commitment but at later moments it could be abandoned, translated, or even contextualized in terms of further legal fictions.

In contrast, the netting law embraced the global markets by simply mirroring back these markets' virtual quality (Carrier and Miller 1998; Comaroff and Comaroff 2000; Miller 2003; Miyazaki 2005). At its core the netting law was empty, and for this very reason its potential content was infinite, everything and nothing, to be determined as necessary, in time, by the relevant authorities. Its very form, therefore, signaled infinite potential but generated nothing much more concrete than that. In its formal symmetry with other netting statutes in jurisdictions around the world, moreover, it evoked a transnational dimension of legality, something that could be posted on a Web site in an English version, as if it could be made sense of immediately and without recourse to some localizing act of translation. The aesthetics of this form of knowledge therefore invoked an image of Japan as one of a number of similarly situated jurisdictions, rather than an image of Japan as a culturally distinct, and therefore unique, entity.

Rethinking the New Realism

In regulatory reform debates, the notion that the law should reflect market and social realities as closely as possible is taken pretty much as common sense, true dogma across the political spectrum—such that any deviation from this position seems almost silly. Who would dare to claim that the law should be out of touch with the market, that it should have its own separate logic? On the right, there are loud and repeated calls for getting away from lawyerly syllogisms and analogies in favor of "simple rules for a complex world." At the center and on the left likewise, a movement is afoot to bring Realism back as a theoretical resource for addressing current economic and social problems, under the banner of a New Legal Realism (Garth 2006; Mertz and Mitchell 2006; Miles and Sunstein 2007).

But if the netting law screams Realism in its law and economics pedigree and its pro-market ambitions, it is anything but realistic. As we have seen, it is rather a quite virtual form of regulation, one that signals transparency as a way of being opaque. This law is truly "reflexive" in the terms of Gunther Teubner: it does no more than describe itself (2004b).

So it turns out that the Realist reformists and reforms are not all that realistic after all.

So should we denounce the netting law as a sham—faux Realism exposed? In fact, one of the insights to be gained from looking closely at legal technique in global economic governance is that the very purpose of law is often precisely to achieve a certain virtualism, a certain distance from reality. Indeed, the point of John Henry Wigmore's (1897) evolutionary tale about the development of the law of collateral with which this book began was that the very existence of markets depends upon the evolution of legal fictions—of ways of thinking about the market that are *not* realistic in any straightforward sense. For example, as we saw in the previous chapter, the very purpose of collateral as a legal technique is to set limits on the realities (social, economic, political) that market participants must take into account. The purpose of collateral is to substitute something for those realities—a set of legal fictions I call placeholders (chapter 4). From this point of view it is stunning how empirically inadequate, how utterly unrealistic, is the classic Realist description of legal technicalities as a kind of naïve blind faith, believed by no one but law professors and judges, and contradicted entirely by actual market practice.

Realists argue that there is nothing inherently special about legal knowledge—that it is just another version of managerial expertise. Therefore any attempts to separate law from reality are exercises in obfuscation and muddleheadedness (Posner 1987). I want to suggest, instead, that what is special about legal knowledge is precisely its own claim to be set apart from, collateral to, realities. Indeed, one of the fundamental problems with Realist critiques of various stripes is their failure to take seriously the appreciation of form, in its own right, independent of crude instrumentalist definitions of formalism's political and other functions.

If, as is fairly generally acknowledged, the "certainty" of legal formalism is a kind of veneer, we need to understand the features of this veneer, how and why it garners the commitment of scholars and practitioners it does, and, most important, what uses various kinds of institutional actors may find for it. As one of the grandfathers of international economic law long ago insisted, the international economic order itself is also an As If economic order (Röpke 1954, 227). Fictions of all kinds proliferate in economic law despite the fact that this is a field in which, according to its own ideology, the law should most closely mirror reality (Hannoun 1995, 84).[28] In fact, to critique law for its distance from reality in my view misses the power and also the transformative promise of law. As we have seen in this chapter and the previous one, the very unreal and reflexive quality of law has real-world effects. It sets in motion new ways of collaborating that have profound transformative effects.

Social scientists have always felt more at home with the technocrat, who sees him- or herself as immersed in realities, than with the back-office lawyer whose self-image is more collateral. But the insight of this material is that what sociolegal studies and cognate forms of empirical work in the law are trying to do, by continually linking law to social reality, is ultimately at cross purposes with what legal knowledge *in reality* often is. That is, the connections between legal practice and market practice that sociolegal scholars would want to show—the chains of relations between documents, theories, and persons I have described in the chapters of this book—are often premised on a shared task of holding back social and economic realities.

On Virtual Transparency

From this point of view we can reflect further on the law's entanglement in the politics of global markets. In particular, this account raises questions about the politics of transparency, and about whether transparency in market regulation is always and everywhere inherently a good. Recently legal commentators have pointed out that transparency is in fact a contradiction, perhaps even an impossibility. The fantasy of eliminating the "distance between state and public" belies the reality of an inherently complex, contradictory, and incommunicative state. As a matter of actual bureaucratic work—of paper and procedures—"transparency is an ideal that can undercut itself in practice" (Hull 2008, 515). The very ideals of risk management and transparency in financial regulation are by definition tragic opposites (Westbrook 2010) that aim for opposite visions of the regulatory good and thwart one another in practice. As Daniel Tarullo has put it somewhat ironically, "While there is agreement that more transparency in emerging financial markets is desirable, there is considerably less agreement as to how useful that transparency will be" (2001, 648).

Virtual transparency is a quietly ironic, but nevertheless powerful, response to this impossible mandate. Certainly, as we have seen, the statute generated the *effect* of global market standards; it aesthetically produced the indicia of its own effectiveness. The statute was also an ingenious bureaucratic response to the onslaught of "global standards"—a way of hiding what is crucially important, well understood, and yet cannot be expressed in straightforward terms (such as the relations and obligations that make possible informal solutions to banking crises) within the very emptiness of its opposite, transparency. In other words, this denunciation of traditional legal knowledge in favor of a hollow placeholder—an empty statute—actually recaptures the As If orientation of legal knowledge by hiding it, rather than making of it an analytical edifice. The Japanese netting law was rather more like the case of the German Bundestag, the beautiful modern German parliament building made of pure glass, as described by Bruno Latour: Something you can see right through, but that somehow does not reveal anything at all (Latour and Weibel 2005). Legal reforms that seem at first blush to capitulate to global demands for the privatization of state power therefore can serve as a kind of shield from the pressures to do things the globally standard way.

When one approaches questions of the power and legitimacy of states in their relationship with global markets in their lived detail, one episode of privatization at a time, moreover, one finds that weighty political matters often turn on something far away from the vocabulary for theorizing neoliberalism in social theory and law—the aesthetics of legal knowledge. What animated dialogue and collaborative effort for these reformers were not simply instrumentalist concerns (who would benefit from this arrangement, and why) but also a shared appreciation of the form of legal argument and of legal rules. Many of the lawyers working for banks I knew experienced the work of drafting a statute or making arguments for the enforceability of a netting agreement as more interesting and engaging than their ordinary work for their banks, something outside of the ordinary drudgery of "papering the transactions." These reformers' ideological commitment to what they viewed as the rule of law and promarket reform was matched by a subtle orientation toward the aesthetic propensities of legal argumentation and rule making. If, at the level of explicit arguments and claims, the advocates of the netting law viewed the turn to rules as an instrumental goal, they found in the form of the law a new point of inspiration, a subject worthy of commitment, a pleasurable source of reflection, as well as a means of achieving requisite instrumental ends. That is, legal knowledge is effective because of the particular form that it takes.

This suggests that questions of regulatory form deserve as much attention as questions of regulatory substance. The form of law enrolls and engages different actors in different ways. We have seen, for example, how legal form can inspire, or allow people to compare themselves with others, or signal certain ideas to oneself or to others. The choice of form, therefore, has implications for how law, and law reform, engages the attention and aspirations of the people whose daily life work it must become to build and implement it, and for the intended and unintended consequences and possibilities law may engender below the political radar.

Notes

1. The close-out netting clause of the ISDA Master Agreement (1992, § 6e) reads:

> The amount payable in respect of an Early Termination date will be calculated as follows: If there is a Defaulting Party, the Defaulting Party will pay to the other party the excess, if a positive number, of (A) the sum of (i) the amount determined in accordance with Agreement Value—Limited Two Way Payments, calculated on the basis of Aggregation (or, if the Aggregate Market Quotation calculated in determining such amount is less than zero, the amount by which such Aggregate Market Quotation is less than zero, expressed as a negative number) and (ii) the Unpaid Amounts due to the other party over (B) the Unpaid Amounts due to the Defaulting Party.

Prior to the promulgation of the netting law, the only government pronouncement on the issue was a 1994 Ministry of Finance Ordinance (*shorei*). That ordinance presented a "strange tautology," as one legal affairs specialist in a derivatives group put it. It states that netting agreements are enforceable if the agreements themselves state that they are effective.

2. See Shindo 1996a, 157. Although a swap contract mutually obligates each side to complete the contract, Shindo argues in the first opinion that the Master Agreement stipulates that debts are to be consolidated and netted out for each payment date and for each currency. He argues that this is evidenced by the fact that in clause 2(c) of the Master Agreement the word "replaced" is used to describe this process. In addition, this clause only refers to the payment date, he points out. See ISDA 1992, § 2(c):

> If on any date amounts would otherwise be payable (i) in the same currency; and (ii) in respect of the same Transaction, by

each party to the other, then, on such date, each party's obligation to make payment of any such amount will be automatically satisfied and discharged and, if the aggregate amount that would otherwise have been payable by one party exceeds the aggregate amount that would otherwise have been payable by the other party, replaced by an obligation upon the party by whom the larger aggregate amount would have been payable to pay to the other party the excess of the larger aggregate amount over the smaller aggregate amount.

3. The problem here was that the bankruptcy law expressly forbade setoff under certain circumstances (Bankruptcy Law of Japan 1922). Article 104 read,

Setoff shall not be effected in any of the following cases: (1) Where a creditor in bankruptcy has assumed obligation due to the bankrupt estate subsequent to the adjudication of bankruptcy; (2) Where a creditor in bankruptcy assumed obligation due to the bankrupt estate with the knowledge that there has been suspension of payment or that petition for bankruptcy has been filed; provided, however, that this shall not apply if the assumption is based on causes provided for in laws, or if it is based on causes which had arisen prior to the time creditor in bankruptcy had become aware of suspension of payment or of petition for bankruptcy having been filed, or on causes which had arisen one year or more prior to the time of adjudication of bankruptcy; (3) Where a[n] obligor of the bankrupt has acquired other person's claims in bankruptcy after adjudication of bankruptcy; (4) Where an obligor of the bankrupt has acquired a claim in bankruptcy with the knowledge that there has been suspension of payment or that petition for bankruptcy has been filed; provided however, that this shall not apply in cases where the acquisition is based on causes provided for in laws, or on causes which had arisen prior to the time the obligor had become aware of suspension of payment or of petition for bankruptcy having been filed, or on causes which had arisen one year or more prior to the time of adjudication of bankruptcy.

4. One interesting attempt to bring formalist aesthetics to the forefront of academic debate is Ernest Weinrib's (1993, 958–62) defense of formalism. In his understanding,

Form is the ensemble of characteristics that constitute the matter in question as a unity identical to that of other matters of the same kind and distinguishable from matters of a different kind.

Form is not separate from content but is the ensemble of characteristics that marks the content as determinate, and therefore marks the content as a content. . . . [F]orm is a principle of structure or unity. The thing that has a form is a single entity, characterized by the ensemble of attributes that make it what it is. . . . Legal formalism postulates that the law's content can be understood in and through itself by reference to the mode of thinking that shapes it from inside.

5. Langenbucher (1998, 482) points out that "the civil law tradition does not view analogies with statutes as usurpation of 'legislative power' by an overactive judiciary but, on the contrary, as especially faithful adherence to the *volonté générale*."

6. For example, the first problem for Shindo's argument raised by the analogy of close-out netting to off-setting is that Civil Code Article 505(1) suggests that, in order for off-setting to be valid, the opposing rights have to be of the same kind. Article 505(1) (Setoff) reads, "In cases where two persons mutually owe to the other any obligation with the same kind of purpose, if both obligations are due, each obligor may be relieved from his/her own obligation by setting off each value thereof against the corresponding amount of the obligation of the other obligor; provided, however, that, this shall not apply to the cases where the nature of the obligation does not permit such set-off" (Civil Code 1896). Shindo acknowledges that because the opposing rights in swap transactions are determined in different currencies, it might be argued that they create different "kinds" of obligations and therefore are ineligible for off-setting (Shindo 1996a, 144). He addresses this problem through an analogy to Civil Code Article 403, which states that a debtor can pay foreign denominated obligations in Japanese yen, and concludes that, applying this reasoning, it is possible to net each individual swap transaction into a single payment flow.

7. The second opinion addresses close-out netting in transactions involving stock options, commodity options, and options on bonds with delivery clauses.

8. Shindo further argues that the exchange-traded commodities specified in Article 61 are very similar to options on securities with delivery clauses: there are objective markets for these products, there is an element of speculative trading to them, and options must be exercised within a specified period of time. Moreover, the same rationale for the rule—to prevent the trustee from engaging in speculative activities—applies (Shindo 1996b, 194). He therefore argues that this rationale should be extended to reorganization proceedings, even though the company reorganization law lacks an equivalent to Article 61 of the bankruptcy law.

9. Figure 7 depicts only a small portion of the total argument.

10. If it is advantageous to do so, he notes, the trustee will exercise the option. The result of exercising the option might be understood in one of two ways. Under the first theory, a bilateral contract is created; under the second theory, the result is a unilateral contract. Under the first theory, the administrator will request execution under Article 59, and the seller will acquire an opposing entitlement. If one views the option as a unilateral contract, the administrator will acquire a monetary credit. In the first theory, the monetary gain is the difference between the market price of the stock and the payment for that stock. In the second theory, the monetary gain is the actual monetary credit. In principle, the economic value of the monetary gain under either of these two theories is the same as the amount gained from close-out netting, Shindo argues; therefore the enforcement of a close-out netting clause would not cause any substantial damage to the trustee's resources (Shindo 1996b, 186).

11. Samuel gives the example of categories such as "person," "damage," "thing," and "fault" which the law treats as facts, and which social actors treat as social categories, but which are actually legal categories. Some kinds of damage may not amount to "damage," while some types of things may not amount to a "thing." As he explains,

> the idea that legal science is a discourse that has its object in actual factual situations is to misunderstand, fundamentally, legal thought. . . . [Law] functions as much within the world of fact as within the world of law and it is this dual role that endows it with its capacity to create virtual facts. Lawyers, like scientists, do not work directly on reality but construct rationalized models of this reality, and it is these models that become the "objects" of legal discourse. (Samuel 2004, 74)

12. Bankruptcy Law Article 59 reads, in relevant part, "If the bankrupt and the other party have not yet both completed performance of a bilateral contract at the time of adjudication of bankruptcy, the administrator in bankruptcy may, at his option, either rescind the contract, or perform [the] obligations of the bankrupt [party] and demand of the other party performance of obligations."

13. The opinion cites as important authority a Supreme Court judgment holding that when a debtor goes bankrupt while still owing the creditor debts that have not yet reached maturity, the creditor's rights are entitled to priority. See *State v. Shinwa Bank* 1970 . Shindo likewise disposes of authority that runs counter to his argument by distinguishing it on the facts and the law. For example, in a 1982 Supreme Court case, a party applying for reorganization was in possession of a machine purchased from another company on installment. The seller of the machine demanded that the installment contract be canceled and the machine be returned. The Court ruled that to do so would frustrate the company's

intention to reorganize. See *Shintoa Koeki vs. The Trustee of Tanaka Tekkin* (1982). Shindo disposes of the case by arguing that the 1982 judgment concerned rights to collateral, not off-setting (1996a, 153).

14. Cf. Dezalay and Garth (1996, 34–40), who apply Pierre Bourdieu's understanding of analytical positions as the outcomes of "palace wars" within a social "field." Dezalay and Garth's account of a struggle between the "Grand Old Men" of international arbitration and the "Technocrats"—their young disciples who seek to overturn them through their commitment to more formalized procedures and their affinity for the Anglo-American legal culture, closely parallels the struggles over formalism described here.

15. ISDA's model netting act is in turn modeled on New York banking law (Cunningham and Werlen 1996).

16. According to the ordinance later issued by those ministries, transactions covered by the netting law included "OTC derivatives transactions and the leasing of money or securities as collateral for these transactions"; "financial derivatives transactions and transactions in collateral for those transactions"; "the leasing of securities and transactions in collateral related to those transactions"; options on securities; and "transactions in foreign exchange futures and collateral related to those transactions" (Ministerial Ordinance on Netting Law 1998).

17. These are banks, long-term trust banks, securities firms, and foreign securities firms. Absent from this list, or from the text of the law, were foreign banks. In an opinion letter to the British Bankers Association, Mr. Wani took the view that Japanese branches of foreign banks were covered by the law and that in cases in which the foreign financial institution's counterparty is a Japanese financial institution, the netting law could be invoked by both sides. However, in other cases, he argued that foreign banks could not count on the netting law and would need to continue to rely on the Shindo opinions. Industry representatives involved in lobbying efforts surrounding the netting law suggested to me that the effect of this regulation was to incentivize foreign financial institutions that wished to sell derivatives products to nonfinancial institutions such as corporations or private parties to do so through a Japanese financial institution.

18. "When a reason for close-out netting arises for one party engaged in a specified financial transaction according to the master agreement, regardless of the intentions of the parties concerned, at the time of the occurrence of the reason for close-out netting, for all specified financial transactions engaged in according to the relevant master agreement, a valuation of each specified transaction is made, and each value is added up, and the total becomes one single entitlement or obligation."

The separate Cabinet Order concerning close-out netting initially listed the other relevant financial institutions as insurance companies or foreign insurance companies, credit cooperatives, the Central Bank for Agriculture and Forestry, the Shoko Chukin Bank, securities financing companies, and nonbank lending institutions (Office of the Prime Minister and Ministry of Finance 1998) .

19. Article 2-4 states that "reasons for close out netting (*ikkatsu seisan jiyu*)" are applications for "bankruptcy or the beginning of company reorganization procedures."

20. These clauses refer to the "property or entitlements of the bankruptcy estate" as specified in the Bankruptcy Law (1922) and "property or entitlements of the public company or cooperative financial institution at the time of commencing reorganization" as specified in the Company Reorganization Law (1952) and the Special Treatment of Financial Institutions Law (1996). A "cooperative financial institution" is defined as a credit cooperative association, credit union, or labor credit association in Article 2-2 of the Special Treatment of Financial Institutions Law.

21. A new insolvency law for financial institutions allowed the government to nationalize banks and to inject cash into failing banks (Financial Institutions Rehabilitation Law 1998). See also Hattori and Henderson 1983, chap. 11, p. 3.

22. In most cases, counterparties had anticipated LTCB's possible failure or nationalization and therefore had protected themselves with acceleration clauses and by collateralizing obligations.

23. Ronald Dore (1999, 71) reports a similar attitude surrounding the government's effort to crack down on manipulation in the futures markets in January 1998:

> This brought forth a resounding denunciation from the Democratic Party questioning the government's true commitment to freedom and openness: "against the world trend toward open market reform," the "real problem is lack of transparency and blockage of information reduces foreigners' faith in our markets." The party's resort to "what will the foreigners think?" arguments is a clear indication of how far Japanese opinion is in the grip of the reigning ideology of the international financial community.

24. As I have suggested in an earlier project, many aspects of international human rights law, and of the transnational issue networks that advocate for human rights, share something of the same quality (Riles 2000).

25. He notes that this argument raises problems about how to deal with multiple transactions, for example (Shindo et al. 1994).

26. In invoking the notion of lawyer as translator, Shindo appeals to an old professional metaphor (e.g., Cunningham 1992).

27. As Mitchel Lasser has argued (2004) the claim that civilian legal reason-

ing is not transparent belies a lack of appreciation for the way legitimacy is con-structed and politics is revealed in the "discursive sphere" of lawyers, jurists, and academics among whom such arguments are intended to circulate .

28. What the legal fictions of international economic law foreground in Han-noun's terms are not economic "realities" but the effects of legal practice ("effets de la pratique") (1995, 93).

From Design to Technique in Global Financial Governance

This book aims to democratize the practice of global financial regulation by making it at once *more technical* and *more political*. Unlike most of the policy and academic debate, which is framed for an audience of bureaucrats, legislators and their advisors in the think tanks, the academy, and the world of lobbyists, this book begins from the assumption that finance's many publics—from consumers to traders to regulators—can and must be brought into the political debate at a sophisticated level, the kind of level that defines conversation among self-styled insiders. It seeks to engage a broader audience about the very aspect of financial regulatory practice that is usually seen as inaccessible to outsiders—its technical quality. Indeed, the central argument of the book is that the technicalities of regulation are its core element. And if this is so, then to eliminate the technicalities from popular debate is to subtly cut the broader public out of the conversation.

At the same time, to begin a wider conversation about global financial governance through legal technicalities is finally to see legal technicalities as not simply "mere" technicalities—but as profoundly political practices. If technicalities are at the core of regulatory practice, then they must be understood as political moves, with broad constituencies and consequences. The point of the book, then, is to broaden the political debate about global financial regulation not by rendering it less technical, but by placing the technicalities in their appropriate frame—a larger political and theoretical conversation about markets and about democracy.

The argument of the book is that, viewed from this perspective, financial governance does not just happen in legislatures and bureaucracies.

Indeed, it does not mainly happen there. When we put the technical aspects of regulatory practice at the center of the analysis, as market insiders do, we come to see that many more kinds of agents—from financiers to back-office administrative staff to ordinary retail investors, and including even computer programs and legal documents—are indispensable agents of market governance. This book is not just for the policymakers and their advisors, therefore. It is aimed at all of us who govern the market by being involved in it every day.

The previous chapters have presented many new frames for thinking about markets and new ideas for thinking about what regulation is and what it should be. But they have also asked the reader to think about the larger political, social, and ethical implications of the current financial crisis. They have been about finance and its regulation, but they have always also been about something larger. The larger concern of the book has been how to use the present moment of crisis, and the broad reflection about current practices it has spawned around the globe, in order to imagine an alternative kind of politics that is not utopian, but rather that begins from where we are now. Imagining alternative "knowledge practices," as I call them, requires beginning from existing knowledge practices. And that in turn requires understanding what existing technical knowledge does, what it achieves, and what latent possibilities it might hold. This book is meant as a work of legal and political theory, then, but it is theory through the material, because this is what the moment demands (Mitchell 2002, 8).

I have traced the practices surrounding the governance of the global financial markets through one motif—the uses of collateral. In one sense it is only an example, a core theme in day-to-day regulatory practice as I observed it in fieldwork. But its ubiquity in the market points to the way that it is not just any example. Collateral, at the nexus of the law of property and contract, is the paradigmatic private regulatory device, and yet it is also the subject of numerous forms of state regulation. Hence it provides a unique vantage point on the tug-of-wars over private versus public governance of the markets. Moreover collateral is, by its very terms, "collateral," on the sidelines of financial activity, somewhat under the radar screen. And yet the markets cannot exist without it. In this respect it is paradigmatic of the way law operates in the market. But it is also paradigmatic of a class of low-profile, mundane, but indispensable activities and practices that are too often ignored as we think about how markets should work and how they should be governed. Collateral and similar devices are not marginal. Rather, they are core sites of the techniques and politics of global financial governance.

An Alternative to New Architecture Talk

Everywhere one turns today one hears calls for the creation of a "New Financial Architecture" (Crotty and Epstein 2008; Eichengreen 2009; Stiglitz 2009; World Economic Forum 2009). Along with these calls comes a parallel focus on "Institutional Design." The idea here is that to be a reformist is to be an architect and a designer, someone who creates something bold and new, from the ground up. Indeed, so ubiquitous is the call for new architecture that it often seems that there are only two positions in the current regulatory debate—either you are an architect or you are an apologist for the financial industry, someone who just wants to squander the opportunity for reform in favor of entrenched interests and the status quo (Kahneman, Knetsch, and Thaler, 1991). This simple opposition of architecture to intransigence is spurred by the financial industry itself, which has so far largely responded to all regulatory proposals by throwing up standard and stale arguments against any form of regulation as, alternatively, impeding financial innovation, or creating national regulatory differences that will only push the financial markets off-shore (e.g., Larsen 2009).

However, given the significance of the reform of the regulation of the global derivatives markets, and given the sheer number of individuals and institutions now devoting themselves to thinking about how to reform global financial governance, the range of policy proposals generated to date is remarkably narrow. There are proposals to standardize derivatives contracts as much as possible and to trade standardized contracts on an organized exchange (Burns 2010; Lynch and Ng 2009), countered by proposals from the financial industry to clear standardized contracts through a private clearinghouse (*New York Times* 2009). There are proposals to ensure that more information is available about the capitalization of institutions engaged in derivatives trading so that market participants can have greater confidence that their swap partners can meet their obligations—ranging from reducing reliance on private rating agencies (Partnoy 2008a) to requiring better disclosure about swap positions and capitalization to government regulators. There are proposals to bring the activities of derivatives traders into existing regulatory frameworks, including, in the United States, granting the Federal Reserve or some other regulatory body greater authority to investigate fraudulent activity, treating certain swaps as securities subject to securities regulation (Scannell and Ng 2008), or treating certain swaps as insurance, subject to insurance regulation (Van Duyn, Chung, and Scholtes 2008). There are calls to break up institutions that are "too big to fail" tempered by calls to create "wind down plans" for such institutions. There are calls for banning certain categories of derivatives altogether (Soros 2009; see also Van Duyn 2009). Finally, there are proposals from the industry, led by the International Swaps and Derivatives Association, to create new private "protocols" for addressing defaults (Sakoui, Mackenzie, and Bullock 2009).

What the two sides in this debate—the architects and the industry apologists—share is a remarkably simple view of the divide between public and private governance, between regulation and deregulation. In this view, either you bring derivatives into the ambit of state regulation, or you don't. They disagree, of course, as to which side they are on, but they are clear that there are two sides. In contrast, much current research in legal studies, economic sociology (e.g., Eisner 2009), anthropology (Das and Poole 2004; Dunn 2008; Ferguson and Gupta 2002; Ong and Collier 2005; Roitman 2004b; Sharma and Gupta 2006) and cognate fields suggests that such a simple divide between the market and the regulatory state—between public and private governance—is far too crude to be truly helpful for thinking through regulatory options.

It is clear, then, that we need a new vocabulary for thinking about governance and markets, one that moves beyond the battles over public and private. Building on anthropological research into the nature of states and markets, one of the contributions of this book has been to present a more sophisticated and nuanced view of public and private governance, and ultimately to present a fresh set of conceptual categories derived from my observations of day-to-day market governance that do not owe their allegiance to the public/private genealogy whatsoever.

By now the criticisms of industry insiders have been well developed in the academic and journalistic literature (Akerlof and Shiller 2009; Partnoy 2008b; Tett 2009). Since I don't largely dispute these criticisms, let me focus instead on the current fascination with financial regulatory design and the construction of a new regulatory architecture. Chapters 2, 3, and 4 described what I termed "technocratic knowledge"—the kind of thought that has defined regulatory practice in the twentieth century. Although I was sympathetic to the political ambitions of many technocratic projects, I argued, based on my own ethnographic research as well as the research of many other anthropologists working in diverse regulatory contexts around the world, that technocratic knowledge ultimately faces certain limits and can in fact have serious unintended consequences.

The objects and clients of regulatory designs have a way of disrupting the best of technocratic plans; they don't live and act, in practice, as the architects of regulatory systems often think they can make them do (Boyer 1983, 9–32). It is simply an empirical reality that with every proposal to build a new clean system for derivatives trading there is already talk among market participants about how one would get around such a system. For example, as I am finishing this text, the *Financial Times* reports that Goldman Sachs and other investment banks are already marketing financial products that will allow banks to get around the higher capital adequacy rules for banks proposed by the G20 by converting one class of assets into another for bookkeeping purposes (Guerrera and Sender 2010). Although it is tempting to suggest that this is simply the problem with finance, that market participants cannot be trusted as worthy partners in the regulatory process because of this mindset, research on technocracies of various kinds tells similar stories of what happens when the subjects of regulation are set apart from regulatory design.[1]

This leads me to introduce a note of caution that may not meet with enthusiasm from progressive reformer colleagues. Simply put, new architectures historically have never worked at the level of design. Where regulatory reforms have succeeded, it has been because, in one way or another, they enroll the targets or clients of regulation in the regulatory mission and encourage them to take responsibility for the regulatory problem. Architectures do not build themselves.

Furthermore, new architectures reflect the necessarily limited understanding and biases of the architects, who may not appreciate all that is valuable about existing practices. We may look back one day on certain aspects of existing market practices with regret that we allowed their well-intended destruction. Now, I realize that to say this is to risk being misunderstood as supporting market participants' own self-serving intransigence. But the fact that finance is a world of privilege, wealth, and power, and of course the fact that the consequences of the financial crisis have been felt so deeply and broadly in our societies may have deadened our usual common sense about the possible collateral damage of regulatory initiatives. Of course, valuing what works in existing market practices does not mean devaluing the seriousness of the problems or condoning abusive, short-sighted, or unscrupulous practices. The choice is not simply new architecture or unfettered laissez-faire. Rather, *good* design (that is, workable design) requires active collaboration with its targets, however unpopular or distasteful such collaboration may be, in order to be effective in the long run (Healey 1997). It should work organically with the practices already in place, as the building blocks of—not a new, but a transformed architecture (Buntrock 2002; Ellin 2006).

From this point of view, the problem with the current focus on institutional design and the creation of new architectures of financial regulation is that they suffer from the paternalist tendency of technocratic thought—the tendency to imagine oneself, the designer, as somehow outside and above the grand architecture one is creating. In this view, market participants become targets of intervention (Cohen 2008, 506), not collaborators. The result is both the instantiation of the biases and bounded rationality of regulators, and also the intransigence and lack of buy-in of market participants.

So this book argues that it is time to stop thinking solely in terms of new architectures and institutional design. We need to abandon the idea of policymakers as a separate class of designers, apart from the market, in favor of a more modest and participatory understanding of governance as knowledge practice. That is, what we principally need is not a new architecture but a new way of thinking through existing techniques for governing the market, and a full appreciation of their potentialities.

Legal Techniques

In contrast, when one begins ethnographically, from day-to-day practice in the market, a number of strange artifacts that have nothing at all to do with current regulatory debates—placeholders, documents, theories, dreams, fictions, analogies, and many others described in the previous chapters—surface as central terms, core elements of financial governance. So what are these artifacts? I call them *techniques*—fundamentally legal techniques—that is, means, not ends. And I argue that the essence of private governance is governance according to such techniques, and associated epistemological, ethical, and political commitments. For the most part, unlike grand regulatory designs and policies, these techniques deflect attention rather than drawing attention to themselves. They work under the radar, albeit in plain view for anyone who bothers to observe day-to-day practice. Their uses by private parties with particular interests and political agendas should not blind us to the fact that these techniques are means, not ends—they are not inherently tethered to any particular policy outcome or political point of view.

The centrality of these techniques in global governance admittedly runs counter to the ideological claims legal elites often make about the nature of legal expertise. Modern lawyers, in both the private and public worlds, like to think of themselves as dedicated to particular ends— whether those are the grand ends of justice, efficiency, and democracy, or just improving the bottom line for one's clients. In this ideological view, legal technique is really just *collateral* to the more important political and economic decisions happening elsewhere. But the materials in the previous chapters demonstrate how the ends often fade in the background, while the means assume center stage in the "meantime" of practical day-to-day governance (Vaihinger 2001). It is the means—how to structure a good legal argument, how to draft a statute—that inspired, motivated, and created conflicts among many of the people I have described. This is true even as they dutifully rehearsed the ends all their activity could be understood to serve (chapter 2).

This deceptively simple cultural reality deserves a bit more attention. The notion of law as tool assumes that the user of the tool is completely in control of the purpose, process, and outcome of the tool's use. It assumes that the legal tool is really nothing but collateral knowledge, on the way to achieving certain stated objectives, defined in other terms. But legal tools, as I have described them, are more interesting than this. They sometimes, mysteriously, overtake their users (Latour 2002a). And the "users" (perhaps we dare say "collaborators with") such tools are neither completely aware, nor completely unaware, of the agency of "their" tools. Again, it is one of those collateral realities that lies under the radar, and yet in plain view for all to see. It is not simply that the means sometimes define the ends and vice versa (Dewey 1998; Dorf and Sabel 1998, 284–85). Rather, we are dealing with something more mysterious and profound: in the "meantime," the means often occlude the ends and overtake the instrument's user. There are intriguing political possibilities in this too-often-unacknowledged technical reality.

When we rethink private governance, it is this technique, in all its practical, theoretical, and political possibilities, we should be thinking about, I want to suggest. Doing so gives us a new set of metaphors for understanding regulation and deregulation, and it directs our attention to a different set of aspects or dimension of regulatory practice. As I have described them throughout the book, the core aspects of private governance that deserve practical and theoretical attention are its *epistemology*—the kinds of subtle claims private law makes about what is true, what is real, for whom and in what conditions; its *aesthetics*—the variety of forms private law techniques can take, from sets of mutually reinforcing analogies to empty cores of statutory form without content (chapter 5) and many more; its *materiality*—the way legal theories, policies and arguments become reified or objectified in documentary practices, and the institutional relations such documents may set in motion; and its *virtual sociality*—the way legal technique enables thin but nevertheless robust sociotechnical relations among individuals and machines in different institutions, cities and countries, and the way it enables comparisons and translations among jurisdictions—how, for example, it becomes possible for central bankers from around the world to meet at a conference, discuss regulatory policy for a weekend, and understand one another to be talking about much the same thing.[2]

Understanding private governance as a practice of legal technique is important for progressive regulatory projects in part because it finally and definitively demystifies the private. Many current proposals for regulatory design propose various kinds of partnerships between public and private entities in the governance project, in order to move from "command and control" to "coordinated regulation" (Braithwaite 2002) and to encourage market participants to collaborate better with one another and with regulators (Benkler 2009; Schneiberg and Bartley 2008). These projects usefully emphasize that public and private need not be seen as in opposition, that there are many more possibilities than simply public or private forms of regulation, many hybrids of the two. However, there is a certain implicit defensiveness to these efforts to hybridize public and private; they are often presented as a response to the Hayekian critiques of planning discussed in chapter 4 (e.g., Braithwaite 1999, 90) and to the public choice critiques of bureaucratic accountability discussed in chapter 3 (e.g., Dorf and Sabel 1998, 273). In the process of responding to these critiques with new regulatory designs, these approaches unwittingly buy into a certain Hayekian mystique of the private—a sense that it is important to involve private actors in regulation because there is something about human motivation in the private sphere that is fundamentally different and often superior. The power of private regulation, in this view, is that it is fundamentally founded in the self-interest of private actors. Hence the only means of improving public sector regulation is by imitating private sector management practices and their incentive structures (Harrington and Turem 2006). In contrast, the argument of this book is that it is not human motivation that is fundamentally different in the private sphere. Rather, what differentiates private governance is the fact that legal technique has been the primary mechanism of such governance.

I am aware that for the mainstream of legal theory, which is aimed primarily at a technocratically oriented bureaucracy and judiciary, a focus on legal technicality as the core of governance and as something to be celebrated and redeployed on other terrains is profoundly odd, if not politically suspect. For a century, legal technicality has been an epithet in the law, something to be destroyed, swept away, cleansed from the system. Indeed, the sheer staying power of legal technicalities, in the face of this century of assault, might give us some indication of their robust and consequential nature.

This distrust of legal form, and its preference instead for legal informality, has made a strong imprint on policymaking—so strong that it is hard for us to imagine market governance in other terms. As discussed in chapters 2 and 3, technocratic knowledge often makes sophisticated use of legal expertise, but its attitude toward legal technique is ultimately one of denigration. In the technocratic mindset, legal knowledge is rigid, inflexible, antiparticipatory, and old-fashioned. As Schneiberg and Bartley summarize the view,

> the interest in soft law also derives from concerns about rigidity and legalism in American regulation. Going by the book and applying fixed and universal environmental standards to industries of heterogeneous firms was, by this account, an exercise doomed to inefficiency. (2008, 47)

This is where the now-fashionable focus on regulatory design and new architectures comes in. Design is perceived as innovative precisely because it mixes legal technique with tools from the social sciences and policy studies into a style of regulation that is purposely not purely legal.

In conversations with colleagues I have come to realize that it is not technicality as such that bothers many mainstream legal theorists, social scientists, and policymakers. Most of all, it is the very fictional quality of the technicality. The fact that it openly flaunts empiricist mantras that law should be in touch with and reflect "reality" seems both unserious and dangerous at once. In responses to the current financial crisis, once again, we hear that the fictional quality of finance and its regulation is ultimately the problem.

But what if we were to accept that fiction is at the core of market practice—indeed at the core of human interaction? This would require a very different kind of social science and a very different kind of political and legal strategy. It would require abandoning the caricatured and derogatory view of legal technique, embracing its epistemological and aesthetic sophistication, and its practical and theoretical importance (see also Knop, Michaels, and Riles 2009). As I have suggested throughout this book, there is nothing inherently private about legal technique, nothing to stop regulators, judges, politicians, and other agents of the state from harnessing its power. It is just that in the modern era, the technocrats have controlled our public institutions, and as a result legal technique has been devalued in state regulatory practice. It need not be so in the future.

So the larger point here is that we need to give far more attention to the *form* of regulation, and not simply its content. In particular, we need more attention to legal form, legal technique. In existing policy debates, the proposals are all proposals about the content of regulations—should derivatives be traded on an exchange or not? Should banks have to report their trades or not? Who should have authority to set rules—local authorities, national authorities, transnational authorities? But there are many different forms the same regulatory proposal could take. In chapter 5, for example, we followed an intense internal debate in Japan about what form a given reform should take—should it take the form of a statute or a legal interpretation of existing law? Too often, regulatory form is treated as an afterthought—something to be left to lower-tier implementers, or even to market participants themselves.

A New Approach to Market Governance

In sum, this book shares the ambition of many current proposals to make financial regulation more stable, effective, and democratic. But where most current proposals for reforming financial regulation aim to achieve this by making regulation more informal, in contrast, I suggest that financial regulation might become more just and efficient if it redeployed legal formality in particular ways. By legal formality I do not mean rigid rules set by legislatures or regulatory agencies. Rather, in the previous chapters I have drawn attention to legal techniques, tricks of the formal legal trade, deployed thousands of times a day by ordinary actors in the financial market that together add up to regulatory governance from the ground up. Ultimately, it is always these techniques that stabilize markets, and top-down rules and designs—formal or informal—are only mechanisms for encouraging legal practice on the ground. A securities law requiring certain kinds of filings, for example, ultimately works by encouraging a myriad acts of self-accounting by an army of professionals trained into the production of the specific documents mandated by the filing requirements of securities law and the practical tools and ways of doing things that have grown up around these requirements.

The previous chapters give a number of real-world examples of how such techniques and practices can be and are in fact deployed, drawn from extensive fieldwork in the practical governance of the financial markets. I will mention only three here.

Compliance

In chapter 1 I focused on the material practices of document production and exchange that are the unnoticed core of ISDA's private governance regime. Commentators have begun to pay particular attention to the consequences of standardized contracts such as the ISDA documents for the authority, legitimacy, and power of law in a global market.[3] We saw that these material practices are culturally and socially "thin"— they do not depend upon thick social networks or deep relations of trust. The material practices surrounding collateral relations script a different kind of global collaborative project in which social relations and informational complexity are rendered largely superfluous. From this point of view, one proposal would be to expand these practices, and to consider how else they might be used, and for what other purposes, beyond those envisioned by the derivatives industry itself.

So how might a policymaker do this practice? As an example, let's take the problem of compliance. At its root, every regulatory problem comes down to a problem of compliance: how to get people in the market—the clients, or targets of regulation—to conform to a certain regulatory agenda. To take some examples from recent headlines: how to get traders, bankers, and shareholders to think in terms of longer-time horizons as they assess the costs and benefits of their actions, rather than focusing on making short-term gains that might have disastrous longer-term consequences? Or, how to make individual market participants more aware of, and willing to take into account the systemic consequences of their actions—to realize that the market is a kind of public good whose strength and vitality is in everyone's wider self-interest? Or, in formulating new rules, say, for the capital adequacy of banks involved in derivatives trading, how to encourage market participants to bring their conduct into line with the spirit and purpose of the regulation, rather than seeking loopholes or other ways of circumventing the regulation through financial engineering? All this is what we mean by compliance—how do we get people to bring their conduct into line? The key word here, of course, is *people*: markets are made up of people, social actors within institutions, and all regulation has as its ultimate goal to change the actions of real people. Ultimately, it is only the ordinary, mundane, day-to-day acts of market participants that can make markets more stable, efficient, and just. The entire efforts of regulation are only means to this end, tools for changing what market participants do—whether it is the behavior of traders or the behavior of consumers or anyone in between.

Now despite the fact that compliance is at the heart of all regulatory projects, remarkably, it is hardly discussed at all. Most discussion of current financial regulatory reform, as of other regulatory projects, focuses rather on the content of regulation. It is as if we naively assume that policies will be enforced, obeyed, and implemented, and in predictable, transparent ways—even though one of the key lessons of the recent financial crisis surely should have been that this could not be further from the truth.

In a recent Brookings Institution paper, Kent Weaver outlined the state of the art in thinking about compliance: policymakers, he argues, have basically three options at their disposal. They can admonish market participants to behave in a certain way (think of President Obama's speech on Wall Street urging financial industry executives to act responsibly); they can incentivize them (think of proposals to put limits on bonuses, or to institute "claw-back provisions" that would reduce bonuses if it turned out they were earned because of short-term gains that ultimately turned into long-term losses); and they can prohibit or require certain conduct (think of proposals to require certain levels of capitalization before banks can engage in derivatives trading, or again of certain duty-of-care standards for fund managers that create private causes of action *ex post*). As Weaver points out, the utility of these options turns, ultimately, on one's theory of what motivates human behavior. And here, the standard has long been the rational actor model. The assumption has been that market participants rationally pursue their own self-interest. If this is true, then policymakers should be able to influence market participants' behavior by creating policies that bring individual self-interest into line with policy interests. Proposals to place a cap on traders' bonuses, for example, reflect the rational actor model's assumption that when it is no longer in traders' individual pecuniary interest to take unduly risky positions they will cease to do so.

Weaver further points out that a more recent view of human nature—the so-called behavioral economics model—qualifies the rational actor in two ways. First, it fills out the rational actor model with an account of where preferences (long taken as extraneous to economic analysis) come from. Second, it critiques the rational actor model by pointing out cognitive sources of bias. The implication of this is that incentives may not work as well as the rational actor model assumes. As Cass Sunstein and Richard Thaler have suggested in their book *Nudge* (2009), the implication is that policymakers can and should structure choices in order to skew preferences toward optimal outcomes. Another implication is that if incentives do not work so well, government may need to do more prohibiting and requiring.

This is the state of the art on compliance. And yet, from the point of view of what we have learned in this book, it is a breathtakingly crude, impressionistic, abstract, even conjectural account of the most crucial aspect of policymaking—the question of how any regulatory change actually translates into real change in the market. What is left out is all the complexity of the regulatory process, of the relationship between public and private actors, institutions, individuals, documents, ways of thinking, ways of identifying, that policies must go through on their way to becoming "compliance." That is, solutions like limits on bonuses are not wrong—they are just very crude beginnings. There are so many more possibilities, many more subtle possibilities, that regulators could have at their disposal.

Indeed, from the point of view of the most sophisticated regulators I had the privilege of shadowing for this study, the problem with the existing options—admonish, incentivize, prohibit, or require—is that they are not nearly ambitious enough because they tackle one behavioral change, one incentive or prohibition at a time. The greater ambition, rather, should be to fundamentally change the culture of financial practice, to create a world in which actors of their own will, indeed before even being admonished, incentivized, pushed or prodded by regulators, make socially optimal choices, the very choices regulators would enshrine in regulation. The goal is to enroll actors in the regulator's way of thinking about the market. This is the greater meaning of "internalizing the costs of one's behavior." When market participants take on the goals and values of the regulator, governance takes far less political capital. Market participants already choose to do what is best, without being monitored at every turn.

Sounds too good to be true? In fact, we already have examples of this approach to governance at work. Doug Holmes's ethnography of central bankers' uses of policy statements (Holmes 2009), for example, demonstrates that the purpose of these statements is to change market behavior in just this way. Another example is the use of reporting requirements in regulation. Reporting requirement are not simply ways of getting information—they are means of structuring an internal conversation within an institution that can lead to rethinking policies and perhaps internal change. For example, Holmes describes how the Central Bank of New Zealand's innovative requirement that market participants submit their own wind-up plans aims at encouraging an internal conversation within financial institutions about their own fallibility.

Another example of how this might be done involves operationalizing existing social relations in the market, as regulators do in Japan. This book has highlighted the tremendous achievements that can come from professional relationships between individual regulators and back office staff, relationships framed around shared legal expertise, and the social connections, such as shared alma maters, shared research interests and shared social networks, that come with this expertise. Now, at first, this seems nonsensical: is it not the job of the ethical regulator to keep a certain personal distance from market participants? But as we saw, Japanese government regulators were nevertheless skilled at working with lawyers in the market—whether in private law firms or in the back office of financial institutions—to effectuate change. Through joint study groups, research fellowships within government institutions, and informal social contacts, regulators turned these individuals into collaborators, in the best sense of the term. The principle here is simple: prestige is a form of social capital, and receiving a prestigious government fellowship, or participating in a selective study group, matters to lawyers in the market just as much as it matters to anyone else. Most of these individuals, as we saw, were just like everyone else in one other sense: they longed to make a difference, to have a career that had some wider meaning. Indeed, many of my back-office informants sought to tell the story of their career to an outsider like myself in just such terms—as the story of someone who championed reform as much as possible, patiently, from the inside. When these individuals begin to see a wider role they can play in encouraging market reform from the inside, they can become effective advocates and collaborators—skilled navigators of internal institutional politics, expert evaluators of where change is most required and how it might best be achieved.

How else might we encourage compliance? The core insight of this book is that there are aspects of private regulatory governance that work, that can be emulated and appropriated by governments for the benefit of wider interests, and that can provide new kinds of levers of government intervention, new possibilities for public-private collaboration. In particular, the legal dimensions of markets—the aspects of market practice that deploy legal expertise—have proven to have a vitality and a solidity that deserve greater attention, even when there is very little actual threat of sanction, public or private, to back up particular norms and practices. Why is this so? As we saw, legal expertise is a kind of world unto itself, a set of institutional and expert practices that add up to their own boot-strapped reality. The experts that tend to these practices have a deep commitment to them—in essence, their expert identities depend on them—and they stick with them even when the rational actor model tells us they should not. This was the case with collateral calls in the recent financial crisis when, rather than abandon their legal obligations, institutions (that is, the people within those institutions) stuck with those legal obligations to the bitter end (even as they disputed valuation and other financial aspects of these same deals).

In particular, we saw that documents, and committees, and protocols, and all the other mundane aspects of international private governance really do matter. In failing fully to appreciate this, the architects of regulatory reform are missing a golden opportunity for intervention. Current regulatory proposals coming out of national governments focus on such things as the amount of collateral that banks will be required to post to trade, but they often leave the procedures for posting, the documents to be produced, the kinds of expertise and training required of back-office staff and all the rest to the private sector. And yet, as we have seen in this book, this is really where much of the action is.[4] Indeed, the materials in the previous chapters suggest that regulators should go beyond narrowly envisioning collateral, netting, and the like as fuse boxes—ways of ensuring that when disaster strikes it will be contained—and instead recognize the role of such practices as what I have termed "private constitutions," that is, building blocks of the kind of cultural change I alluded to above. I have shown in the previous chapters how this is exactly the role these practices have played for private governance to date.

For example, if the goal of policy is to encourage private actors to monitor one another more closely so that the market as a whole takes appropriate corrective action in response to unexpected events, then regulators might want to work more closely with private organizations such as ISDA to produce different kinds of protocols surrounding valuation and margin calls. Or if the goal is to ensure that banks, securities firms, and hedge funds have more sophisticated wind-down plans, then one could imagine working with ISDA and other such organizations to require parties to specify more detailed and concrete scenarios for privately handling a variety of different default situations, beyond the current contractual terms that simply give the parties the ultimate right to rescind the agreement in certain conditions of default without specifying what they might actually do when faced with such a situation.

Some sectors of the financial industry might object that these are private contracts and that government should not interfere in their revision. But recall that as a result of ISDA's own intensive lobbying efforts, ISDA documents are ultimately rendered enforceable in many jurisdictions through legislation—whether it is amendments to U.S. bankruptcy law or the creation of a new Japanese netting law. To date, the industry has lobbied for these very dramatic delegations of state power to its own private regulatory system with little input from other interest groups, despite the substantial distributive implications of these laws. It is reasonable to expect that in exchange for such a large delegation of state power to a private authority, the state would in turn receive a commitment to certain kinds of private governance procedures.

But from my own interviews with back office staff and ISDA leaders in Japan, at least, I suspect that after perhaps some initial ideological push-back the industry might ultimately welcome this kind of public-private collaboration. Because ISDA's own procedures in default situations specify little else than the rights of the parties to exercise what one informant called "the nuclear option"—abandonment of the agreement. In practice, such an option is rarely in anyone's interest, and it might be quite helpful to have, ready at hand, a range of more delicate and diverse possibilities that are familiar to all involved in advance for renegotiating and winding down.

Glitches in the System

In light of all of the talk of the fluidity of global capital, and the notion that one of the problems facing modern financial regulation is the speed of circulation of capital, I have sought to call attention to how different this activity often looks from the inside. We saw that rather than fluid connections, markets often were experienced as a world of endless disconnects—the quantitative people don't understand the legal people, Bank A has a different culture than Bank B, the computer systems can't be synchronized because they are set to different time zones, the document doesn't get filed because employee X was out for the day, and so on. And rather than a world of instantaneous trading, of the excessive compression of time and space (Scheuerman 2004, 107), the problem of derivatives was precisely the sense of an expanded present, the "meantime" between the opening and closing out of positions in which one lives with uncertainty and risk. These are not simply descriptive corrections to the dominant understanding of market governance—they have implications for governance practice. For example, Marc Schneiberg has recently argued that one core problem facing financial regulation is the problem of "tightly coupled systems" in which a problem in one area of the markets quickly spreads to others. In response, he proposes regulatory design aimed at inserting "stopgaps in the system," in essence to slow down the speed with which problems might spread.

Many commentators have suggested that the recent financial crisis was precipitated by a "herd mentality" in which decisions, too often made in an instant rather than with adequate reflection, often come down to copying what others are doing. This is a bad thing for several reasons. It is bad if one believes that the strength of markets depend on the existence of diversity—a diversity of products and approaches. It is also bad because it suggests an absence of rational judgment. Now, from this point of view, ironically, glitches in the system can be a good thing: when people in one unit must consult with people in another unit, rather than relying merely on seamless electronic communication, they also must take time to explain their initiatives and the rationales behind them. Such a small glitch may be frustrating to people on the inside; it may feel like a waste of time. But sometimes, slowing down makes room to think (Miyazaki n.d.). And sometimes the questions of uninitiated outsiders, such as back-office staff who do not understand the all the financial details and don't belong to the social world of financial traders, can provoke fundamental opportunities for rethinking—why *do* we do things this way?

One insight of my fieldwork is that there are already many such glitches or stopgaps in current practice. Building on Schneiberg's suggestion, then, it would be possible to scan the range of existing practices to find points at which the system does get tripped up, become redundant, or otherwise disconnected. Glitches—points at which the expertise does not match up perfectly, at which the technologies create speed-bumps in the road—might be seen as sources of regulatory opportunity. They might be exploited as organic, indigenous firewalls of a sort, not embarrassing failures. Perhaps before we redesign the regulatory system to introduce such redundancies and stopgaps, we might be interested in working with the robust ones that have already developed *sui generis* within it.

Placeholders

Another example of the possible uses of legal technicalities in market governance is what I term the "placeholder" (chapter 4). As we saw, lawyers in the financial markets routinely make use of certain working fictions, or placeholders, to govern relations in the near future among market participants. These placeholders are provisional agreed truths— Party X has certain rights vis a vis Party Y, *for the moment*, until it turns out not to be case that Party X has such rights, for whatever factual or legal reasons. I showed how, contrary to the stereotypes of legal formalism, these working fictions perform a highly sophisticated and subtle epistemological, political, aesthetic, and ethical stance.

I have argued that such placeholders—and we explored many different versions and types deployed by both private and public actors—are key mechanisms by which real-world financial market participants handle the two core challenges of financial markets. These are the problem of time, and the unknowability of the future and related problems of risk on the one hand, and the problem of the political legitimacy of their governance mechanisms, ranging from the legitimacy of states to the legitimacy of international governance institutions, to the basis for trust among individual market participants on the other. Placeholders already achieve what John Braithwaite describes as one of the core goals of his institutional designs for experimental governance: "to inculcate trust while institutionalizing distrust" (1999, 92). In other words, such placeholders are already bearing a heavy quotidian burden of governance in the markets.

This then raises questions about how else such placeholders might be deployed, in the service of other regulatory agendas, by a wider range of actors. In chapter 5, I offered one example of such an application—a statute with a hollow core, in which all the key terms are left unspecified. Now, as national regulators seek to devise new forms of global financial regulation that will provide sufficient global uniformity but preserve room for diversity, and that will place real limits on certain market practice while preserving room for necessary flexibility, they might consider the form of the indexical statute as one way of achieving this. Such tools are not culturally specific precisely because they are understood by all to be nothing more than placeholders, to be fictional. They perform regulatory convergence and do not claim to do more. While some would view such a statute as a formalist sham, and others would view it as valuable only because it leaves the key terms to experimental deliberation among private and public actors, I suggested that the way such a statute signals and ultimately channels future action can itself be extremely valuable. This form of regulation has important applications in the context of transnational governance problems in which multiple jurisdictions, and constituencies with nothing but a very thin understanding of one another, must be engaged. But this is only one public application of the placeholder technique. There are many more. The first task is simply to recognize such devices and to appreciate the governance work they already do.

Responses to Possible Criticisms

Before concluding, I want to take a moment to address two principal lines of criticism that may legitimately be directed at this argument. The first is essentially a political criticism. The claim would be that I have it all backwards: legal technicalities are not foundations of governance

whose agentive power deserves our attention and analysis. Legal technicalities are rather merely the tools, among other tools, of unscrupulous
people, entrenched interests in the financial markets, individuals who
are so absorbed into free market fundamentalism that they are unable to
see how their behavior leads to massive economic instability or, worse,
are willing to undermine the long-term stability of the market as a whole
in order to make a quick buck for themselves. For example, the financial
journalist (and anthropologist) Gillian Tett (2009) has recently given us
a book-length account of the creation of ISDA as essentially the scheme
of a few greedy insiders who recognized that in order to make derivatives as profitable for themselves as possible they needed to be sure that
national governments did not interfere. From this point of view, my focus
on private governance techniques sounds like just another apology for industry business as usual. In this vein, Ed Balleisen (2009) has questioned
the euphoria surrounding private governance as partaking in a logic of
"civic republicanism" in which communities consent to their own internal governance rules. He points out that such arguments for "home rule"
have an ugly history in the American history of segregation as justifications for avoiding wider democratic accountability for local oligarchy.

The view of existing market self-regulatory organizations as simply
expedient mechanisms for avoiding government regulation is, of course,
in one respect accurate. But the previous chapters suggest that, whatever
the reasons for ISDA's original creation, by now it is no longer just the
political tool of a small group of insiders in New York and London—it
is also a constellation of durable material and institutional practices engaged in by people and institutions very far away indeed from those original insiders (Morgan 2008). Private global governance is, as I have suggested throughout this book, a routinized set of knowledge practices, a
set of techniques that enroll a wide range of political actors (Roitman
2004a). These practices are forms or pathways or scripts for thought that,
as we saw in the example of the Bank of Japan's use of legal fictions in
chapter 4, are not inherently public or private, not inherently conservative or progressive. But they are established building blocks for a transformed and yet workable financial architecture. I recognize that at this
moment the argument that there is something of value in the practices
of financial self-governance to be nurtured and redeployed will strike
many as improbable, if not preposterous. But one view of the causes of
the crisis, from the point of view of this book, is that public entities abandoned the most powerful tools of governance entirely to private-sector

insiders—that the most robust governance techniques were deployed only by one side, in the service of one set of interests.

A second possible criticism is more practical than political. Assuming that one accepts the description I have provided of how governance actually happens on a quotidian level in the financial markets, can such techniques, with names like "placeholders," "unwinding," and "empty circles," really be seriously deployed in regulatory practice? Can they truly be turned into policy proposals? Or are they simply beyond the scope of the kinds of form of action we can imagine government taking? How might one actually use the insights of this book, as a regulator, a legislator, a judge, or anyone involved in the regulatory policy process?

I have tried to address this concern in this chapter with some concrete examples of how such devices are already used in actual regulatory policy and how they might be used in the future to address problems on the horizon. But while I believe there is room for creative rethinking of regulatory design along these lines, I also want to emphasize that the most significant uses of this material may not be at the level of regulatory design at all.

In recent months, there has been much interesting discussion in academic and policy spheres about the importance of creating a robust professional regulatory culture—of creating a kind of esprit de corps among regulators, a sense of confidence and professionalism that would enable them to take on financial fraud, as for example in the early years of the Securities and Exchange Commission (Balleisen 2009; Ernst 2009). In this Weberian view of professionalism, institutions produce professional roles, and it is personal connections among regulators, and social capital (in the form of prestigious academic degrees, or the prestige of the regulatory position itself) that enables regulators to confront marketeers.

But as Weber himself recognized, institutions are really just routines for doing particular things—they are just scripted and materialized knowledge practices. Bureaucratic discipline, for example, is a practice based in the deployment of certain formal frames of thought, certain technical tools. Thus while professionalism is indeed key to governance, the notion that professionals must be people with positions in certain institutions gets it backwards. The core of any particular kind of professionalism is rather a way of thinking and acting, a set of knowledge techniques. What is interesting about legal technique in this respect is that it can be deployed by an astounding range of persons, including, in Japan, many who lack any formal professional qualification as lawyers at all

(Riles and Uchida 2009). Thus while we often think of what is "technical" as a barrier to general access, in fact, these particular technicalities are easily learned and taught, diffused and taken on by countless anonymous agents of indigenous market governance around the world.

One of the insights of this book is that the most important regulatory work—public and private—is often not at the level of policy design. Regulation also takes place in practices of enforcement, information collection and management, and bureaucratic routine. And when we broaden our scope of inquiry, we discover that legal technicalities are not simply the tools of a policy-designing class. In practice, a broad range of market participants engage in these mundane practices. Thus ultimately the audience for this project is not simply policy designers but back-office staff, regulators, market participants, academics—all of us who see ourselves as acting in the world of the market and not simply building a framework for it from the outside.

The larger message of this book is that lawyers and legal professionals of all kinds—from secretarial and paralegal staff to back-office managers to legal academics and judges and everyone in between—have a role to play in financial stability. They already occupy a strategic place in the chain of market transactions—as both insiders/advisors and as translators to wider constituencies, facilitators of transactions, and coaches for a structured form of reflection on the larger consequences of individual market activity. Legal professionals already have at their disposal the day-to-day professional tools and techniques for inserting stability into the system, one transaction, one investment decision, one disclosure at a time. This fact—and hence the special responsibilities of lawyers not so much to the ethics of the lawyer-client relationship, but to doing their part to create a more stable market "commons"—rarely gets the attention it deserves from regulators, from commentators, even from lawyers themselves.

What would market reform look like if, instead of investing all our political energies in a policy-driven search for the perfectly calibrated regulatory architecture, we focused more attention on developing and redirecting the practical legal techniques that are already contributing in practical, day-to-day ways to market stability? This is a radically different vision of market reform—one that places lawyers, back-office staff, and risk managers in private practice at the center rather than on the periphery of market stability. But if it is a radical change in perspective, it requires no new laws, no new policies, not even a change in these lawyers' existing roles. It simply requires that all of us individually take action to exploit the options and possibilities we already have, as part of our professional portfolio and repertoire, every day, to create more breathing room, more space, and hence more practical stability in the system. The tricks and techniques and strategies for this kind of legal intervention will vary from one practice to another. As such this kind of reform must be a personal project of the individual professional. At the same time, it can be comparatively instructive and motivating to think about how to go about doing this in conversation with others.

Could we think of this as a market movement, along the lines of the other movements that have traditionally been more social or political in character? In all such movements, the actual direction of progress is always unclear, and for everyone involved, ambivalence, mixed motives, and compromised interests are par for the course. Our own professional doubts about how we might "balance," for example, a desire to do well with a desire to do good, or about whether the "right" thing to do is to encourage or discourage a certain form of risk-taking on the part of clients, are not only inevitable, they are actually the engine of such a movement. In such a condition, hope comes from creating small opportunities for change, small spaces for reflection, and then letting those opportunities unfold. It involves deploying the skills and tools we already have, in the context in which we already find ourselves, in ordinary ways that reshuffle the deck just a little in order to open up opportunities for different individual and institutional choices, to create space for reflection, to make room for transformative possibilities.

Conclusion

As we ponder how to respond to the current crisis in the financial markets and their regulation, our attention is necessarily drawn first to the problems, the weaknesses, the shortcomings in existing practices. But we might also do well to pause to focus for a moment on what remains standing in financial governance when all else collapses, for this might provide a lesson about how to rebuild.

As we do this, we may have to accept that those aspects of governance that remain most robust, that is, most able to enlist participants' continued commitment, are not necessarily those that legal theory, or policy design, or sociolegal studies tell us are most important or valuable. And yet, this is where we should be looking for new ideas that are nevertheless not simply utopian dreams but are already put into practice, have already have earned the commitments of market participants. The argument of this book is that legal technique is just such an element. Precisely because it is so epistemologically subtle as a legal fiction, and yet so materially concrete as a pre-printed standardized contract, it continues to inspire, to interest, to demand commitment, and to serve as the basis for collaboration.

What I have presented in this book, then, is a different kind of project and approach to financial regulation. Rather than a new design I have sought to understand existing technique; rather than a front and center program for a new financial architecture, I have offered up collateral knowledge. That is, I have suggested that legal governance is ultimately not so much a matter of grand designs as it is a set of lived practices and techniques—techniques that are often disparaged or ignored but in fact are far more interesting, subtle, and full of transformative potential than we habitually recognize.

Ultimately, derivatives markets and their regulation are not some entirely separate and mysterious world. What the previous chapters show is that they are made up of very ordinary, mundane practices, techniques, theories, ethical positions, and subjects, very much like those found in other aspects of law and markets or indeed, of social life more broadly. Hence, ultimately, a radical rethinking of financial regulation demands— and holds out the promise of—a radical rethinking of democratic governance more broadly. This is the challenge of this moment, to forego the impulse to simply recreate out of the rubble yet another version of the same old regulatory state, or its nemesis, free market opportunism, and to appreciate the alternatives already before us that went unnoticed before.

Notes

1. Medical anthropologists studying public health policy for example repeatedly have found that in systems that assign sole responsibility for health problems to medical experts, other stakeholders are inadvertently discouraged from taking an ownership stake in finding solutions to such problems. A patient may wait for a doctor to prescribe a sophisticated and invasive form of treatment, for example, rather than to realize that only she has the psychological and emotional resources necessary to improve her condition by taking difficult quotidian measures such as quitting smoking.

2. Note that none of these four elements is unique to financial regulation. And neither in fact are the two core problems financial regulation must address, as I have described them—the problem of time and the problem of political legitimacy. Rather, these problems are at the core of all political engagement, and these elements of legal practice are relevant to the way law addresses them everywhere.

3. For example, Schmitthoff long ago identified "the contribution which standard contract forms and general conditions of business . . . can make to the unification or harmonisation of the law of international trade" (1968, 551). He emphasized the aura of "realism" about this "unifying activity" owing to the fact that the rules are created by the business community rather than by government (555). More recently, Klaus Peter Berger celebrates standardized contracts as examples of "the changing paradigm of international commercial law" toward "privatized law-making" (Berger 1999, 27). Ronit and Schneider (2000, 1, 23) distinguish between private legal authority, which is delegated to the private lawmaking institution by a state, and private legal authority, which is autonomously claimed or built by nonstate forces. However, they overstate the distinction where they fail to consider how private regulatory authority may in fact constitute a delegation of authority from the state. Ralf Michaels has instead analyzed these issues as a matter of the accommodation of global private law regimes by the state. Michaels usefully dissects these forms of accommodation into three distinct kinds, all of which enter into the play with standardized contracts—deference, incorporation, and delegation (2005, 1209).

4. Recent accusations by the former head of AIG give a concrete example of how changes in ISDA documentation can have a significant impact. Hank Greenberg maintains that the fall of AIG was precipitated by the fact that ISDA (presumably at the request of certain swap dealers) changed the protocols to require that credit default swaps mark to market rather than being assessed at maturity.

References

Secondary Sources

Abolafia, Mitchel Y. 1996. *Making markets: Opportunism and restraint on Wall Street*. Cambridge: Harvard University Press.

Ahdieh, Robert B. 2006. The strategy of boilerplate. *Michigan Law Review* 104:1033–73.

Akerlof, George A., and Robert J. Shiller. 2009. *Animal spirits: How human psychology drives the economy, and why it matters for global capitalism*. Princeton, N.J.: Princeton University Press.

Alexander, Larry. 1999. "With me, it's all 'er nuthin'": Formalism in law and morality. *University of Chicago Law Review* 66 (3): 530–65.

Alexander, Gregory S. 1997. *Commodity and propriety: Competing visions of property in American legal thought, 1776–1970*. Chicago: University of Chicago Press.

Alexander, Gregory, and Eduardo Penalver. 2008. Properties of community. Paper presented at Property and Community Conference. Tel Aviv University, January 2–4.

Aman, Alfred C. 2004. *The democracy deficit: Taming globalization through law reform*. New York: New York University Press.

American Banker. 1997. Is there a private global bank in your future? May 12, 44–48.

Anderson, Christopher W., and Terry L. Campbell. 2000. Corporate governance of Japanese banks. Working Paper. http://ssrn.com/abstract=231950.

Anderson, Elizabeth. 2008. How should egalitarians cope with market risk? *Theoretical Inquiries in Law* 9:239–70.

Andrews, Edmund L., and Peter Baker. 2009. Bonus money at troubled AIG draws heavy criticism. *New York Times*, March 15.

Angelini, Paolo. 1998. An analysis of competitive externalities in gross settlement systems. *Journal of Banking and Finance* 22 (1): 1–18.

Appelbaum, Richard P., William L. F. Felstiner, and Volkmar Gessner, eds. 2001. *Rules and networks: The legal culture of global business transactions.* Oxford: Hart.

Arendt, Hannah. 1979. *The origins of totalitarianism.* New York: Harcourt.

Asia Pulse. 1998. New legislation, reforms set to shake banking in Japan. April 2.

Atiyah, Patrick S., and Robert S. Summers. 1987. *Form and substance in Anglo-American law: A comparative study of legal reasoning, legal theory, and legal institutions.* New York: Clarendon Press.

Austin, J. L. 1975. *How to do things with words.* Cambridge: Harvard University Press.

Avanzato, Paul. 1998. How to use the collateral carousel. *International Financial Law Review* 17 (1): 29–32.

Azfar, Omar, Young Lee, and Anand Swamy. 2001. The causes and consequences of corruption. *Annals of the American Academy of Political and Social Science* 573:42–56.

Balleisen, Edward. 2009. The prospects for effective "co-regulation" in the United States: An historian's view from the early twenty-first century. In *Government and markets: Toward a new theory of economic regulation,* ed. Edward Balleisein and David Moss, 443–81. Cambridge: Cambridge University Press.

Bamberger, Kenneth. 2010. Technologies of compliance: risk and regulation in a digital age. *Texas Law Review* 88 (4): 669–740.

Banerjee, Abhijit, Rema Hanna, and Sendhil Mullainathan. 2009. Corruption. MIT Department of Economics. http://econ-www.mit.edu/files/3848 (accessed June 3, 2009).

Bank for International Settlements. 1993. *Payment system in the Group of Ten countries.* Basel: Bank for International Settlements.

———. 2002. Second working paper on securitisation (December 20). Basel: Bank for International Settlements.

Bank of Japan. 1996. Nihon Ginko toza yokin kessai no "RTGS-ka" ni tsuite [About the move to RTGS for the settlement of deposits at the Bank of Japan]. http://www.boj.or.jp/type/release/zuiji/kako01/set9612a.htm (accessed July 12, 2010).

———. 1998. The framework for restructuring BOJ-NET JGB services. Public statement, September 4. http://www.boj.or.jp/en/type/release/zuiji/kako01/set9809a.htm (accessed July 14, 2010).

———. 2001a. RTGS–Hantoshikan no keiken to hyoka [RTGS—Six months' experience and evaluation]. http://www.boj.or.jp/type/ronbun/ron/research/ron0108b.htm.

———. 2001b. Real-time gross settlement (RTGS) in Japan: An evaluation of the first six months. *Bank of Japan Quarterly Bulletin* (November). http://www.boj.or.jp/en/type/ronbun/ron/research/ron0111a.htm.

———. 2005. Nihon Ginko toza yokin kessai ni okeru jisedai RTGS no tenkai [New developments regarding next-generation RTGS for Bank of Japan current deposits]. http://www.boj.or.jp/type/release/zuiji/set0511a.htm (accessed July 14, 2010).

———. 2006. Jisedai RTGS koso no jitsugen ni mukete [Toward the realization of the concept of next-generation RTGS]. http://www.boj.or.jp/type/ronbun/ron/research/data/ron0609a.pdf. English version: http://www.boj.or.jp/en/type/ronbun/ron/research/data/ron0610a.pdf (accessed August 24, 2009).

———. 2007–8. Payment and settlement systems report, 2007–2008. http://www.boj.or.jp/en/type/ronbun/psr/data/psr2007.pdf (accessed May 29, 2009).

Basel Committee on Banking Supervision. 1999. A new capital adequacy framework. http://www.bis.org/publ/bcbs50.pdf (accessed July 9, 2010).

———. 2003. The compliance function in banks. http://www.bis.org/publ/bcbs103.pdf (accessed July 9, 2010).

Bataille, Georges. 1991. Sacrifices and the wars of the Aztecs. In *The accursed share*, vol. 1, *Consumption*, trans. Robert Hurley, 45–62. New York: Zone Books. (Orig. pub. 1949.)

Bateson, Gregory. 1980. *Mind and nature: A necessary unity*. New York: Bantam Books.

Beaulier, Scott, Peter J. Boettke, and Christopher J. Coyne. 2004. Knowledge, economics, and coordination: Understanding Hayek's legal theory. *NYU Journal of Law and Liberty* 1 (Fall): 209–24.

Bebchuk, Lucian Arye, and Jesse M. Fried. 1996. The uneasy case for the priority of secured claims in bankruptcy. *Yale Law Journal* 105:857–934.

Beck, Thorsten, Asli Demirgüç-Kunt, and Ross Levine. 2006. Bank supervision and corruption in lending. *Journal of Monetary Economics* 53 (8): 2131–63.

Beck, Ulrich. 1992. *Risk society: Towards a new modernity*. London: Sage Publications.

Benkler, Yochai. 2009. Law, policy, and cooperation. In *Government and markets: Toward a new theory of regulation*, ed. Edward Balleisein and David Moss, 299–332. Cambridge: Cambridge University Press.

Berger, Adolf. 1953. *Encyclopedic dictionary of Roman law*. Philadelphia: American Philosophical Society.

Berger, Klaus Peter. 1999. *The creeping codification of the Lex Mercatoria*. Boston: Kluwer Law International.

Berman, Paul Schiff. 2005. From international law to law and globalization. *Columbia Journal of Transnational Law* 43:485–556.

Biagioli, Mario. 2006. Documents of documents: Scientists' names and scientific claims. In *Documents: Artifacts of modern knowledge*, ed. Annelise Riles, 127–57. Ann Arbor: University of Michigan Press.

Bishop, William. 1997. Agency cost and administrative law. In *The new Palgrave dictionary of economics and the law*, ed. P. Newman, 21–26. London: Palgrave Macmillan.

Blair, Margaret M., and Lynn A. Stout. 2001. Trust, trustworthiness, and the behavioral foundations of corporate law, business, economics, and regulatory law. Working Paper 241403. http://www.ssrn.com (accessed April 18, 2009).

Bockman, Johanna, and Gil Eyal. 2002. Eastern Europe as a laboratory of economic knowledge. *American Journal of Sociology* 108 (2): 310–52.

Bohannan, Paul, and Laura Bohannan. 1968. *Tiv economy*. Evanston: Northwestern University Press.

Borchers, Patrick J. 1998. Choice of law relative to security interests and other liens in international bankruptcies. *American Journal of Comparative Law* 46:165–95.

Borio, C. E. V., and P. Van den Bergh. 1993. The nature and management of payment system risks: An international perspective. BIS Economic Papers 36.

Born, Georgina. 1995. *Rationalizing culture: IRCAM, Boulez, and the institutionalization of the musical avant-garde*. Berkeley: University of California Press.

Borovoy, Amy. 2001. Recovering from codependence in Japan. *American Ethnologist* 28 (1): 94–118.

Bowley, Graham. 2010. Goldman deal-maker now advocates regulation. *New York Times*, March 10. http://www.nytimes.com/2010/03/11/business/11cftc.html (accessed April 16, 2010).

Boyer, M. Christine. 1983. *Dreaming the rational city: The myth of American city planning*. Cambridge, Mass.: MIT Press.

Bradley, Caroline. 2005. Private international law-making for the financial markets. *Fordham International Law Journal* 29:127–80.

Braithwaite, John. 1999. Accountability and governance under the new regulatory state. *Australian Journal of Public Administration* 58 (1): 90–97.

———. 2002. *Restorative justice and responsive regulation*. New York: Oxford University Press.

Brenneis, Donald. 1988. A propos des "research proposals." *Actes de la Recherche en Sciences Sociales* 674:82.

———. 2006. Reforming promise. In *Documents: Artifacts of modern knowledge*, ed. Annelise Riles, 41–70. Ann Arbor: University of Michigan Press.

Bridge, Michael. 2002. *Personal property law*. Oxford: Oxford University Press.

Buchanan, Ruth. 1994–95. Border crossings: NAFTA, regulatory restructuring, and the politics of place. *Indiana Journal of Global Legal Studies* 2:371–93.

Buchanan, James M., and Gordon Tullock. 1962. *The calculus of consent: Logical foundations of a constitutional democracy*. Ann Arbor: University of Michigan Press.

Bull, Ryan E. 2000. Operation of the new Article 9 choice of law regime in an international context. *Texas Law Review* 78:679–718.

Buntrock, Dana. 2002. *Japanese architecture as a collaborative process: Opportunities in a flexible construction culture.* London: E&F Spon.

Burns, Judith. 2010. Obama: Dodd's financial overhaul "essential." *Wall Street Journal*, March 20. http://online.wsj.com/article/SB10001424052748704550004575133243203437802.html (accessed April 24, 2010).

Buxbaum, Hannah L. 2000. Rethinking international insolvency: The neglected role of choice-of-law rules and theory. *Stanford Journal of International Law* 36:23–71.

Cain, Maureen E., and Christine B. Harrington. 1994. Introduction. In *Lawyers in a postmodern world: Translation and transgression*, ed. M. E. Cain and C. B. Harrington, 1–12. New York: New York University Press.

Calavita, Kitty. 1998. Immigration, law, and marginalization in a global economy: Notes from Spain. *Law and Society Review* 32 (3): 529–66.

Calder, Kent E. 1989. Elites in an equalizing role: Ex-bureaucrats as coordinators and intermediaries in the Japanese government-business relationship. *Comparative Politics* 21 (4): 379–403.

———. 1991. *Crisis and compensation: Public policy and political stability in Japan, 1949–1986.* Princeton, N.J.: Princeton University Press.

———. 1993. *Strategic capitalism private business and public purpose in Japanese industrial finance.* Princeton, N.J.: Princeton University Press.

Callon, Michel. 1998a. An essay on framing and overflowing: Economic externalities revisited by sociology. In *The laws of the markets*, ed. M. Callon, 244–69. Oxford: Blackwell.

———. 1998b. Introduction: The embeddedness of economic markets in economics. In *The laws of the markets*, ed. Michel Callon, 1–57. Oxford: Blackwell.

Campbell, John L. 1998. Institutional analysis and the role of ideas in political economy. *Theory and Society* 27 (3): 377–409.

Cardozo, Benjamin N. 1921. *The nature of the judicial process.* New Haven: Yale University Press.

Carnell, Richard Scott. 2010. Regulator's incentives. Make markets be markets report. Roosevelt Institute. http://makemarketsbemarkets.org/modals/report_regulatory.php.

Carpenter, Susan. 2003. *Special corporations and the bureaucracy: Why Japan can't reform.* New York: Palgrave Macmillan.

Carrier, James G., and Daniel Miller. 1998. *Virtualism: A new political economy.* New York: Berg.

Carruthers, Bruce G., and Terence C. Halliday. 2000. Professionals in systemic reform of bankruptcy law: The 1978 U.S. Bankruptcy Code and the English Insolvency Act 1986. *American Bankruptcy Law Journal* 74:35–76.

Carruthers, Bruce G., and Arthur L. Stinchcombe. 1999. The social structure of liquidity: Flexibility, markets, and states. *Theory and Society* 28 (3): 353–82.

Carruthers, Bruce G., Sarah L. Babb, and Terence C. Halliday. 2001. Institutionalizing markets, or the market for institutions? Central banks, bankruptcy law, and the globalization of financial markets. In *The rise of neoliberalism and institutional analysis*, ed. J. L. Campbell and O. K. Pedersen, 94–126. Princeton, N.J.: Princeton University Press.

Centeno, Miguel Ángel. 1994. *Democracy within reason: Technocratic revolution in Mexico*. University Park: Penn State Press.

———. 1998. The politics of knowledge: Hayek and technocracy. In *The politics of expertise in Latin America*, ed. Miguel Ángel Centeno and Patricio Silva, 36–51. New York: St. Martin's Press.

Cerny, Philip G. 2000. Embedding global financial markets. In *Private organizations in global politics*, ed. K. Ronit and V. Schneider, 59–82. New York: Routledge.

Chakrabarty, Dipesh. 2000. *Provincializing Europe: Postcolonial thought and historical difference*. Princeton, N.J.: Princeton University Press.

Chiba, Masaji. 1989. *Legal pluralism: Toward a general theory through Japanese legal culture*. Tokyo: Tokai Press.

Chie, Nakane. 1972. *Japanese society*. Berkeley: University of California Press.

Choi, Stephen J., and G. Mitu Gulati. 2006. Contract as statute. *Michigan Law Review* 104:1129–73.

Clark, D. S. 2002. Pragmatism's instrumental view of moral reasoning. *Essays in Philosophy* 3 (2): 1–19.

Clarke, Lee. 1999. *Mission improbable: Using fantasy documents to tame disaster*. Chicago: University of Chicago Press.

Cohen, Amy J. 2008. Negotiation, meet new governance: Interests, skills, and selves. *Law and Social Inquiry* 33 (2): 503–62.

Cohen, Morris R. 1927. Property and sovereignty. *Cornell Law Quarterly* 13:8–30.

Colebrooke, William. 1883. *A treatise on the law of collateral securities: As applied to negotiable, quasi-negotiable, and non-negotiable choices in action*. Chicago: Callaghan.

Coiley, James. 2001. New protections for cross-border collateral arrangements: Summary and analysis of draft E.U. directive on financial collateral. *Journal of International Banking Law* 16 (5): 119–24.

Comaroff, John L., and Jean Comaroff, eds. 2001. *Millennial capitalism and the culture of neoliberalism*. Durham, N.C.: Duke University Press.

Committee on Payment and Settlement Systems of the Central Banks of the Group of Ten Countries. 1990. Lamfalussy report on interbank netting schemes of central banks. http://www.bis.org/publ/cpss04.pdf?noframes=1 (accessed May 31, 2009).

———. 1997. Real-time gross settlement systems. March. http://www.bis.org (accessed July 6, 2010).

Cook, Walter W. 1924. The logical and legal bases of the conflict of laws. *Yale Law Journal* 33:457–88.

Council Report. 2001. The Justice System Reform Council, Recommendations of the Justice System Reform Council for a Justice System to Support Japan in the twenty-first century. http://www.kantei.go.jp/foreign/judiciary/2001/0612report.html (accessed July 14, 2010).

Counterparty Risk Management Policy Group II. 2005. Toward greater financial stability: A private sector perspective. July 27. http://www.crmpolicygroup.org/crmpg2/.

Coutin, Susan B. 2005. Being en route. *American Anthropologist* 107 (2): 195–206.

Coutin, Susan B., Bill Maurer, and Barbara Yngvesson. 2002. In the mirror: The legitimation work of globalization. *Law and Social Inquiry* 27:801–43.

Craig, Albert. 2009. *Civilization and enlightenment: The early thought of Fukuzawa Yukichi.* Cambridge: Harvard University Press.

Crosman, Penny. 2008. Collateral damage; The quiet backwater of collateral management has been stirred up by Bear Stearns' collapse, Lehman's bankruptcy, AIG's near-death and ongoing turmoil in the credit markets. *Wall Street and Technology,* December 1.

Crotty, James, and Gerald Epstein. 2008. Proposals for effectively regulating the U.S. financial system to avoid yet another meltdown. Political Economy Research Institute Working Paper Series 181 (October).

Cunningham, Daniel. 1992. The lawyer as translator, representation as text. *Cornell Law Review* 77:1298–1387.

Cunningham, Daniel P., and Dr. Thomas J. Werlen. 1996. The model netting act: A solution for insolvency uncertainty. *Futures and Derivatives Law Report* 16 (9): 7.

Cutler, A. Claire. 2003. *Private power and global authority: Transnational merchant law in the global political economy.* New York: Cambridge University Press.

Cutler, A. Claire, Virginia Haufler, and Tony Porter. 1999. Private authority and international affairs. In *Private authority and international affairs,* ed. A. C. Cutler and V. Haufler, 3–30. Albany: SUNY Press.

Dagan, Hanoch, and Michael A. Heller. 2001. The liberal commons. *Yale Law Journal* 110:549–623.

Danzig, Richard. 1975. A comment on the jurisprudence of the Uniform Commercial Code. *Stanford Law Review* 27 (3): 621–35.

Das, Veena, and Deborah Poole. 2004. The state and its margins: Comparative ethnographies. In *Anthropology in the margins of the state,* ed. Veena Das and Deborah Poole, 3–34. Santa Fe: School of American Research Press.

David, René. 1983. On the concept of western law. *Cincinnati Law Review* 52 (1): 126–35.

Davis, Kevin E. 2006. The role of nonprofits in the production of boilerplate. *Michigan Law Review* 104:1075–1103.

de Goede, Marieke. 2005. *Virtue, fortune, and faith: A genealogy of finance.* Minneapolis: University of Minnesota Press.

De Soto, Hernando. 2000. *The mystery of capital: Why capitalism triumphs in the West and fails everywhere else.* New York: Basic Books.

———. 2009. Toxic assets were hidden assets. *Wall Street Journal* (Eastern ed.), March 25, 2009, A13.

De Man, Paul. 1979. *Allegories of reading: Figural language in Rousseau, Nietzsche, Rilke, and Proust.* New Haven: Yale University Press.

Dewey, John. 1998. The place of habit in conduct. In *The essential Dewey*, vol. 2, *Ethics, logic, psychology*, ed. L. A. Hickman and T. M. Alexander, 24–49. Bloomington: Indiana University Press. (Orig. pub. 1922.)

Dezalay, Yves, and Bryant Garth. 1995. Merchants of law as moral entrepreneurs: Constructing international justice from the competition for transnational business disputes. *Law and Society Review* 29 (1): 27–64.

———. 1996. *Dealing in virtue: International commercial arbitration and the construction of a transnational legal order.* Chicago: University of Chicago Press.

———. 2002. *The internationalization of global palace wars: Lawyers, economists, and the contest to transform Latin American states.* Chicago: University of Chicago Press.

Dickie, Mure. 2009. War on the samurai. *Financial Times* (Asia ed.), June 30, 2009, 8.

Dimock, Marshall. 1968. *The Japanese technocracy: Management and government in Japan.* New York: Walker/Weatherhill.

Donagan, Alan. 1979. *The theory of morality.* Chicago: University of Chicago Press.

Dore, Ronald. 1999. Japan's reform debate: Patriotic concern or class interest? Or both? *Journal of Japanese Studies* 25 (1): 65–89.

Dorf, Michael C., and Charles F. Sabel. 1998. A constitution of democratic experimentalism. *Columbia Law Review* 98 (2): 267–371.

Douglas, Mary, and Aaron Wildavsky. 1983. *Risk and culture: An essay on the selection of technological and environmental dangers.* Berkeley: University of California Press.

Drucker, Peter. 1998. In defense of Japanese bureaucracy. *Foreign Affairs* 77 (5): 68–81.

Dunn, Elizabeth Cullen. 2008. Postsocialist spores: Disease, bodies, and the state in the Republic of Georgia. *American Ethnologist* 35 (2): 243–58.

Eames, S. Morris. 1977. *Pragmatic naturalism: An introduction.* Carbondale: Southern Illinois University Press.

Edelman, Lauren B., Christopher Uggen, and Howard S. Erlanger. 1999. The endogeneity of legal regulation: Grievance procedures as rational myth. *American Journal of Sociology* 105 (2): 406–54.

Edwards, Franklin R., and Edward R. Morrison. 2005. Derivatives and the bankruptcy code: Why the special treatment? *Yale Journal on Regulation* 22:91–122.

Eichengreen, Barry. 2009. Out of the box thoughts about the international financial architecture. *International Monetary Fund.* http://imf.org/external/pubs/ft/wp/2009/wp09116.pdf.

Eisenbeis, Robert. 1997. International settlements: A new source of systemic risk? *Federal Reserve Bank of Atlanta Economic Review* (Second Quarter): 44–50.

Eisner, Marc. 2009. Markets in the shadow of the state: An appraisal of deregulation and implications for future research. http://www.tobinproject.org/conference_theory/papers/TobinProject_EisnerMarc.pdf (accessed June 25, 2010).

Ellickson, Robert C. 1991. *Order without law: How neighbors settle disputes.* Cambridge: Harvard University Press.

Ellin, Nan. 2006. *Integral urbanism.* New York: Routledge.

Epstein, Richard. 1999. Hayekian socialism. *Maryland Law Review* 58:271–99.

———. 2000. *The legacy of Friedrich von Hayek*, vol. 2, *Hayekian socialism.* Indianapolis: Liberty Fund.

Ernst, Daniel. 2009. Lawyers, bureaucratic autonomy and securities regulation during the New Deal. http://scholarship.law.georgetown.edu/cgi/viewcontent.cgi?article=1117&context=fwps_papers (accessed June 25, 2010).

Espeland, Wendy. 1994. Legally mediated identities: The National Environmental Policy Act and the bureaucratic construction of interests. *Law and Society Review* 28 (5): 1149–79.

———. 2000. Bureaucratizing democracy, democratizing bureaucracy. *Law and Social Inquiry* 25:1077–1109.

Espeland, Wendy, and Berit Irene Vannebo. 2007. Accountability, quantification, and law. *Annual Review of Law and Social Science* 3:21–43.

Fackler, Martin. 2010. Japan leader aims to root out bureaucrats. *New York Times*, March 24. http://www.nytimes.com/2010/03/25/world/asia/25japan.html (accessed April 18, 2010).

Feldman, Eric. 2006. The culture of legal change: A case study of tobacco control in twenty-first-century Japan. *Michigan Journal of International Law* 27 (3): 743–822.

Ferguson, James. 1990. *The anti-politics machine: "Development," depoliticization, and bureaucratic power in Lesotho.* Cambridge: Cambridge University Press.

———. 2005. Seeing like an oil company: Space, security and global capital in neoliberal Africa. *American Anthropologist* 107 (3): 377–82.

Ferguson, James, and Akhil Gupta. 2002. Spatializing states: Towards an ethnography of neoliberal governmentality. *American Ethnologist* 29 (4): 981–1002.

Fife, Wayne. 1995. The look of rationality and the bureaucratization of consciousness in Papua New Guinea. *Ethnology* 34:129–41.

Finance System Research Council. 1997. Summary of the report regarding the reform of the Japanese financial system. http://www.fsa.go.jp/p_mof/english/tosin/e1a602f11.htm (accessed July 12, 2010).

Financial Times. 1998. Japan's plan to form financial inspection agency faces setback. February 11.

———. 2009. AIG's billions. March 16. http://global.factiva.com (accessed April 21, 2010).

Firth, Raymond. 1939. Problems of primitive economics. In *Primitive Polynesian Economy*, 1–31. London: Routledge.

Fischer, Frank. 1990. *Technocracy and the politics of expertise.* Newbury Park, Calif.: Sage Publications.

Fligstein, Neil. 2001. *The architecture of markets: An economic sociology of twenty-first-century capitalist societies.* Princeton, N.J.: Princeton University Press.

Flitner, Michael. 1998. Biodiversity: Of local commons and global commodities. In *Privatizing nature: Political struggles for the global commons*, ed. Michael Goldman, 144–66. New Brunswick, N.J.: Rutgers University Press.

Florini, Ann M. 1999. Does the invisible hand need a transparency glove? The politics of transparency. Paper prepared for ABCDE Conference, April 28–30. http://siteresources.worldbank.org/INTWBIGOVANTCOR/Resources/florini.pdf.

Folkerts-Landau, David, Peter Garber, and Dirk Schoenmaker. 1996. The reform of wholesale payment systems and its impact on financial markets. Occasional Papers 51. Washington, D.C.: Group of Thirty.

———. 1997. The reform of wholesale payment systems. *Finance and Development* 34 (2): 25–29.

Foy, Agnes. 1999. The ISDA Master Agreement—Managing legal risk: Jurisdictions and counter-parties. *Commercial Law Practitioner* (April): 104–10.

French, Peter. 1979. The corporation as a moral person. *American Philosophical Quarterly* 16:207–15.

Friedman, Lawrence M. 1966. On legalistic reasoning—a footnote to Weber. *Wisconsin Law Review* 1966 (1): 148–71.

Fujimura, Joan. 1992. Crafting science: Standardized packages, boundary objects, and "translation." In *Science as practice and culture*, ed. A. Pickering, 168–211. Chicago: University of Chicago Press.

Fuller, Lon L. 1930a. Legal fictions. *Illinois Law Review* 25 (4): 363–99.

———. 1930b. Legal fictions part III. *Illinois Law Review* 25 (4): 877–910.

Fukuzawa, Yukichi. 1931. *Bunmeiron no gairyaku* [*An outline of a theory of civilization*]. Tokyo: Iwanami Shoten.

Fung, Archon, Mary Graham, David Weil, and Elena Fagotto. 2004. The political economy of transparency: What makes disclosure policies effective? Ash Institute for Democratic Governance and Innovation, Kennedy School of Government, Harvard University, OPS-03-04. http://www.hks.harvard.edu/taubman center/transparency/downloads/effectiveness.pdf (accessed May 29, 2009).

Galanter, Marc. 1974. Why the "haves" come out ahead: Speculations on the limits of legal change. *Law and Society Review* 9 (1): 95–160.

Gangahar, Anuj. 2002. How to trade collateral. *International Securities Finance* 44:23–25.

Garrard, Glen. 1938. The pledge as a security device. *Virginia Law Review* 24: 355–80.

Garsten, Christina, and Monica Lindh de Montoya, eds. 2008. *Transparency in a new global order*. Cheltenham: Edward Elgar Publishing.

Garth, Bryant G. 2006. Introduction: Taking new legal realism to transnational issues and institutions. *Law and Social Inquiry* 31 (4): 939–45.

Geertz, Clifford. 1973. *The interpretation of cultures*. New York: Basic Books.

Gelpern, Anna, and G. Mitu Gulati. 2007. Public symbol in private contract: A case study. *Washington University Law Review* 84 (7): 1627–1716.

General Committee of the Securities and Exchange Council. 1996. Summary of discussions, November 29. http://www.fsa.go.jp/p_mof/english/tosin/e1a501f1 .htm (accessed August 3, 2010).

Gibney, Frank. 1998. Introduction. In *Unlocking the bureaucrat's kingdom: Deregulation and the Japanese economy*, ed. Frank Gibney, 1–18. Washington, D.C.: Brookings Institution Press.

Giddens, Anthony. 1991. *Modernity and self-identity: Self and society in the late modern age*. Stanford, Calif.: Stanford University Press.

Gilmore, Grant. 1951. The secured transactions article of the Commercial Code. *Law and Contemporary Problems* 16 (1): 27–48.

Goode, Roy. 2005. Rule, practice, and pragmatism in transnational commercial law. *International and Comparative Law Quarterly* 54:539–62.

Goodfellow, D. M. 1939. *The applicability of economic theory to so-called primitive communities in principles of economic sociology*. Westport, Conn.: Negro Universities Press.

Gooding, David, Trevor Pinch, and Simon Schaffer. 1989. *The uses of experiment: Studies in the natural sciences*. Cambridge: Cambridge University Press.

Graziadei, Michele. 2006. Comparative law as the study of transplants and receptions. In *The Oxford handbook of comparative law*, ed. R. Zimmermann and M. Reimann, 441–75. Oxford: Oxford University Press.

Greenhouse, Carol J. 1996. *A moment's notice: Time politics across cultures.* Ithaca, N.Y.: Cornell University Press.

Grey, Thomas C. 1991. What good is legal pragmatism? In *Pragmatism in law and society*, ed. M. Brint and W. Weaver, 9–48. Boulder, Colo.: Westview Press.

Grossman, Emiliano, Emilio Luque, and Fabian Muniesa. 2008. Economies through transparency. In *Transparency in a new global order: Unveiling organizational visions*, ed. Christina Garsten and Monica Lindh de Montoya, 97–121. Cheltenham: Edward Elgar Publishing.

Guerrera, Francesco, Nicole Bullock, and Julie MacIntosh. 2008. Wall Street "made rod for own back." *The Financial Times*, October 31. Factiva. http://global.factiva.com (accessed April 12, 2010).

Guerrera, Francesco, and Henny Sender. 2010. Goldman Sachs splash. *The Financial Times*, April 17. Factiva. http://global.factiva.com (accessed April 24, 2010).

Gunning, J. Patrick. 2003. *Understanding democracy: An introduction to public choice.* Taiwan: Nomad Press.

Guyer, Jane. 2007. Prophecy and the near future. Thoughts on macroeconomic, evangelical, and punctuated time. *American Ethnologist* 34 (3): 409–27.

Guynn, Randall D. 1996. Modernizing securities ownership, transfer and pledging law. A Discussion paper on the need for international harmonization with responding comments by Professor James Steven Rogers (USA), Professor Kazuaki Sono (Japan) and Dr. Jürgen Than (Germany): I.B.A. Capital Markets Forum 1996, Section on Business Law, International Bar Association. http://www.davispolk.com/iba.modernization.pdf (accessed June 25, 2010).

Guynn, Randall D., and Margaret Tahyar. 1996. The importance of choice of law and finality to PvP, netting and collateral arrangements. *Journal of Financial Regulation and Compliance* 4 (2): 170–77.

Hagan, John. 2003. *Justice in the Balkans: Prosecuting war crimes in the Hague tribunal.* Chicago: University of Chicago Press.

Hagan, John, and Ron Levi. 2005. Crimes of war and the force of law. *Social Forces* 83:1499–1534.

Hale, R. L. 1923. Coercion and distribution in a supposedly non-coercive state. *Political Science Quarterly* 38:470–94.

Haley, John O. 1986. Administrative guidance versus formal regulation: Resolving the paradox of industrial policy. In *Law and trade issues of the Japanese economy: American and Japanese perspectives*, ed. G. R. Saxonhouse and K. Yamamura, 108–9. Seattle: University of Washington Press.

———. 1987. Governance by negotiation: A reappraisal of bureaucratic power in Japan. *Journal of Japan Studies* 13:343–57.

———. 1995. Japan's postwar civil service: The legal framework. In *The Japanese civil service and economic development: Catalysts of change*, ed. Hyung-Ki

Kim, Michio Muramatsu, and T. J. Pempel, 77–101. Oxford: Clarendon Press.

———. 1998. Whence, what and whither Japan? *Comparative Labor Law and Policy Journal* 19:475–84.

Hall, Rodney Bruce, and Thomas J. Biersteker, eds. 2002. *The emergence of private authority in global governance.* Cambridge: Cambridge University Press.

Hannoun, Charley. 1995. Les fictions en droit économique. *Droits* 21:83–93.

Hardin, Garrett. 1968. The tragedy of the commons. *Science* 162:1243–48.

Hargadon, Andrew, and Robert I. Sutton. 1997. Technology brokering and innovation in a product development firm. *Administrative Science Quarterly* 42 (4): 716–49.

Harootunian, Harry. 2000. *Overcome by modernity: History, culture, and community in interwar Japan.* Princeton, N.J.: Princeton University Press.

Harrington, Christine B., and Z. Umut Turem. 2006. Accounting for accountability in neoliberal regulatory regimes. In *Public accountability: Designs, dilemmas and experiences,* ed. Michael Dowdle, 195–219. Cambridge: Cambridge University Press.

Harris, Steven L., and Charles W. Mooney. 1994. A property-based theory of security interests: Taking debtors' choices seriously. *Virginia Law Review* 80:2021–72.

Hart, Herbert L. A. 1961. *The concept of law.* London: Oxford University Press.

Haselmann, Rainier, Katharina Pistor, and Vikrant Vig. 2006. How law affects lending. Columbia Law and Economics Working Paper 285. http://ssrn.com/abstract=846665 (accessed July 27, 2010).

Hattori, Takaaki, and Dan Henderson. 1983. *Civil procedure in Japan.* New York: M. Bender.

Hayashida, Kiyoaki. 1995. Kokyo sentaku to ho—higekiteki sentaku [Public choice and law—a tragic decision]. *Hogaku Semina* 40:98–101.

Hayek, F. A. 1948a. Economics and knowledge. In *Individualism and economic order,* 35–56. Chicago: University of Chicago Press. (Orig. pub. 1936.)

———. 1948b. The use of knowledge in society. In *Individualism and economic order,* 77–91. Chicago: University of Chicago Press. (Orig. publ. 1945.)

———. 1952. *The counter-revolution of science: Studies on the abuse of reason.* Glencoe, Ill.: Free Press.

———. 1975. *The rule of law.* Menlo Park, Calif.: Institute for Human Studies.

———. 1976a. *Denationalisation of money: An analysis of the theory and practice of concurrent currencies.* London: The Institute of Economic Affairs.

———. 1976b. *Law, legislation, and liberty.* Chicago: University of Chicago Press.

Healey, Patsy. 1997. Collaborative planning: Shaping places in fragmented societies. London: Macmillan.

Heidegger, Martin. 1977. *The question concerning technology and other essays.* New York: HarperCollins.

Heimer, Carol. 2006. Conceiving children: How documents support case versus biographical analyses. In *Documents: Artifacts of Modern Knowledge*, ed. A. Riles, 95–126. Ann Arbor: University of Michigan Press.

Hein, Laura. 1994. In search of peace and democracy: Japanese economic debate in political context. *Journal of Asian Studies* 53 (3): 752–78.

———. 2004. *Reasonable men, powerful words: Political culture and expertise in twentieth-century Japan*. Ewing, N.J.: University of California Press and the Woodrow Wilson Center Press.

Henare, Amiria J. M., Martin Holbraad, and Sari Wastell. 2006. *Thinking through things: Theorising artefacts in ethnographic perspective*. New York: Routledge.

Henderson, Kathryn. 1999. On line and on paper: Visual representations, visual culture, and computer graphics in design engineering. Cambridge, Mass.: MIT Press.

Hendricks, Darryll. 1994. Netting agreements and the credit exposures of OTC derivative portfolios. *Federal Reserve Bank New York Quarterly Review* 19:7–18.

Herskovits, Melville J. 1952. Economizing and rational behavior. In *Economic anthropology*, 3–24. New York: Knopf.

Hertzog, Esther. 1999. *Immigrants and bureaucrats: Ethiopians in an Israeli absorption center*. New York: Berghahn Books.

Herzfeld, Michael. 1992. *The social production of indifference*. Chicago: University of Chicago Press.

Hetherington. 2008. Populist transparency: The documentation of reality in rural Paraguay. *Journal of Legal Anthropology* 1 (1): 45–69.

Hevia, James L. 1968. The archive state and the fear of pollution: From the opium wars to Fu-Manchu. *Cultural Studies* 12 (2): 234–64.

Hillman, Robert A., and Jeffrey J. Rachlinski. 2002. Standard-form contracting in the electronic age. *New York University Law Review* 77 (2): 429–95.

Hindess, Barry. 2001. Good government and corruption. In *Corruption and anti-corruption*, ed. Peter Larmour and Nick Wolanin, 1–10. Canberra: Asia Pacific Press.

Hirai, Yoshio. 1991. *Zoku horitsugaku kisoron oboegaki* [*Notes on the fundamental theory of law, continued*]. Tokyo: Yuhikaku.

Ho, Karen. 2009. Disciplining investment bankers, disciplining the economy: Wall Street's institutional culture of crisis and the downsizing of corporate America. *American Anthropologist* 111 (2): 177–89.

Holmes, Douglas R. 2009. Economy of words. *Cultural Anthropology* 24 (3): 381–419.

Holmes, Douglas R., and George E. Marcus. 2005. Cultures of expertise and the management of globalization: Toward the refunctioning of ethnography.

In *Global assemblages: Technology, politics, and ethics as anthropological problems*, ed. A. Ong and S. J. Collier, 235–52. Oxford: Blackwell.

Hope, Wayne. 2006. Global capitalism and the critique of real time. *Time and Society* 15:275–302.

Horwitz, Morton J. 1977. *The transformation of American law, 1780–1860*. Cambridge: Harvard University Press.

———. 1992. *The transformation of American law, 1870–1960: The crisis of legal orthodoxy*. New York: Oxford University Press.

Hoskin, Keith. 1996. The 'awful idea of accountability': Inscribing people into the measurement of objects. In *Accountability: Power, ethos and the technologies*, ed. Rolland Munro and Jan Mouritsen, 265–81. London: International Thompson Business Press.

Hull, Matthew. 2008. Ruled by records: The expropriation of land and the misappropriation of lists in Islamabad. *American Ethnologist* 35 (4): 501–18.

Hval, Nina. 1997. Credit risk reduction in the international over-the-counter derivatives market: Collateralizing the net exposure with support agreements. *International Lawyer* 31 (Fall): 801–22.

International Swaps and Derivatives Association (ISDA). 1987. Interest Rate Swap Agreement. New York: International Swap and Derivatives Association.

———. 1992. Master Agreement (multicurrency, cross-border). New York: International Swap and Derivatives Association.

———. 1993. User's Guide to the 1992 ISDA Master Agreements. New York: International Swap and Derivatives Association.

———. 1994. 1994 ISDA Credit Support Annex (Security Interest—New York Law). New York.

———. 1995. Credit Support Annex for security interest subject to Japanese law. New York: International Swap and Derivatives Association.

———. 1999a. Instructions to external counsel from the ISDA Collateral Documentation Working Group, 1–40. New York: International Swaps and Derivatives Association.

———. 1999b. ISDA guidelines for collateral practitioners. New York: International Swaps and Derivatives Association.

———. 2000. ISDA collateral survey 2000. New York: International Swaps and Derivatives Association.

———. 2001. ISDA margin provisions and user's guide. New York: International Swaps and Derivatives Association.

———. 2002a. Master Agreement (multicurrency, cross-border). New York: International Swaps and Derivatives Association.

———. 2002b. Model Netting Act. http://www.isda.org/docproj/netact.pdf (accessed June 10, 2009).

———. 2002c. Preliminary draft convention on the law applicable to certain

rights in respect of securities held with an intermediary. http://www.isda.org/
c_and_a/pdf/HagueResponseMay02Final.pdf (accessed July 8, 2010).

———. 2005. 2005 ISDA collateral guidelines. New York.

———. 2006. Model Netting Act (Version 2.0). http://www.isda.org/docproj/pdf/
Model-Netting-Act101007.pdf (accessed June 5, 2009).

———. 2007. ISDA Margin Survey.

———. 2010a. ISDA announces further industry commitments to increase robust-
ness of OTC derivatives markets. Press release, March 1. http://www.isda.org/
media/press/2010/press030110fed.html (accessed April 7, 2010).

———. 2010b. Market review of OTC derivative bilateral collateralization practices (2.0). ISDA Collateral Steering Committee, March 1. http://www.isda
.org/c_and_a/pdf/Collateral-Market-Review.pdf (accessed April 12, 2010).

Ito, Mitsutoshi. 1995. Administrative reform. In *The Japanese civil service and
economic development: Catalysts of change*, ed. Hyung-Ki Kim, Michio Muramatsu, and T. J. Pempel, 235–58. Oxford: Clarendon Press.

James, William. 2000. What pragmatism means. In *Pragmatism and classical American philosophy: Essential readings and interpretive essays*, ed.
J. J. Stuhr, 193–202. New York: Oxford University Press.

Johnson, Chalmers. 1982. *MITI and the Japanese miracle: The growth of industrial policy, 1925–1975*. Stanford, Calif.: Stanford University Press.

Johnson, Christian A. 1997. Derivatives and rehypothecation failure: It's
3:00 pm, do you know where your collateral is? *Arizona Law Review* 39 (3):
949–1001.

———. 2000. *Over-the-counter derivatives documentation*. New York: Bowne.

Johnson, Omotunde. 1998. *Payment systems, monetary policy, and the role of
the Central Bank*. Washington, D.C.: International Monetary Fund.

Jolls, Christine, Cass R. Sunstein, and Richard Thaler. 1998. A behavioral approach to law and economics. *Stanford Law Review* 50:1471–1550.

Jones, Leonard A. 1881. *A treatise on the law of mortgages of personal property*.
Boston: Houghton Mifflin.

Jorges, Christian, and Jürgen Neyer. 1997. From intergovernmental bargaining
to deliberative political processes: The constitutionalisation of comitology.
European Law Journal 3 (3): 273–99.

Kahan, Marcel, and Michael Klausner. 1997. Standardization and innovation in
corporate contracting (or "The economics of boilerplate"). *Virginia Law Review* 83:713–70.

Kahn, Charles M., and William Roberds. 1998. Demandable debt as a means of
payment: Banknotes versus checks. Public Affairs Department Working Paper 98-5. Atlanta: Federal Reserve Bank of Atlanta.

Kahn, Charles M., James Andrews, and William Roberds. 1999. Settlement risk
under gross and net settlement. Working Paper 99-10a. Atlanta: Federal Reserve Bank of Atlanta.

Kahneman, Daniel, Jack L. Knetsch, and Richard H. Thaler. 1991. Anomalies: The endowment effect, loss aversion, and status quo bias. *Journal of Economic Perspectives* 5 (1): 193–206.

Kanda, Hideki. 1994. Nettingu no hoteki seishitsu to tosanho o meguru mondaiten [Issues surrounding the legal character of netting and its relationship to the bankruptcy law]. *Kinyu Homu Jijo* no. 1386 (May 5): 7–15.

———. 1996. Finance bureaucracy and the regulation of financial markets in Japan. In *Japan: Economic success and legal system*, ed. Harold Baum, 305–19. New York: de Gruyter.

———. 1998. Ikkatsu seisanho no seiritsu [The enactment of the close-out netting law]. *Kinyu Homu Jijo* no. 1517 (June 15): 18–21.

———. 2002. Japan. In *Cross border collateral: Legal risk and the conflict of law*, ed. R. Potok, 366–79. London: Butterworths.

Kanda, Hideki, Hideyuki Kobayashi, and Takashi Uchida. 1986. "Ho to keizaigaku" de naniga dekiruka [What can we do with "law and economics"?]. *Hogaku Semina* 396:24–41.

Kapstein, Ethan. 1992. Between power and purpose: Central bankers and the politics of regulatory convergence. *International Organization* 46 (1): 265–87.

Karmel, Roberta S., and Claire R. Kelly. 2009. The hardening of soft law in securities regulation. *Brooklyn Journal of International Law* 34 (3): 883–951.

Kaufman, George G. 1996. Comment on financial crises, payment system problems, and discount window lending. *Journal of Money, Credit and Banking* 28 (4): 825–31.

Kaufmann, Daniel, Aart Kraay, and Massimo Mastruzzi. 2006 . Measuring governance using cross-country perceptions data. In *International handbook on the economics of corruption*, ed. Susan Rose-Ackerman, 52–104. Cheltenham: Edward Elgar Publishing.

Kawahama, Noboru. 1993a. "Ho to keizaigaku" to hokaishaku no kankei ni tsuite (1) [The relationship between "law and economics" and interpretation of the law (1)]. *Minshoho Zasshi* 108 (6): 820–49.

———. 1993b. "Ho to keizaigaku" to hokaishaku no kankei ni tsuite (2) [The relationship between "law and economics" and interpretation of the law (2)]. *Minshoho Zasshi* 109 (1): 1–35.

———. 1993c. "Ho to keizaigaku" to hokaishaku no kankei ni tsuite (3) [The relationship between "law and economics" and interpretation of the law (3)]. *Minshoho Zasshi* 109 (2): 207–34.

———. 1993d. "Ho to keizaigaku" to hokaishaku no kankei ni tsuite (4—kan) [The relationship between "law and economics" and interpretation of the law (4—complete)]. *Minshoho Zasshi* 109 (3): 413–43.

Keeler, Theodore E. 1984. Theories of regulation and the deregulation movement. *Public Choice* 44 (1): 103–45.

Keizai Shingikai (Economic Council). 1996. Roku-bunya no keizai kozo kaikaku [Six areas of economic structural reforms]. Proposal of the Economic Council, December. http://www5.cao.go.jp/j-j/keikaku/pl6-1-j-j.html (accessed July 12, 2010).

Kelly, John D. 1991. *A politics of virtue*. Chicago: University of Chicago Press.

Kelsen, Hans. 1941. The law as a specific social technique. *University of Chicago Law Review* 9:75–97.

———. 1967. *Pure theory of law*. Translated by Max Knight. Berkeley: University of California Press.

Kennedy, David. 2004. *The dark sides of virtue: Reassessing international humanitarianism*. Princeton, N.J.: Princeton University Press.

Kennedy, Duncan. 1997. *A critique of adjudication* [Fin de Siècle]. Cambridge: Harvard University Press.

Kennedy, Duncan, and Frank Michelman. 1980. Are property and contract efficient? *Hofstra Law Review* 8:711–70.

Kettering, Kenneth C. 1999. Repledge and pre-default sale of securities collateral under revised Article 9. *Chicago-Kent Law Review* 74:1109–54.

Knop, Karen, Ralf Michaels, and Annelise Riles. 2009. International law in domestic courts: A Conflict of laws approach. *American Society of International Law Proceedings* 103.

Knorr-Cetina, Karen, and Urs Bruegger. 2002. Traders' engagement with markets: A postsocial relationship. *Theory, Culture, and Society* 19 (5/6): 161–85.

Kodres, Laura E. 1996. Foreign exchange markets: Structure and systemic risks. *Finance and Development* 33 (4): 22–25.

Koh, Byung Chul. 1989. *Japan's administrative elite*. Berkeley: University of California Press.

Komine, Yoshio. 2001. Shijo e no impakuto RTGS donyugo sankagetsu. [The impact of RTGS on the market three months on]. *Kinyu Zaisei Jijo* no. 2450 (March 19): 62–63.

Konczal, Mike. 2010. Progressive values, financial reform and sunlight. Rortybomb blog, comment posted March 15. http://rortybomb.wordpress.com.

Korobkin, Russell B. 2000. Behavioral analysis and legal form: Rules vs. standards revisited. *Oregon Law Review* 79:23–60.

Koschmann, Julien Victor. 2002. Rule by technology, technologies of rule. In *Knowledge and institutions of total war, 1935–55*, ed. Sakai Naoki, 139–71. Tokyo: Iwanami Shoten.

Kramer, Lawrence. 1991. Return of the renvoi. *New York University Law Review* 66:979–1044.

Krugman, Paul. 1998. What happened to Asia? http://web.mit.edu/krugman/www/DISINTER.html (accessed on April 17, 2009).

———. 2009. Reform or bust. *New York Times*, September 21.

Kurokawa, Kazumi. 1998. Goriteki tsuiju to kanryo kodo: Goriteki sentaku to shite no tsuiju [Rational conformity and bureaucratic behavior: Compliance as rational choice]. *Kokyo Sentaku no Kenkyu* 30:32–42.

Lambsdorff, Johann Graf, Markus Taube, and Matthias Schramn, eds. 2005. *The new institutional economics of corruption.* New York: Routledge.

Landis, James. 1938. *The administrative process.* New Haven: Yale University Press.

Langenbucher, Katja. 1998. Argument by analogy in European law. *Cambridge Law Journal* 57:481–521.

Langer, Maximo. 2004. From legal transplants to legal translations: The globalization of plea-bargaining and the Americanization thesis in criminal procedure. *Harvard International Law Journal* 45:1–64.

Langevoort, Donald C. 1996. Selling hope, selling risk: Some lessons for law from behavioral economics about stockbrokers and sophisticated customers. *California Law Review* 84:627–702.

Langley, P., and H. S. Simon. 1981. The central role of learning in cognition. In *Cognitive skills and their acquisition,* ed. J. R. Anderson, 361–80. Hillsdale, N.J.: Lawrence Erlbaum Associates.

Lanyi, Anthony, and Young Lee. 1999. Governance aspects of the East Asian financial crisis. Working Paper, IRIS Center, University of Maryland, College Park. http://www.iris.umd.edu (accessed June 3, 2009).

Larmour, Peter, and Nick Wolanin. 2001. *Corruption and anti-corruption.* Canberra: Asia Pacific Press.

Larner, Wendy, Richard Le Heron, and Nicholas Lewis. 2007. Co-constituting after neoliberalism? Political projects and globalising governmentalities in Aotearoa New Zealand. In *Neo-liberalization: States, networks, people,* ed. Kim England and Kevin Ward, 223–47. Oxford: Blackwell Publishing.

Larsen, Peter Thal. 2009. U.K. banks liquidity overhaul facing opposition. *Financial Times* (Europe ed.), March 12, 22.

Lasser, Mitchel. 2004. *Judicial deliberations: A comparative analysis of judicial transparency and legitimacy.* Oxford Studies in European Law. Oxford: Oxford University Press.

Latour, Bruno. 1987. *Science in action: How to follow scientists and engineers through society.* Milton Keynes: Open University Press.

———. 1990. Drawing things together. In *representation in scientific practice,* ed. M. Lynch and S. Woolgar, 19–68. Cambridge, Mass.: MIT Press.

———. 1996. *Aramis, or, the love of technology.* Cambridge: Harvard University Press.

———. 2002a. *La fabrique du droit: Une ethnographie du conseil d'état.* Paris: La Découverte.

———. 2002b. Morality and technology: the end of the means. *Theory, Culture and Society* 19 (5–6): 247–60.

———. 2004. Scientific objects and legal objectivity. In *Law, anthropology, and the constitution of the social: Making persons and things*, ed. A. Pottage and M. Mundy, 73–114. New York: Cambridge University Press.

Latour, Bruno, and Peter Weibel, eds. 2005. *Making things public: Atmospheres of democracy*. Cambridge, Mass.: MIT Press.

Latour, Bruno, and Steven Woolgar. 1986. *Laboratory life: The construction of scientific facts*. Princeton, N.J.: Princeton University Press. (Orig. pub. 1979.)

LeClair, E. E. 1962. Economic theory and economic anthropology. *American Anthropologist* 64 (6): 1179–1203.

Legrand, Pierre. 1997. The impossibility of legal transplants. *Maastrict Journal of European and Comparative Law* 4:111–24.

Leight, Jessica. 2010. Public choice: A critical reassessment. In *Government and markets: Toward a new theory of regulation*, ed. Edward Balleisen and David Moss, 213–55. New York: Cambridge University Press.

Lepinay, Vincent-Antonin. 2007. Decoding finance: Articulation and liquidity around a trading room. In *Do economists make markets?: On the performativity of economics*, ed. Donald A. MacKenzie, Fabian Muniesa, and Lucia Siu, 87–127. Princeton, N.J.: Princeton University Press.

Levi, R., and M. Valverde. 2001. Knowledge on tap: Police science and common knowledge in the legal regulation of drunkenness. *Law and Social Inquiry–Journal of the American Bar Foundation* 26 (4): 819–46.

Levit, Janet K. 2005. A bottom-up approach to international lawmaking: The tale of three trade finance instruments. *Yale Journal of International Law* 30:125–210.

Leyshon, Andrew, and Nigel Thrift. 1997. *Money/space: Geographies of monetary transformation*. New York: Routledge.

Lipset, Seymour, and Gabriel S. Lenz. 2000. Corruption, culture, and markets. In *Culture matters*, ed. Lawrence E. Harrison and Samuel E. Huntington, 112–25. New York: Basic Books.

LiPuma, Edward, and Benjamin Lee. 2004. *Financial derivatives and the globalization of risk*. Durham, N.C.: Duke University Press.

Llewellyn, Karl N. 1931. Some realism about realism: Responding to Dean Pound. *Harvard Law Review* 44:1222–64.

———. 1938. Through title to contract and a bit beyond. *New York University Law Quarterly Review* 15 (2): 159–209.

———. 1948. Problems of codifying security law. *Law and Contemporary Problems* 13:687–702.

———. 1951. *The bramble bush: On our law and its study*. New York: Oceana Publications.

Luhmann, Niklas. 1985. *A sociological theory of law*. Translated by E. King and M. Albrow. London: Routledge and Kegan Paul.

Lynch, Michael. 1993. *Scientific practice and ordinary action: Ethnomethodology and social studies of science.* New York: Cambridge University Press.

Lynch, Sarah N., and Serena Ng. 2009. U.S. moves to regulate derivatives trade—Geithner lays out plans of framework for multitrillion-dollar market; agency consolidation? *Wall Street Journal,* May 14, C1.

Mabuchi, Masaru. 1993. Deregulation and legalization of financial policy in political dynamics. In *Contemporary Japan,* ed. G. D. Allinson and Y. Sone, 13–54. Ithaca, N.Y.: Cornell University Press.

Macaulay, Stewart. 1963. Non-contractual relations in business: A preliminary study. *American Sociological Review* 28 (1): 55–67.

———. 1976–77. Elegant models, empirical pictures and the complexities of contract. *Law and Society Review* 11 (3): 507–28.

Macaulay, Stewart, John Kidwell, William Withford, and Marc Galanter. 1995. *Contracts: Law in action.* Charlottesville, Va.: Michie Co.

Macey, Jonathan. 1989. The political science of regulating bank risk. *Ohio State Law Journal* 49 (5): 1277–98.

MacLennan, Carol A. 1997. Democracy under the influence: Cost-benefit analysis in the United States. In *Meanings of the market: The free market in western culture,* ed. James G. Carrier, 195–224. Oxford: Berg Publishers.

Malinowski, Bronislaw. 1961. Introduction. In *Law and order in Polynesia,* ed. H. I. Hogbin, xvii–xxii. Hamden, Conn.: The Shoe String Press, Inc. (Orig. pub. 1934.)

Maine, Henry Sumner. 1931. *Ancient law.* London: Oxford University Press.

Mann, Ronald J. 1995. Bankruptcy and the entitlements of the government: Whose money is it anyway? *New York University Law Review* 70:993–1058.

———. 1997. Explaining the pattern of secured credit. *Harvard Law Review* 110:625–83.

Mapother, Bill. 1998. Get double duty from collateral. *Credit Union Magazine* 64 (2): 74.

Marcus, G. E., and F. R. Myers. 1995. The traffic in art and culture: An introduction. In *The traffic in culture: Refiguring art and anthropology,* ed. G. E. Marcus and F. R. Myers, 1–51. Berkeley: University of California Press.

Marcuse, Herbert. 1964. *One-dimensional man.* Boston: Beacon.

Marin, Dalia, and Monika Schnitzer. 2002. *Contracts in trade and transition: The resurgence of barter.* Cambridge, Mass.: MIT Press.

Marsh, R. M. 2000. Weber's misunderstanding of traditional Chinese law. *American Journal of Sociology* 106:281–302.

Martin, Emily. 1994. *Flexible bodies: Tracking immunity in American culture from the days of polio to the age of AIDS.* Boston: Beacon Press.

Massumi, Brian. 2002. *Parables for the virtual: Movement, affect, sensation.* Durham, N.C.: Duke University Press.

Matsuo, Takumi. 2003. *Seisankikan ni yoru maruchirateraru nettingu ni kan-*

suru hoteki ronten (jo) [Legal issues concerning settlement institutions' multilateral netting (pt. 1)]. *NBL* 772:25–32.

———. 2004a. *Seisankikan ni yoru maruchirateraru nettingu ni kansuru hoteki ronten* (chu) [Legal issues concerning settlement institutions' multilateral netting (pt. 2)]. *NBL* 777:53–60.

———. 2004b. *Seisankikan ni yoru maruchirateraru nettingu ni kansuru hoteki ronten* (ge) [Legal issues concerning settlement institutions' multilateral netting (pt. 3)]. *NBL* 779:44–47.

Maurer, Bill. 2005a. Due diligence and "reasonable man," offshore. *Cultural Anthropology* 20 (4): 474–505.

———. 2005b. *Mutual life, limited: Islamic banking, alternative currencies, lateral reason.* Princeton, N.J.: Princeton University Press.

McBarnet, Doreen. 1994. Legal creativity: Law, capital and legal avoidance. In *Lawyers in a postmodern world: Translation and transgression*, ed. M. E. Cain and C. B. Harrington, 73–84. New York: New York University Press.

———. 2002. Transnational transactions: Legal work, cross-border commerce, and global regulation. In *Transnational legal processes: Globalisation and power disparities*, ed. M. Likosky, 98–113. London: Butterworths.

McVeigh, Brian J. 1998. *The nature of the Japanese state.* New York: Routledge.

Mehrez, Gil, and Daniel Kaufmann. 1999. Transparency, liberalization and financial crises. World Bank Policy Research Working Paper 2286. http://papers.ssrn.com/s013/papers.cfm?abstract_id=258976 (accessed June 3, 2009).

Merry, Sally Engle. 1988. Legal pluralism. *Law and Society Review* 22 (5): 869–96.

Merryman, John Henry. 1985. *The civil law tradition: An introduction to the legal systems of western Europe and Latin America.* 2nd ed. Stanford, Calif.: Stanford University Press.

Mertz, Elizabeth, and Thomas Mitchell. 2006. The empirical turn in the legal academy: A new legal realist perspective. *Law and Society Newsletter* (November 2005): 4–5.

Meynaud, Jean. 1969. *Technocracy.* New York: Free Press.

Michaels, Ralf. 2005. The re-state-ment of non-state law: The state, conflict of laws and the challenge of global pluralism. *Wayne Law Review* 51:1209–59.

Michaels, Ralf, and Nils Jansen. 2006. Private law beyond the state? Europeanization, globalization, privatization. *American Journal of Comparative Law* 54 (4): 843–90.

Mikuni, Akio, and R. Taggart Murphy. 2002. *Japan's policy trap: Dollars, deflation, and the crisis of Japanese finance.* Washington, D.C.: Brookings Institution Press.

Mikuniya, Katsunori. 2009. Speech. High Level Meeting Jointly Organized by the Financial Stability Institute (FSI) and the Executives' Meeting of East Asia–Pacific Central Banks (EMEAP) Working Group on Banking Super-

vision. Financial Services Agency, November 29. http://www.fsa.go.jp/en/
announce/state/20091129.html (accessed April 14, 2010).

Miles, Thomas J., and Cass Sunstein. 2007. The new legal realism. *University of
Chicago Law Review* 75:831–52.

Milhaupt, Curtis J. 1997. The market for innovation in the United States and
Japan: Venture capital and the comparative corporate governance debate.
Northwestern University Law Review 91 (3): 865–98.

Milhaupt, Curtis J., and Mark D. West. 2003. Law's dominion and the market
for legal elites in Japan. *Law and Policy in International Business* 34 (2):
451–98.

———. 2004. *Economic organizations and corporate governance in Japan: The
impact of formal and informal rules.* Oxford: Oxford University Press.

———. 2006. The dark side of private ordering: An institutional and empirical
analysis of organized crime. In *The Japanese legal system: Cases, codes, and
commentary*, ed. J. Mark Ramseyer, Mark D. West, and Curtis Milhaupt,
412–21. New York: Foundation Press.

Miller, Daniel. 2003. The virtual moment. *Journal of the Royal Anthropological
Institute* 9 (1): 57–75.

———. 2005. *Materiality.* Durham, N.C.: Duke University Press.

Miller, Geoffrey, P. 1996. Decision-making at the Bank of Japan in law and policy. *International Business* 28 (1): 1–48.

Ministry of Finance Japan. 1997. Financial system reform—Toward the early
achievement of reform. June 13. http://www.fsa.go.jp/p_mof/english/big-bang/
ebb32.htm (accessed July 6, 2010).

———. 1999a. About the financial system reform (The Japanese version of the
Big Bang). http://www.fsa.go.jp/p_mof/english/big-bang/ebb1.htm (accessed
July 14, 2010).

———. 1999b. The originator of the Big Bang, England. http://www.fsa.go.jp/
p_mof/english/big-bang/ebb24.htm (accessed July 14, 2010).

Mitchell, Timothy. 1998. Fixing the economy. *Cultural Studies* 12 (1): 82–101.

———. 2002. *Rule of experts: Egypt, techno-politics, modernity.* Berkeley: University of California Press.

Miyamoto, Masao. 1998. Deregulating Japan's soul. In *Unlocking the bureaucrat's kingdom: Deregulation and the Japanese economy*, ed. Frank Gibney,
69–78. Washington, D.C.: Brookings Institution Press.

Miyazaki, Hirokazu. 2003. The temporalities of the market. *American Anthropologist* 105 (2): 255–65.

———. 2005a. From sugar cane to "swords": Hope and the extensibility of the gift
in Fiji. *Journal of the Royal Anthropological Institute* 11 (2): 277–95.

———. 2005b. The materiality of finance theory. In *Materiality*, ed. D. Miller,
165–205. Durham, N.C.: Duke University Press.

———. 2006a. Documenting the present. In *Documents: Artifacts of modern knowledge*, ed. Annelise Riles, 206–25. Ann Arbor: Michigan University Press.

———. 2006b. Economy of dreams: Hope in global capitalism and its critiques. *Cultural Anthropology* 21 (2): 147–72.

———. Forthcoming. *Arbitraging Japan: Traders as Critics of Capitalism.* Berkeley: University of California Press.

Miyazawa, Setsuo, and Hiroshi Otsuka. 2002. Legal education and the reproduction of the elite in Japan. In *Global prescriptions: the production, exportation, and importation of a new legal orthodoxy*, ed. Y. Dezalay and B. G. Garth, 162–208. Ann Arbor: University of Michigan Press.

Moe, Terry M. 1984. The new economics of organization. *American Journal of Political Science* 28 (4): 739–77.

Morgan, Glenn. 2008. Market formation and governance in international financial markets: The case of OTC derivatives. *Human Relations* 61:637–60.

Morgenson, Gretchen, and Louise Story. 2010. Testy conflict with Goldman helped push AIG to precipice. *New York Times*, February 7. http://www.nytimes.com/2010/02/07/business/07goldman.html (accessed April 16, 2010).

Morris-Suzuki, Tessa. 1994. *The technological transformation of Japan: From the seventeenth to the twenty-first century.* Cambridge: Cambridge University Press.

Mueller, Dennis. 1989. *Public choice II.* Cambridge: Cambridge University Press.

Muniesa, Fabian. 2000. Performing prices: The case of price discovery automation in the financial markets. In *Facts and figures: Economic representations and practices*, ed. Herbert Kalthoff, Richard Rottenburg, and Hans-Jürgen Wagener, 289–312. Jahrbuch Ökonomie und Gesellschaft 16. Marburg: Metropolis.

Muramatsu, Michio, and Ellis Krauss. 1987. The conservative policy line and the development of patterned pluralism. In *The political economy of Japan*, vol. 1, ed. Kozo Yamamura and Yasukichi Yasuba, 516–54. Stanford, Calif.: Stanford University Press.

Nader, Laura. 1996. Introduction: Anthropology inquiry into boundaries, power, and knowledge. In *Naked science*, ed. Laura Nader, 1–28. New York: Routledge.

Nakagawa, Takehisa. 2000. Administrative informality in Japan: Governmental activities outside statutory authorization. *Administrative Law Review* 52 (1): 175–211.

Nakajima, Masashi. 2007. Nichi-Ou de dojishinko suru jisedai RTGS purojekuto. [Coincidental developments of the two "next generation RTGS projects" in Europe and Japan]. *Reitaku International Journal of Economic Studies* 15 (1): 79–92.

———. 2008. Global trends of payment systems and the next-generation RTGS Project in Japan. In *Cyberlaw for global E-business: Finance, payments, and dispute resolution*, ed. Takashi Kubota, 109–27. Hershey, Pa.: Information Science Reference.

Nakamoto, Michiyo, and Gillian Tett. 1998. Battle for top job at Japan's Central Bank. *Financial Times*, March 16.

Nakasone, Yasuhiro. 1998. Politicians, bureaucrats, and policymaking in Japan. In *Unlocking the bureaucrat's kingdom: Deregulation and the Japanese economy*, ed. Frank Gibney, 41–52. Washington, D.C.: Brookings Institution Press.

Nelkin, David. 2006. Signaling conformity: Changing norms in Japan and China. *Michigan Journal of International Law* 27:933–72.

New York Times. 2009. European Union proposes to police derivatives trading. July 4, B3.

Nice, Julie A. 1995–96. The new private law: An introduction. *Denver University Law Review* 73 (4): 993–99.

Nickel, Rainer. 2006. Participatory transnational governance. In *Constitutionalism, multi-level governance, and social regulation*, ed. Christian Joerges and Ernst-Ulrich Petersmann, 209–50. Oxford: Hart Publishing.

Niskanen, William. 1971. *Bureaucracy and representative government*. Chicago: Aldine, Atherton.

Ogura, Takeshi. 2008. Jugatsu ni kado suru jisedai RTGS no eikyo wa genteiteki. [Next-generation RTGS to be put into operation in October will have limited effect]. *Kinyu Zaisei Jijo* no. 2808 (October 6): 62–63.

O'Harrow, Robert, Jr., and Brady Dennis. 2008. Downgrades and downfall; How could a single unit of AIG cause the giant company's near-ruin and become a fulcrum of the global financial crisis? Straying from its own rules for managing risk and then failing to anticipate the consequences. *Washington Post*, December 31. Factiva. http://global.factiva.com (accessed April 12, 2010).

Okimoto, Daniel. 1989. *Between MITI and the market: Japanese industrial policy for high technology*. Stanford, Calif.: Stanford University Press.

Ong, Aihwa. 2006. *Neoliberalism as exception: Mutations in citizenship and sovereignty*. Durham, N.C.: Duke University Press.

Ong, Aihwa, and Stephen J. Collier. 2005. *Global assemblages: Technology, politics, and ethics as anthropological problems*. Malden: Blackwell Publishing.

Ono, Masaru, Hideki Kanda, Yukihiro Tanaka, Seichi Yamada, and Akihiro Wani. 1998. Kinyu shisutemu kaikaku o meguru hoteki shomondai [Legal problems surrounding the financial system reforms]. *Kinyu Homu Jijo* no. 1522 (August 5): 26–52.

Ouchi, William G., and Alan L. Wilkins. 1985. Organizational culture. *Annual Review of Sociology* 11:457–83.

Partnoy, Frank. 1999. The Siskel and Ebert of financial markets? Two thumbs down for the credit rating agencies. *Washington University Law Quarterly* 77:619–712.

———. 2001. The shifting contours of global derivatives regulation. *University of Pennsylvania Journal of International Economic Law* 22:421–95.

———. 2008a. Do away with rating-based rules. *Financial Times* (London ed.), July 9, 15.

———. 2008b. Hubris is thy name Richard Fuld? *Financial Times* (Asia ed.), September 15, 9.

Patrick, Hugh. 1962. *Monetary policy and central banking in contemporary Japan*. Bombay: University of Bombay Press.

Patrikis, Ernest. 1998. Japan's big bang financial reforms. *Brooklyn Journal of International Law* 24 (2): 557–92.

Pempel, T. J. 1987. The unbundling of Japan, Inc.: The changing dynamics of Japanese policy formation. *Journal of Japan Studies* 13 (2): 271–306.

Pempel, T. J., and Michio Muramatsu. 1995. The Japanese bureaucracy and economic development: Structuring a proactive civil service. In *The Japanese civil service and economic development: Catalysts for change*, ed. Hyung-Ki Kim, Michio Muramatsu, T. J. Pempel, and Kozo Yamamura, 19–76. Oxford: Oxford University Press.

Penalver, Eduardo. 2005. Property as entrance. *Virginia Law Review* 91:1889–1972.

Penalver, Eduardo, and Sonia Katyal. 2007. Property outlaws. *University of Pennsylvania Law Review* 155:1095–1186.

Piccioto, Sol. 1996–97. Networks in international economic integration: Fragmented states and the dilemmas of neo-liberalism. *Northwestern Journal of International Law & Business* 17:1014–56.

Pickering, Andrew. 1997. Concepts and the mangle of practice: Constructing quaternions. In *Mathematics, science, and postclassical theory*, ed. B. H. Smith and A. Plotnitsky, 40–82. Durham, N.C.: Duke University Press.

Pistor, Katherina, and Philip Wellons. 1998. *The role of law and legal institutions in Asian economic development, 1960–1995*. Oxford: Oxford University Press.

Polanyi, Karl. 1944. *The great transformation*. New York: Beacon Press.

———. 1968. *Primitive, archaic, and modern economies*, ed. George Dalton. Garden City, N.Y.: Anchor Books.

Pomerleano, Michael. 1998. Corporate finance lessons from the East Asian crisis: Public policy for the private sector. *World Bank Public Policy Journal* 155 (October). http://rru.worldbank.org/documents/publicpolicyjournal/155pomer.pdf (accessed July 16, 2010).

Pope, Jeremy, ed. 1997. *The TI source book*. Berlin: Transparency International.

Porter, Michael, and Takeuchi Hirotaka. 1999. Fixing what really ails Japan. *Foreign Affairs* 78 (3): 66–81.

Posnak, Bruce. 1988. Choice of law: Interest analysis and its "new crits." *American Journal of Comparative Law* 36:681–728.

Posner, Richard A. 1987. The decline of law as an autonomous discipline, 1962–1987. *Harvard Law Review* 100:761–80.

———. 1995. *Overcoming law*. Cambridge: Harvard University Press.

Potok, Richard. 1999. Legal certainty for securities held as collateral. *International Financial Law Review* 18 (12): 12–16.

Pound, Roscoe. 1908. Mechanical jurisprudence. *Columbia Law Review* 8: 605–23.

———. 1911. The scope and purpose of sociological jurisprudence. *Harvard Law Review* 24:591–619.

———. 1945. Individual interests of substance—Promised advantages. *Harvard Law Review* 59:1–42.

———. 1959. *Jurisprudence*. St. Paul, Minn.: West Publishing.

Powell, M. J. 1993. Professional innovation—Corporate lawyers and private lawmaking. *Law and Social Inquiry–Journal of the American Bar Foundation* 18 (3): 423–52.

Power, Michael. 1997. *The audit society: Rituals of verification*. Oxford: Oxford University Press.

Preda, Alex. 2002. On ticks and tapes: Financial knowledge, communicative practices, and information technologies on nineteenth-century financial markets. Paper presented at the Conference on the Social Studies of Finance, Columbia University, New York.

Rabel, Ernst. 1945. *The conflict of laws: A comparative study*. 4 vols. Ann Arbor: University of Michigan Press.

Raffel, Stanley. 1979. *Matters of fact: A sociological inquiry*. London: Routledge.

Rahman, M. Zubaidur. 1998. The role of accounting disclosure in the East Asian financial crisis: Lessons learned. *Transnational Corporations* 7 (3): 1–52.

Ramseyer, Mark J., and Minoru Nakazato. 1998. *Japanese law: An economic approach*. Chicago: University of Chicago Press.

Reddy, Sanjay G., and Antoine Heuty. 2008. Global development goals: The folly of technocratic pretensions. *Development Policy Review* 26 (1): 5–28.

Richman, Barak D. 2006. How community institutions create economic advantage: Jewish diamond merchants in New York. *Law and Social Inquiry* 31(2): 383–420.

Riles, Annelise. 1994. Representing in-between: Law, anthropology and the rhetoric of interdisciplinarity. *University of Illinois Law Review* (3): 597–650.

———. 2000. *The network inside out*. Ann Arbor: University of Michigan Press.

———. 2003. Law as object. In *Law and empire in the Pacific: Fiji and Hawai'i*, ed. Sally Merry and Don Brenneis, 187–212. Sante Fe, N.M.: SAR Press.

———. 2004a. Property as legal knowledge: Means and ends. *Journal of the Royal Anthropological Institute* (n.s.) 10:775–95.

———. 2004b. Real time: Unwinding technocratic and anthropological knowledge. *American Ethnologist* 31:392–405.

———. 2006a. [Deadlines]: Removing the brackets on politics in bureaucratic and anthropological analysis. In *Documents: Bureaucratic authorship, academic collaboration, ethnographic response*, ed. A. Riles, 71–92. Ann Arbor: University of Michigan Press.

———. 2006b. Introduction: In response. In *Documents: Artifacts of modern knowledge*, ed. A. Riles, 1–38. Ann Arbor: University of Michigan Press.

———. 2009. Ho ni okeru kibo towa nanika? [What kind of hope does law entail?] In *Kibogaku* [Hope studies], ed. Genda Yuji and Uno Shigeki, 27–56. Tokyo: University of Tokyo Press.

Riles, Annelise, and Takashi Uchida. 2009. Reforming knowledge? A sociolegal critique of the legal education reforms in Japan. *Drexel Law Review* 1:3–51.

Rochet, Jean-Charles, and Jean Tirole. 1996. Interbank lending and systemic risk. *Journal of Money, Credit and Banking* 28 (4): 733–63.

Roitman, Janet L. 2004a. *Fiscal disobedience: An anthropology of economic regulation in Central Africa*. Princeton, N.J.: Princeton University Press.

———. 2004b. Productivity in the margins: The reconstitution of state power in the Chad basin. In *Anthropology in the margins of the state*, ed. Veena Das and Deborah Poole, 191–224. Santa Fe, N.M.: School of American Research.

Romano, Roberta. 1996. A thumbnail sketch of derivative securities and their regulation. *Maryland Law Review* 55:1–83.

Ronit, Karsten, and Volker Schneider. 2000. Private organizations and their contribution to problem-solving in the global arena. In *Private organizations in global politics*, ed. K. Ronit and V. Schneider, 1–33. New York: Routledge.

Rorty, Richard. 1989. *Contingency, irony, and solidarity*. Cambridge: Cambridge University Press.

Röpke, William K. 1954. Economic order and international law. *Recueil des cours* 86:202–71.

Rose, Nikolas. 1999. *Powers of freedom: Reframing political thought*. Cambridge: Cambridge University Press.

Rose-Ackerman, Susan. 1997. The political economy of corruption. In *Corruption and the global economy*, ed. Kimberly Ann Elliott, 31–60. Washington, D.C.: Institute for International Economics.

———. 1998. Corruption. In *The new Palgrave dictionary of economics and the law*, ed. Peter Newman, 517–22. London: Macmillan.

———. 1999. *Corruption and government*. Cambridge: Cambridge University Press.

Rosenbluth, Frances McCall. 1989. *Financial politics in contemporary Japan.* Ithaca, N.Y.: Cornell University Press.

Ross, Alf. 1957. Tu-Tu. *Harvard Law Review* 70:812–25.

Ross, Dorothy. 1991. *The origins of American social science.* New York: Cambridge University Press.

Roszak, Theodore. 1969. *The making of a counter culture: Reflections of the technocratic society and its youthful opposition.* Garden City, N.Y.: Anchor Books/Doubleday.

Rubin, Edward. 2002. Public choice, phenomenology, and the meaning of the administrative state: Keep the bathwater, but throw out that baby. *Cornell Law Review* 87 (2): 309–61.

Sahlins, Marshall. 1972. *Stone age economics.* Piscataway, N.J.: Aldine Transaction Publishers.

Saito, Eikichi. 1994. Japan. In *Payment systems of the world*, ed. Robert Effros, 217–38. New York: Oceana Publications.

Sakakibara, Eisuke. 1998. Reform, Japanese style. In *Unlocking the bureaucrat's kingdom: Deregulation and the Japanese economy*, ed. Frank Gibney, 79–90. Washington, D.C.: Brookings Institution Press.

Sakoui, Anousha, Michael Mackenzie, and Nicole Bullock. 2009. CDS Sector responds to criticism with shake-up. FT.com, April 8, 2009. http://www.ft.com/cms/s/0/20495de0-23d2-11de-996a-00144feabdc0.html (accessed July 16, 2010)

Samuel, Geoffrey. 2004. Epistemology and comparative law: Contributions from the sciences and social sciences. In *Epistemology and methodology of comparative law*, ed. M. V. Hoecke, 35–77. Portland, Ore.: Hart.

Samuels, Richard. 1986. *The business of the Japanese state: Energy markets in comparative and historical perspective.* Ithaca, N.Y.: Cornell University Press.

Santos, Boaventura de Sousa. 2002. *Toward a new legal common sense: Law, globalization, and emancipation.* London: Butterworths.

Sassen, Saskia. 2004. De-nationalized state agendas and private norm-making. In *Public governance in the age of globalization*, ed. K.-H. Ladeur, 51–67. Hants: Ashgate.

Sato, Makoto. 1998. Central Bank targets financial system risk: Plan to introduce real-time settlement forces restructuring. *Nikkei Weekly*, September 21.

Scalia, Antonin. 1989. The rule of law as a law of rules. *University of Chicago Law Review* 56:1175–88.

Scannell, Kara, and Serena Ng. 2008. Market rescue: SEC plans to probe credit-default swaps. *Wall Street Journal*, September 20, B5.

Schaede, Ulrike. 1995. The "old boy" network and government-business relationship in Japan. *Journal of Japanese Studies* 21 (2): 293–317.

Scheuerman, William E. 2004. Democratic experimentalism or capitalist synchronization? Critical reflections on directly deliberative polyarchy. *Canadian Journal of Law and Jurisprudence* 17 (1): 101–27.

Schmitthoff, Clive M. 1968. The unification or harmonisation of law by means of standard contracts and general conditions. *International and Comparative Law Quarterly* 17:551–70.

Schneiberg, Marc, and Timothy Bartley. 2008. Organizations, regulation, and economic behavior: Regulatory dynamics and forms from the nineteenth to twenty-first century. *Annual Review of Law and Social Science* 4:31–61.

——. 2010. Regulating or redesigning finance? Market architectures, normal accidents, and dilemmas of regulatory reform. In *Markets on trial: The economic sociology of the U.S. financial crisis*, ed. M. Lounsbury and P. Hirsh, 30A:281–307. Research in the sociology of organizations. Bingley: Emerald Press.

Schuck, Peter H. 1992. Legal complexity: Some causes, consequences, and cures. *Duke Law Journal* 42:1–52.

Schwarcz, Steven L. 2002. Private ordering of public markets: The rating agency paradox. *University of Illinois Law Review* 2002:1–28.

Schwartz, Frank J. 1998. *Advice and consent: The politics of consultation in Japan*. Cambridge: Cambridge University Press.

Scoles, Eugene F. 2004. *Conflict of laws*. St. Paul: Thomson/West.

Scott, Hal. 2006. *International finance: Transactions, policy and regulation*. New York: Foundation Press.

Scott, Hal, and Philip A. Wellons. 1998. *International finance: Transactions, policy, and regulation*. New York: Foundation Press..

Scott, James. 1972. Patron-client relations and political change in Southeast Asia. *American Political Science Review* 66:91–113.

——. 1998. *Seeing like a state: How certain schemes to improve the human condition have failed*. New Haven: Yale University Press.

Securities and Exchange Council. 1997. Comprehensive reform of the securities market: For a rich and diverse twenty-first century. June 13. http://www.fsa .go.jp/p_mof/english/tosin/e1a505.htm (accessed July 12, 2010).

Sedler, Robert A. 1983. Interest analysis and forum preference in the conflict of laws: A response to the "new critics." *Mercer Law Review* 34 (2): 593–644.

Seidelson, David E. 1981. Interest analysis: The quest for perfection and the frailties of man. *Duquesne Law Review* 19 (2): 207–44.

Shapiro, Martin. 2004. "Deliberative," "independent" technocracy vs. democratic politics: Will the globe echo the EU? *Journal of Law and Contemporary Problems* 68:341–56.

Sharma, Aradhana, and Akhil Gupta. 2006. Introduction: Rethinking theories of the state in an age of globalization. In *The anthropology of the state: A reader*, ed. Aradhana Sharma and Akhil Gupta, 1–42. London: Blackwell.

Shenfield, A. A. 1961. Law. In *Agenda for a free society: Essays on Hayek's*

"*The Constitution of Liberty*," ed. A. Seldon, 51–68. London: Hutchinson of London.

Shiller, Robert. 2010. A crisis of understanding. *Japan Times Online*, March 17. http://search.japantimes.co.jp/cgi-bin/e020100317a1.html?utm _source=feedburner&utm_medium=feed&utm_campaign=Feed%3A+japan times+%28The+Japan+Times%3A+All+Stories%29 (accessed April 16, 2010).

Shindo, Koji. 1996a. Suwappu torihiki ni okeru ikkatsu seisan joko no yukosei: 1987 nenban ISDA kihon keiyaku ni tsuite [The enforceability of the close-out netting clause in swap trading: On the 1987 ISDA Master Agreement]. In *Kinyu torihiki saisentan* [*Frontiers of financial transactions*], ed. Koji Shindo and Masanori Sato, 135–74. Tokyo: Shoji Homu Kenkyukai.

———. 1996b. Kinyu hasei shohin torihiki ni okeru ikkatsu seisan joko no yukosei: 1992 nenban ISDA kihon keiyaku ni tsuite [The enforceability of the close-out netting clause in derivatives trading: On the 1992 ISDA Master Agreement]. In *Kinyu torihiki saisentan* [*Frontiers of financial transactions*], ed. Koji Shindo and Masanori Sato, 175–203. Tokyo: Shoji Homu Kenkyukai.

Shindo, Koji, Hideki Kanda, Junichi Matsushita, Osamu Nomoto, Yoshiyuki Nakamura, Akira Watanabe, Teruo Tanaka, and Akihiro Wani. 1994. Kinyu hasei shohin ni okeru nettingu keiyaku no hoteki yukosei [The enforceability of netting agreements for derivatives products]. *Kinyu Homu Jijo* no. 1386 (May 5): 16–43.

Shirakawa, Masaaki. 2009a. Way out of economic and financial crisis: Lessons and policy actions. Speech at Japan Society in New York, April 23. http://www.boj.or.jp/en/type/press/koen07/ko0904c.htm (accessed July 14, 2010).

———. 2009b. Preventing the next crisis: The nexus between financial markets, financial institutions, and central banks. Speech given by Masaaki Shirakawa, governor of the Bank of Japan, at the London Stock Exchange. May 13. http://www.boj.or.jp/en/type/press/koen07/ko0905b.htm (accessed July 14, 2010).

Shore, Cris, and Susan Wright. 2000. Coercive accountability: The new audit culture and its impact on anthropology. In *Audit cultures: Anthropological studies in accountability, ethics and the academy*, ed. Marilyn Strathern, 57–89. London: Routledge.

Shukuwa, Junichi. 2002. RTGS shisutemu, oguchi haiburiddo kessai shisutemu, koguchi netto kessai shisutemu no kumiawase ga atarashii gurobaru sutandado [RTGS system combined with large volume hybrid settlement system and small volume net settlement system is the new global standard]. *Kinyu Zaisei Jijo* no. 2506 (May 27): 42–46.

Sigman, Harry C., and Christophe Bernasconi. 2005. Myths about the Hague Convention debunked. *International Financial Law Review* 24 (11): 31–35.

Silbey, Susan S. 2005. After legal consciousness. *Annual Review of Law and Social Science* 1:323–68.

Silverstein, Michael, and Greg Urban. 1996. The natural history of discourse. In

Natural histories of discourse, ed. Michael Silverstein and Greg Urban, 1–20. Chicago: University of Chicago Press.

Simon, H. A. 1975. *Learning with understanding*. Columbus, Ohio: ERIC Science, Mathematics and Environmental Education Clearinghouse.

Smith, Dorothy E. 1990. *Texts, facts, and femininity*. London: Routledge.

Snyder, David V. 2003. Private lawmaking. *Ohio State Law Journal* 64:371–450.

Soros, George. 2009. *The crash of 2008 and what it means: The new paradigm for financial markets*. New York: Public Affairs.

Stiglitz, Joseph E. 2009. Reform is needed. Reform is in the air. We can't afford to fail. *The Guardian*, March 27. http://www.guardian.co.uk/commentis free/2009/mar/27/global-recession-reform (accessed July 16, 2010).

Stinchcombe, Arthur L. 2001. *When formality works: Authority and abstraction in law and organizations*. Chicago: University of Chicago Press.

Strathern, Marilyn. 1988. *The gender of the gift: Problems with women and problems with society in Melanesia*. Berkeley: University of California Press.

———. 1990. Artifacts of history: Events and the interpretation of images. In *Culture and history in the Pacific*, ed. J. Siikala, 25–44. Helsinki: Finnish Anthropological Society.

———. 1991. *Partial connections*. Savage, Md.: Rowman and Littlefield.

———. 1995. *The relation: Issues in complexity and scale*. Cambridge: Prickly Pear Press.

———. 1996. Cutting the network. *Journal of the Royal Anthropological Institute* 2 (3): 517–35.

———. 2000a. *Audit cultures: Anthropological studies in accountability, ethics, and the academy*. New York: Routledge.

———. 2000b. The tyranny of transparency. *British Educational Research Journal* 26 (3): 309–21.

Stryker, Robin. 2000. Legitimacy processes as institutional politics: Implications for theory and research in the sociology of organizations. *Research in the Sociology of Organizations* 17:179–223

Suchman, Mark C. 2007. The contracting universe: Law firms and the evolution of venture capital financing in Silicon Valley. University of Wisconsin–Madison. Unpublished.

Suchman, Mark C., and Lauren B. Edelman. 1996. Legal rational myths: The new institutionalism and the law and society tradition. *Law and Social Inquiry* 21:903–41.

Suetens, David. 1995. Collateralization and the ISDA Credit Support Annex. *International Financial Law Review* 14 (8): 15–16.

Sugawara, Sandra. 1998. Japan passes bank-aid bill, but scandals cloud prospects. *International Herald Tribune*, February 17.

Summe, Kimberly. 2001. The European Union's collateral reform initiatives. *Company Lawyer* 22:186–89.

Sunstein, Cass. 2000. Introduction. In *Behavioral law and economics*, ed. Cass Sunstein, 1–10. Cambridge: Cambridge University Press.

———. 2003. Symposium: Empirical legal realism: A new social scientific assessment of law and human behavior: What's available? Social influences and behavioral economics. *Northwestern University Law Review* 97:1295–1338.

Sunstein, Cass, and Richard Thaler. 2009. *Nudge: Improving decisions about health, wealth and happiness.* New York: Penguin.

Takahashi, Tomohiko. 1997. The new Bank of Japan law: Moving toward greater central bank independence. NLI Research Report. http://www.nli-research .co.jp/english/economics/1997/eco9711b.html (accessed July 14, 2010).

Tanase, Takao. 2001. The empty space of the modern in Japanese law. In *Adapting legal cultures*, ed. David Nelken and Johannes Feest, 187–98. Portland, Ore.: Hart.

Tarullo, Daniel. 2001. Rules, discretion and authority in international financial reform. *Journal of International Economic Law* 4 (4): 613–82.

Taylor, Michael. 1998. The search for a new regulatory paradigm. *Mercer Law Review* 49:793–808.

Teixeira, Pedro Gustavo. 2004. Public governance and the co-operative law of transnational markets: The case of financial regulation. In *Public Governance in the Age of Globalization*, ed. K.-H. Ladeur, 305–35. Burlington: Ashgate/Dartmouth.

Tett, Gillian. 1998. Japan's mighty ministry trembles: Prosecutors raid Tokyo's most powerful economic policy-making body. *Financial Times*, January 27, 4.

———. 2009. *Fool's gold: How the bold dream of a small tribe at J. P. Morgan was corrupted by Wall Street greed and unleashed a catastrophe.* New York: Free Press.

Teubner, Gunther. 1997. *Global law without a state.* Brookfield, Vt.: Dartmouth Publishing.

———. 1998. Legal irritants: Good faith in British law or how unifying law ends up in new divergences. *Modern Law Review* 61:11–32.

———. 2004a. Global private regimes: Neo-spontaneous law and dual constitution of autonomous sectors? In *Public governance in the age of globalization*, ed. K.-H. Ladeur, 71–87. Burlington, Vt.: Ashgate/Dartmouth.

———. 2004b. Societal constitutionalism: Alternatives to state-centered constitutional theory? In *Transnational governance and constitutionalism*, ed. Christian Joerges, Inger-Johanne Sand, and Gunther Teubner, 3–28. Oxford: Hart Publishing.

Thrift, Nigel. 2005. Beyond mediation: Three new material registers and their consequences. In *Materiality*, ed. D. Miller, 231–55. Durham, N.C.: Duke University Press.

Tobioka, Ken. 1993. *1993-nen toridoshi no Nihon wa ko naru: Zubari! Keizai, sangyo, shakai 88 no yosoku* [*How Japan will be in 1993: Eighty-eight predictions for the economy, industry, and society*]. Tokyo: Chukei Shuppan.

Traweek, Sharon. 1999. Warning signs: Acting on images. In *Revisioning women, health, and healing: Feminist, cultural, and technoscience perspectives*, ed. Adele Clarke and Virginia Olesen, 187–201. New York: Routledge.

Trubek, David M., and Mark Galanter. 1974. Scholars in self-estrangement: Some reflections on the crisis in law and development studies in the United States. *Wisconsin Law Review* 4:1062–1103.

Tsutsui, William. 1998. *Manufacturing ideology: Scientific management in twentieth-century Japan*. Princeton, N.J.: Princeton University Press.

Twining, William. 1973. *Karl Llewellyn and the Realist movement*. London: Weidenfeld and Nicolson.

———. 2000. *Globalisation and legal theory*. London: Buttersworth.

Unger, Roberto Mangabeira. 1977. *Law in modern society: Toward a criticism of social theory*. New York: Free Press.

———. 1996. *What should legal analysis become?* New York: Verso.

———. 2001. *False necessity—Anti-necessitarian social theory in the service of radical democracy*. London: Verso.

UNIDROIT. 2003. Study LXXVIII – Doc. 8. The UNIDROIT study group on harmonised substantive rules regarding indirectly held securities. Position paper, August. http://www.unidroit.org/english/documents/2003/contents.htm (accessed July 7, 2010).

———. 2005. Study LXXVIII–Doc. 24. Preliminary draft convention on harmonised substantive rules regarding intermediated securities (as adopted by the Committee of Governmental Experts at its first session, held in Rome, May 9–20, 2005). http://www.unidroit.org/english/documents/2005/contents.htm (accessed July 7, 2010).

U.S. Department of Treasury. 2009. Financial regulatory reform: A new foundation. Rebuilding financial supervision and regulation. http://www.financialstability.gov/docs/regs/FinalReport_web.pdf (accessed July 9, 2010).

Upham, Frank K. 1996. Privatized regulation: Japanese regulatory style in comparative and international perspective. *Fordham International Law Journal* 20:396–511.

Vaihinger, Hans. 2001. The philosophy of "as if": A system of the theoretical, practical, and religious fictions of mankind. Translated by C. K. Ogden. New York: Harcourt, Brace. (Orig. pub. 1924.)

Valverde, Mariana. 2003. *Law's dream of a common knowledge*. Princeton, N.J.: Princeton University Press.

———. 2005. Authorizing the production of urban moral order: Appellate courts and their knowledge games. *Law and Society Review* 39 (2): 419–55.

———. 2009. Jurisdiction and scale: Legal "technicalities" as resources for theory. *Social and Legal Studies* 18 (2): 139–57.

Van Duyn, Aline. 2009. U.S. Democrats draft plan to curb CDS trade. *Financial Times* (Europe ed.), January 30, 26.

Van Duyn, Aline, Joanna Chung, and Saskia Scholtes. 2008. Watchdog wants credit derivatives controls. *Financial Times* (USA ed.), May 13, 17.

VanHoose, David D. 1991. Bank behavior, interest rate determination, and monetary policy in a financial system with an intraday federal funds market. *Journal of Banking and Finance* 15 (2): 343–65.

Vishwanath, T., and D. Kaufmann. 1999. Towards transparency in finance and governance. World Bank Policy Research Working Paper. http://sitesources .worldbank.org/INTWBIGOVANTCOR/Resources/tarawish.pdf (accessed August 24, 2009).

Vogel, Steven. 1994. The bureaucratic approach to the financial revolution: Japan's Ministry of Finance and the financial system reform. *Governance* 7 (3): 219–43.

Wagner, Roy. 1977. Analogic kinship: A Daribi example. *American Ethnologist* 4:623–42.

——. 1981. *The invention of culture.* Chicago: University of Chicago Press. (Orig. pub. 1975.)

Wai, Robert. 2002. Transnational liftoff and juridical touchdown: The regulatory function of private international law in an era of globalization. *Columbia Journal of Transnational Law* 40:209–74.

Waldron, Jeremy. 2000. Transcendental nonsense and system in the law. *Columbia Law Review* 100:16–53.

Wall Street Journal. 2009. The future of risk. March 30, R9.

Walters, William. 2004. Some critical notes on "governance." *Studies in Political Economy* 73:27–46.

Walzer, Michael. 1973. Political action: The problem of dirty hands. *Philosophy and Public Affairs* 2:160–80.

Warren, Elizabeth, and Jay L. Westbrook. 2005. Contracting out of bankruptcy: An empirical intervention. *Harvard Law Review* 118:1197–1254.

Watson, Alan. 1993. *Legal transplants: An approach to comparative law.* Athens: University of Georgia Press.

Weber, Max. 1966. *Max Weber on law in economy and society.* Translated by Max Rheinstein. Cambridge: Harvard University Press.

——. 1968. Bureaucracy. In *On charisma and institution building,* ed. and with an introduction by S. N. Eisenstadt, 66–77. Chicago: University of Chicago Press.

——. 1978. *Economy and society: An outline of interpretive sociology.* Translated by Ephraim Fischoff et al. 2 vols. Berkeley: University of California Press. (Orig. pub. 1922.)

Weil, David. 2002. The benefits and cost of transparency: A model of disclosure-based regulation. Working Paper, Transparency Policy Project, A. Alfred Taubman Center for State and Local Government, Kennedy

School of Government, Harvard University. http://ssrn.com/abstract=316145 or DOI: 10.2139/ssrn.316145.

Weinrib, Ernest, J. 1993. The jurisprudence of legal formalism. *Harvard Journal of Law and Public Policy* 16:583–96.

West, Cornel. 1989. *The American evasion of philosophy: A genealogy of pragmatism.* Madison: University of Wisconsin Press.

West, Harry G., and Todd Sanders, eds. 2003. *Transparency and conspiracy: Ethnographies of suspicion in a new world order.* Durham, N.C.: Duke University Press.

West, Mark D. 1994. The pricing of shareholder derivative actions in Japan and the United States. *Northwestern University Law Review* 88:1436–1507.

——. 1997. Legal rules and social norms in Japan's secret world of sumo. *Journal of Legal Studies* 26:165–201.

——. 2006. *Secrets, sex, and spectacle: The rules of scandal in Japan and the United States.* Chicago: University of Chicago Press.

West, William F. 1984. Structuring administrative discretion: The pursuit of rationality and responsiveness. *American Journal of Political Science* 28 (2): 340–60.

Westbrook, David A. 2004a. *City of gold: An apology for global capitalism in a time of discontent.* New York: Routledge.

——. 2004b. Telling all: The Sarbanes-Oxley Act and the ideal of transparency. *Michigan State Law Review* 2004 (2): 441–62.

——. 2010. *Out of crisis: Rethinking our financial markets.* Boulder, Colo.: Paradigm Publishers.

Wheeler, Stanton, and Russell Sage Foundation. 1969. *On record: Files and dossiers in American life.* New York: Russell Sage Foundation.

Wiegman, Robyn. 2000. Feminism's apocalyptic future. *New Literary History* 31 (4): 805–25.

Wigmore, John H. 1897. The pledge idea: A study in comparative legal ideas. *Harvard Law Review* 10 (6): 321–417.

Wilson, James G. 1985. The morality of formalism. *UCLA Law Review* 33:431–84.

Winner, Langdon. 1977. *Autonomous technology: Technics-out-of-control as a theme in political thought.* Cambridge, Mass.: MIT Press.

Wiseman, Zipporah Batshaw. 1987. The limits of vision: Karl Llewellyn and the Merchant Rules. *Harvard Law Review* 100 (3): 465–545.

Wolf, Barney. 1999. The hypermobility of capital and the collapse of the Keynsian state. In *Money and the space economy*, ed. Ron Martin, 227–39. New York: John Wiley.

World Economic Forum. 2009. New financial architecture. http://www.weforum.org/en/initiatives/Scenarios/NewFinancialArchitecture/index.htm.

WuDunn, Sheryl. 1998. Japanese seize central banker in leak of data. *New York Times*, March 12.

Yamana, Norio. 1998. Kinyu kikan ga okonau tokutei kinyu torihiki no ikkatsu seisan ni kansuru horitsu no kaisetsu [An explanation of the law concerning close-out netting in financial trading by financial institutions]. *NBL* 645 (July 15): 20–25.

Yang, Mayfair Mei-hui. 1988. The modernity of power in the Chinese socialist order. *Cultural Anthropology* 3 (4): 408–27.

Yngvesson, Barbara. 2007. Refiguring kinship in the space of adoption. *Anthropological Quarterly* 80 (2): 561–79.

Yoshida, Kazuo. 1998. Nihon no zaisei kaikaku [Japan's fiscal reform]. *Kokyo Sentaku no Kenkyu* 30:27–31.

Yoshii, A. 1998. The Japanese banking system—Past, present, and future. *Yearbook of Law and Legal Practice in East Asia* 3:199–213.

Zaloom, Caitlin. 2006. *Out of the pits: Traders and technology from Chicago to London.* Chicago: University of Chicago Press.

Legal Documents

Bank of Japan. 1997. The Bank of Japan Act. http://www.boj.or.jp/en/type/law/bojlaws/bojlaw1.htm (accessed August 24, 2009).

———. 2003. JGB Book-Entry Regulations. Bank of Japan regulations concerning the JGB Book-Entry System. January 23. http://www.boj.or.jp/en/type/law/furiketsu/fyoryo01.htm (accessed July 14, 2010).

Bankruptcy Law. 1922. *Hasanho.* Law no. 71. In *EHS Law Bulletin* 2, no. 2340. This law has been superseded by Law no. 75, 2004. http://law.e-gov.go.jp/htmldata/H16/H16HO075.html (accessed July 14, 2010).

Civil Code. 1896. *Minpo.* Law no. 89. In *EHS Law Bulletin 2*, no. 2100–2101. http://law.e-gov.go.jp/htmldata/M29/M29HO089.html. English translation: http://www.japaneselawtranslation.go.jp/law/detail/?id=1&vm=04&re=02 (accessed July 14, 2010).

Company Reorganization Law. 1952. *Kaisha koseiho.* Law no. 172. In Nihon Rippo Shiryo Zenshu, no. 47–48 (1994–95). This law has been superseded by the Company Reorganization Law 2002 (*Kaisha koseiho*) Law no. 154. http://law.e-gov.go.jp/htmldata/H14/H14HO154.html (accessed July 14, 2010).

Financial Institutions Rehabilitation Law. 1998. *Kinyu kino no soki kenzenka no tameno kinkyu sochi ni kansuru horitsu* [Law regarding emergency measures for the early rehabilitation of financial functions]. Law no. 143. http://bit.ly/dyPtm7 (accessed August 3, 2010).

Financial Supervisory Agency Establishment Law. 1997. *Kinyukantokucho Seichiho.* Law No. 101 of 1997. This law was superseded by the Act for the Establishment of the Financial Services Agency (*Kinyucho Seichiho*) Law no. 135 of 1998.

Law Concerning the Applications of Laws in General. 1898. *Horei.* Law no. 10. This law has been revised and superseded by the Act on General Rules for

Application of laws (*Ho no tekiyo ni kansuru tsusokuho*), Law No. 78 of 2006.

Ministerial Ordinance on Netting Law. 1998. *Kinyu kikan nado ga okonau tokutei kinyu torihiki no ikkatsu seisan ni kansuru horitsu sekorei [Ordinance regarding the implementation of the law concerning close-out netting in specified financial transactions by financial institutions]*. Ordinance no. 371. http://bit.ly/a2Wht1 (accessed August 3, 2010).

Netting Law. 1998. *Kinyu kikan nado ga okonau tokutei kinyu torihiki no ikkatsu seisan ni kansuru horitsu* [Law concerning close-out netting in financial transactions engaged in by financial and other institutions]. Law no. 108, in *Kanpo Gogai* no. 120, June 15, 1998. The law was subsequently revised several times. The most recent version of the law is available at http://bit.ly/9rFxNe (accessed August 4, 2010).

Office of the Prime Minister and Ministry of Finance. 1998. *Kinyu kikan nado ga okonau tokutei kinyu torihiki no ikkatsu seisan ni kansuru horitsu seko kisoku [Regulations concerning the implementation of the law concerning close-out netting in specified financial transactions by financial institutions]*. Ministerial Ordinance no. 48. http://bit.ly/auXG05 (accessed August 3, 2010).

Penal Code. 1907. *Keiho*. Law no. 45. http://www.cas.go.jp/jp/seisaku/hourei/data/PC.pdf (accessed July 15, 2010).

Special Treatment of Financial Institutions Law. 1996. *Kinyu kikan nado no kosei tetsuzuki no tokurei nado ni kansuru horitsu [Law concerning special rules for reorganization procedures for financial institutions]*. Law no. 95. http://bit.ly/bZg8Tt (accessed August 3, 2010).

Unfair Competition Prevention Act (UCPA). 1993. *Fusei kyoso boshiho*. Law no. 47. Amended April 30, 2009. http://law.e-gov.go.jp/htmldata/H05/H05 HO047.html. English translation: http://bit.ly/gBuOiS (accessed August 3, 2010).

U.S. Bankruptcy Code. 1994. Bankruptcy Code, 11 U.S.C. § 561 (Contractual right to terminate, liquidate, accelerate, or offset under a master netting agreement and across contracts; proceedings under chapter 15). http://www.law.cornell.edu/uscode/uscode11/usc_sec_11_00000561—000-.html. (accessed July 15, 2010).

U.S. Uniform Commercial Code. 1952. Uniform Commercial Code. http://www.law.cornell.edu/ucc/ (accessed July 15, 2010).

Cases

Finance One Public Company Limited v. Lehman Brothers Special Financing, Inc., 414 F. 3d 325 (Second Circuit Court of Appeals, July 12, 2005).

Shintoa Koeki v. Trustee of Tanaka Tekkin, 135 Saibanshu Minji 527 (Supreme Court, March 30, 1982).

State v. Shinwa Bank, 24 Minshu 587 (Supreme Court, June 24, 1970).

Index